Archaeology in Central Europe:
the First 500 Years

WITHDRAWN FROM STOCK

D1826285

- 5 MAY 1999

Archaeology in Central Europe: the First 500 Years

Karel Sklenář

Translated from Czech by Iris Lewitová

With a foreword by
Stuart Piggott

Leicester University Press
St. Martin's Press, New York

1983

BEXLEY LIBRARY SERVICE

CARD	CL. No 936. 3 SKL	
Y		BK
PRICE £6·50	13 MAY 1983	O
MSTAT 2	MAT. TYPE ADBOOK	
KEYER 90	TRACE	LANG	CH	QR

First published in 1983 by Leicester University Press
First published in the United States of America in 1983 by
St. Martin's Press, Inc.
For information, write: St. Martin's Press, Inc.
175 Fifth Avenue, New York, N.Y. 10010

Copyright © Leicester University Press 1983

All rights reserved. No part of this publication may be reproduced, stored in a
retrieval system, or transmitted, in any form or by any means, electronic,
mechanical, photocopying, recording or otherwise, without the prior permission
of the Leicester University Press.

Designed by Arthur Lockwood
Phototypeset in Linotron 202 Times
Printed and bound in Great Britain by The Pitman Press, Bath

British Library Cataloguing in Publication Data

Sklenář, Karel
Archaeology in Central Europe
1. Archaeology – Central Europe
2. Central Europe – Antiquities
I. Title
936.3   CC175

ISBN 0-7185-1204-9

Library of Congress Cataloging in Publication Data

Sklenář, Karel
Archaeology in Central Europe

Bibliography: P.
1. Archaeology – Central Europe – History. 2. Central
Europe – Antiquities. I. Title.
CC101.C36S56   1983   936   82-24104
ISBN 0-312-04721-5

Foreword

As their subject has developed into a modern academic discipline, archaeologists have become increasingly interested in the past history of their own studies, and historians of science and of ideas have seen that antiquarianism, concerned with ancient material culture rather than with the documentary sources of traditional historical enquiry, is an important part of a wider complex, our whole concept of the past. In this context of the general history of ideas, it is clear that even what appears to be a simple antiquarian enquiry, such as the recognition and interpretation of prehistoric cremation-urns, will be conditioned by the climate of thought of the day, and this in turn by social, political and ideological factors which will vary not only from age to age, but from country to country. In this book these changing factors, and their effect upon thinking about the prehistoric past, are studied within an area of great importance and great intricacy, Europe east of the Rhine. Nothing similar has been attempted before, and we have the good fortune that a Czech scholar has presented this pioneer work to us in English.

To those of us interested in the history of British antiquarianism and archaeology in its western European setting, the contrasts are as fascinating as the parallels. The differing cultural content forming diverse patterns in prehistory provided in Central Europe, for instance, a phenomenon absent in this country, the large and numerous cremation-cemeteries of the later Bronze Age, the urns in which, it was originally held, were spontaneously generated by the fecund earth; later they were unwittingly accommodating pawns in a deadly serious ethnic game in which they were used to support the claims of Germans or Slavs to territorial areas of high antiquity. And so with other antiquities and their interpretation: the author traces the dire effects of chauvinistic nationality, at first relatively innocuous, but soon increasingly sinister, which led up to the German prostitution of archaeology and the propagation of Aryan racialism by Kossina and other tools of the Nazis.

Central European antiquarianism, though almost always bedevilled by ethnic fictions centred on Slavs and Germans, seems to have escaped involvement in Celtic nonsense, unlike the west. The Celts in central Europe, important though they are to us today, are after all documented archaeologically, and not by surviving languages, literature or traditions. But, just as the Scots and Welsh of the Romantic Movement helped on their cause by producing the forgeries of James Macpherson or Iolo Morganwg, Old Slavonic heroic epics were similarly invented in 1817–19 to foster ethnic enthusiasm. In the nineteenth century we move decisively into a recognizable international world of co-operation and the rise of the famous schools of archaeology in Vienna or Prague, Budapest or the German states, with figures like Oscar Montelius or Robert Munro moving between them, and attending the now established Congresses or Conferences. The roll of honour of Central European archaeologists is a distinguished one, and here, set out by Dr Sklenář with skill and clarity in their intellectual context, we see them as a product of their times, and can acknowledge their achievements with a new understanding.

STUART PIGGOTT

Contents

viii

Maps and Illustrations

Maps

Illustrations

Introduction:
'Central Europe' – a Brief Definition

This book is the first to attempt an integrated survey of the evolution of archaeology in Central Europe. So defined, this is not the easiest of tasks. At first sight it is obvious that Central Europe is far from being a unified whole. The map of this area is very complicated and has frequently changed in the course of its history. The population is made up mainly of smaller nations, in many respects very different from each other; the language barriers between Slavs, Germani and Finno-Ugrians are considerable. The different national traditions, the social and cultural evolution, have conditioned the different forms which historical interest generally and archaeology in particular took at its inception and during its evolution. Yet in spite of all this, Central Europe is a specific entity existing in history, created by many centuries of proximity and contacts between all these diverse elements.

Yet, what do we mean by Central Europe, exactly? Scholars in different fields will offer different answers. The geologist, the geomorphologist, the botanist, the historian, the archaeologist, the ethnographer, the economist, each will define Central Europe in his own terms – provided he admits that there is any definition. Yet the term exists and is in current use. We must define what is meant by Central Europe for the purposes of this book.

The history of archaeology in Europe has been elaborated to varying degrees of completeness. Best known is the history of archaeology in the North, including the Baltic coast of Germany, and in the West, to which history has bound the Rhine valley and Switzerland. This sets the northern and western limits of our area of interest, where archaeology developed more or less independently, without contact with the West (the North was closer), and therefore beyond the active interests of historians of archaeology, until recently active only in the West. The southern limits of our area are formed naturally by the Alps, while to the south-east lies the belt of what formed the frontier of an alien world in past centuries – the Osman Empire in the northern regions of the Balkans. The eastern limits are set by a sort of no-man's-land between the sphere of consistent Polish interest and that of Eastern European (Russian) archaeology, relatively detached. Thus, by 'Central Europe'

Map 1. Central Europe: some useful geographical terms.

ALS	Alsace	LIT	Lithuania	SIL	Silesia
BAD	Baden	LOM	Lombardy	SLO	Slovenia
BAV	Bavaria	LPO	Lesser Poland	SLOV	Slovakia
BOH	Bohemia	LUS	Lusatia	STY	Styria
BRA	Brandenburg	MAS	Masovia	SWI	Switzerland
CAR	Carinthia	MEC	Mecklenburg	THU	Thuringia
CRO	Croatia	MOR	Moravia	TRA	Transylvania
GAL	Galicia	OLD	Oldenburg	TYR	Tyrol
GPO	Greater Poland	PAL	Palatinate	UAU	Upper Austria
HES	Hesse	POM	Pomerania	UPA	Upper Palatinate
HOL	Holland	PRU	Prussia	VEN	Venetia
HOLS	Holstein	SAL	Salzburg	WES	Westphalia
HUN	Hungary	SAX	Saxony	WOL	Wolhynia
LAU	Lower Austria	SCH	Schleswig	WUR	Württemberg

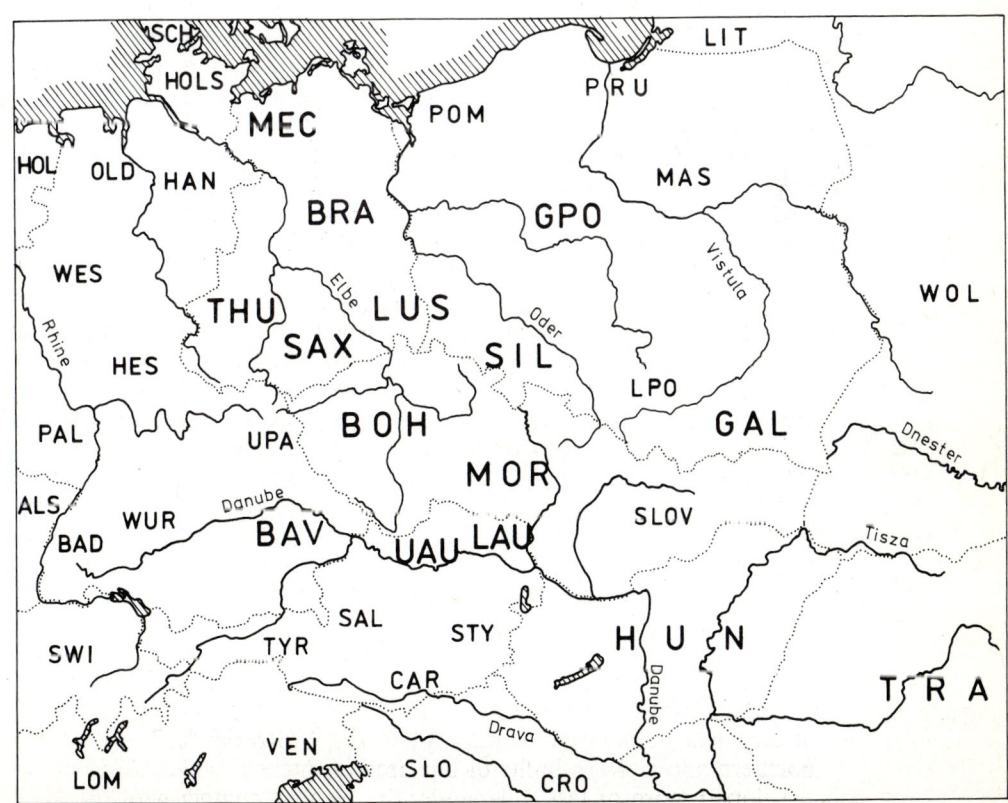

we mean the regions which during the nineteenth century (the decisive period for the evolution of the discipline) formed the territory of the two great empires of Austria (Austro-Hungary) and Germany. Today this region comprises the German Federal Republic except for the Rhine basin, the German Democratic Republic, Poland and the western edge of the Soviet Union, Czechoslovakia, Hungary, Austria; and in the south, part of Yugoslavia (Slovenia and Croatia) and Rumania (Transylvania).

The history of archaeology in Central Europe is rich and complex, yet little known. There are considerable differences between the countries of Central Europe as far as research into the subject goes, no less an obstacle to the historiographer than the language barriers and the scattered nature of the written sources. Elsewhere, however, and especially in the West, Central Europe is *terra incognita* from this point of view, as can be readily seen by glancing at any French or English history of archaeology. Europe seems to end at the Rhine, not intentionally, but from lack of sources and the efforts out of all proportion to results, which would be required to acquire this material. This is of course the fault of the archaeologists of Central Europe. And this is the reason for this book, which as a first attempt makes no claim to be faultless or complete, to be of ideal proportions, to have chosen the best approach or the wisest interpretation; the book is primarily intended to arouse closer interest and to provide a first survey of the subject for readers who are not at all familiar with Central Europe and its history.

Now that we have defined the term 'Central Europe', there are two more terms in the title which require some explanation. By 'archaeology' we mean research into prehistoric times and the earliest period of history, touching only marginally on classical and medieval times; it does not mean archaeology in the narrow sense, but the whole range from the acquisition of material evidence to the interpretation of the historical, economic, social and cultural evolution of mankind. Nor has it been possible to confine our commentary to archaeology alone; in the complex historical conditions of modern society in Central Europe a firm historical framework was felt necessary, a brief account of the mutual relationship between archaeology and the world in which it was born and lives, and from which it cannot be detached. For this reason each chapter begins with a sketch of the historical background, accompanied by a historical map showing the important localities dealt with in the relevant section of the text.

Finally, the '500 years' of the title cover the period from the turn of the fourteenth to fifteenth centuries, the period when we find the first clear evidence of interest in archaeology in Central Europe, up to the first half of the twentieth century, when archaeology as it used to be is giving way to a modern science of the prehistory of man.

A suggested periodization of the evolution of archaeology

I	The antiquarian period		
I.1	Primary analysis (up to the second half of the eighteenth century)		
I.1.1	Classical antiquity	the mythological model	finds as rarities or illustrations
I.1.2	The Middle Ages	the biblical model	to the earliest written records
I.1.3	The Renaissance and its traditions	the classical model	written records given special standing
I.2	Romantic synthesis (late eighteenth – mid-nineteenth century)		
		the Romantic historical (medieval) or static ethnographical model	finds as ethnohistorical evidence; written and material sources complementary

The 'archaeological revolution': the principles of evolution accepted

II	The archaeological period		
II.1	Positivist analysis (up to the 1890s)		
		the evolutionary (ethnographical-dynamic) model	finds as source material for (cultural) anthropology; material sources preferred
II.2	Typological synthesis (up to the Second World War)		
		further elaboration of the model	finds as sources for cultural and ethnic history

The 'historical revolution': mechanical evolutionism outdated

III	The historical period		
III.1	Prehistoric analysis (from the end of the Second World War)		
		a model freed from mechanical analogies	finds as sources for complex history; material sources for prehistory most favoured
III.2	Historical synthesis		

Thunderstones and Magic Crocks:
the Age of Antiquarianism

The historical background I: medieval Central Europe
Central Europe, as an entity, did not appear on the historical scene until
after the fall of the Roman Empire; until then the region was divided
into two parts by the boundaries of the Empire, the sphere of classical
civilization to the south of the Danube, and that of the 'barbarians' and
their culture (which was still in the prehistoric stage) to the north. The
inhabitants of this barbarous region were the Germani, who at the
beginning of the Christian era were victorious over the more civilized
Celts who had ruled there hitherto. When the Roman Empire in the
west collapsed in the fifth century A.D., the 'barbarians' dominated
Central Europe and initiated a new era, known as the Middle Ages.
From the first this term, which came into being during the Renaissance,
was pejorative in tone, for the humanists of the Renaissance agreed with
the Romans in their attitude towards the culture of the native population beyond the pale of the ancient Roman Empire.

Today we take a more favourable view of the Middle Ages, but it
remains a fact that the thought of the time, bound as it was by church
dogma and scholasticism, could not develop an objectively explicable
attitude towards man and nature, and particularly towards the historical
aspect of these phenomena. Archaeology in the true sense of the word
thus did not yet exist between the fifth and the fifteenth centuries; in the
centuries which followed, however, scholars began to turn more and
more to the earliest history of Central Europe, struggling more and
more fervently to understand and explain it.

There is no point in repeating here the well-known facts or theories
about the emergence of feudal society and its crowning period; indeed it

was the towns, the progressive element in that society, already looking outward from the narrow confines of feudalism, which set the tone for the new age in archaeology as well, for in the Renaissance it was the burgher class that produced the first serious interest in the archaeology of Central Europe.

Let us go back once more to the beginning of the Middle Ages, the very varied picture of which was influenced by massive movements of native ethnic groups as well as by periodic penetration of alien ethnic groups from the East. Raids by Asian nomads were destructive in their effect, but as a rule short-lived, like the Hun invasion of the fifth century, the Avars in the seventh or the Mongols in the thirteenth centuries. The invasion of the Slavs was a different matter; this Indo-European ethnic group from somewhere on the north-eastern boundaries of Central Europe gradually pressed westwards and south-wards the weakening Germanic elements, during the fifth to seventh centuries, after the frontiers of the Roman Empire had given way. The Slavs originally penetrated much further than the ethnographical map of Europe today suggests: to the lower Elbe, to the Main, into Bavaria and Austria, then to the Adriatic and into Greece. In the course of the next few centuries, however, they lost much of this territory, being forced out of what is now Germany and Austria by the expansion of the German Empire up to the twelfth century, and out of Hungary by the nomad Magyars about the year 900 A.D.

The Magyars were the third major ethnic group to complete the ethnic picture of Central Europe. Forced westwards by other stronger groups, several Finno-Ugrian tribes arrived in the Carpathian basin from the east right at the end of the ninth century and became a new factor in the political situation in Central Europe. The two major contestants for power here throughout the ninth century had been the Germanic and the Slav states. The former, the eastern Frankish Empire, emerged in 843 when the Frankish Empire was split up between the three grandsons of Charlemagne. The latter, the Great Moravian Empire, was formed about the same time and became the main antagonist of the eastern Franks; it seems to have superseded earlier forms of organization, uniting the Slav tribes for their struggle with the Avars and the Germani as early as the seventh century.

These empires should not be thought of as states in the modern sense. Spread over a wide area but without strong internal structure, they were rather a loosely bound collection of semi-independent territories, often ruled only in name. Relations between the two empires were marked by the persistent efforts of the eastern Franks to expand towards the east, efforts which remained largely ineffectual. Things changed with the arrival on the scene of the Magyars, who brought about the fall of the disunited Great Moravian Empire in 907.

At first the Magyars were as destructive a force as other nomad raiders; they crossed the Rhine and penetrated into Italy as well, wreaking destruction particularly in the eastern Frankish Empire, but after their military power was broken by the united Germans and Czechs in Bavaria, in 955, they did not disappear from the European scene as other nomads had done, but settled in the Carpathian basin. Here they soon formed a state which took an active part in the political and cultural evolution of Central Europe.

The tenth century was the crucial period for the emergence of medieval states formed by the union of related tribes. On the former territory of the Great Moravian Empire it was Bohemia which took the lead; the kingdom was formed in the eleventh century and expanded from the twelfth century onwards, in fairly close relation to the Holy Roman Empire whose rulers attempted to dominate Czech politics with varying success. On her other border Bohemia came up against Poland, the other western Slav state, which became united soon after the

1. Archaeological localities in the Antiquarian Age: the burgwall of Libice, one of the most important seats of Slavic princes in Bohemia in the tenth century, as documented by the artist Karel Škréta in 1668.

Bohemian state and also had frequent trouble with her German neighbours. After the year 907 most of Slovakia remained in the Hungarian lands, united under leaders of the Magyar tribe, who took the title of king from the year 1001. The Hungarian and the German wedge, meeting near the present-day frontier between Austria and Hungary, interrupted the belt of Slav settlement and separated the southern Slavs from those of the West. The former created the Croatian kingdom at the beginning of the tenth century, but after 200 years the kingdom came under the permanent rule of Hungarian kings.

During the eleventh and twelfth centuries all these states had their moments of crisis, and it was not until the thirteenth century that

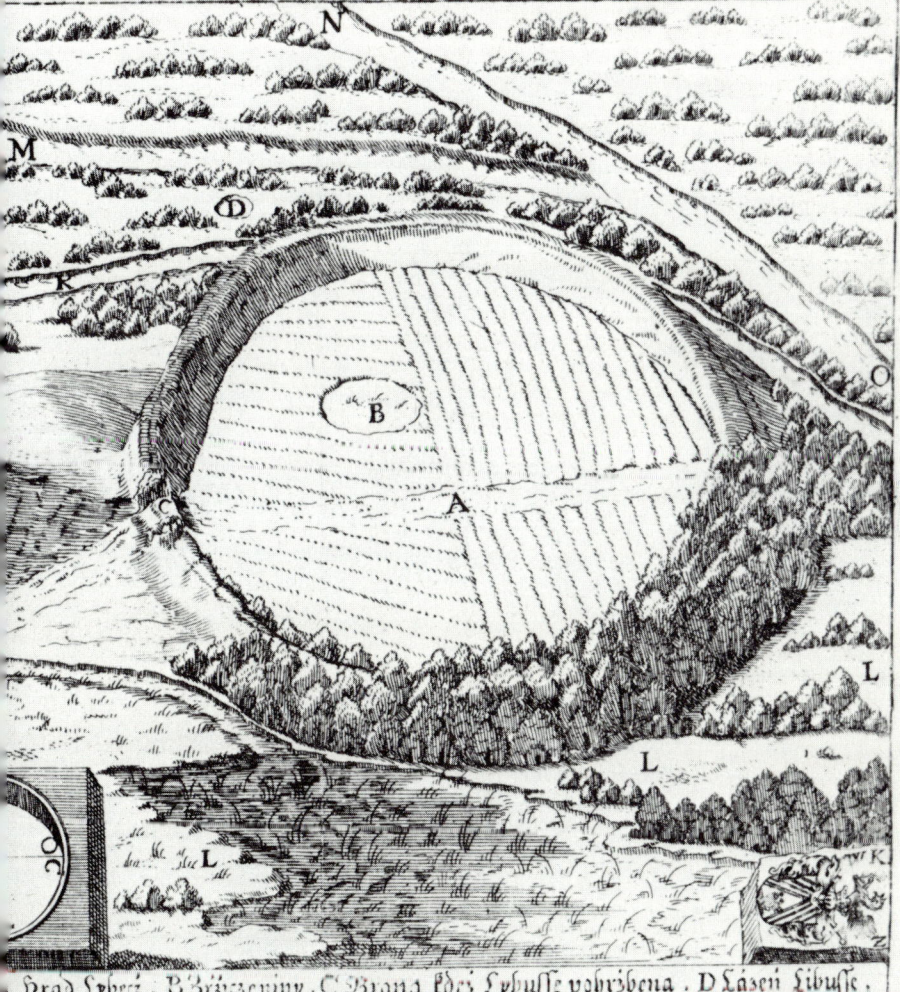

Central Europe attained a measure of stability. This marked the beginning of the High Middle Ages, which lasted into the fifteenth century.

Unlike France and England, Germany did not evolve a centralized feudal monarchy during this period. The Holy Roman Empire was extensive (after the defeat of the Slavs of the Elbe and Baltic regions it covered roughly what is now Germany and Austria together, although of course there were no fixed boundaries), but it was made up of relatively independent and isolated small states ruled by feudal noblemen, while the power of the Emperor was constantly dwindling. Of the princes of the Holy Roman Empire the most important in Central Europe was the King of Bohemia. In 1212 the power of the Czech throne, based on the wealth of the Bohemian silver mines, was given formal expression in the recognition of Czech independent status within

Map 2. Central Europe in the second half of the fourteenth century.

Medieval	5 Buda	*Archaeological*	11 Dargun
universities:	6 Heidelberg	*localities*	12 Steyr
1 Prague	7 Erfurt	*mentioned*	13 Plzeň/Pilsen
2 Cracow	8 Leipzig	*in the text:*	14 Śrem Nochow
3 Vienna		9 Niederndorf	15 Stockerau
4 Pécs		10 Ising	16 Ryczyn

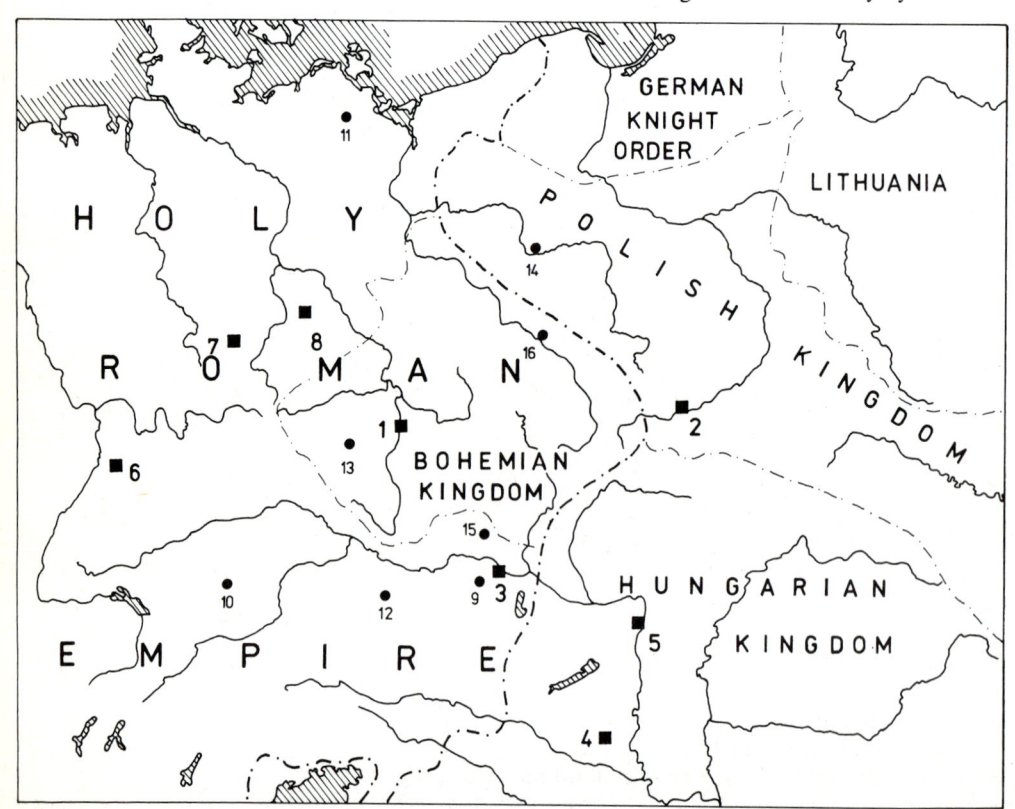

the Holy Roman Empire, and reached its climax in the fourteenth century when the kings of Bohemia ruled the whole Empire. It was also in the more advanced Bohemia that signs of crisis in feudal society first appeared, and were clearest; they led up to the violent upheavals of the first great social and religious reform movement, the Hussite revolution of 1419–34.

Poland attained a position of power at about the same time as Bohemia, after suffering throughout the thirteenth century from fragmentation and from pressure by Germany trying to expand eastwards after the defeat of the Slavs in the Elbe valley. It was during the thirteenth century that the Knights of the Teutonic Order founded their state on the shores of the eastern Baltic. The nucleus of the Polish state was Great Poland, whose interests pressed southwards into Silesia, mainly under Czech rule, and north-eastwards into Lithuania, united with Poland at the beginning of the fifteenth century. Hungary with Croatia also formed a powerful state, but from the fifteenth century onwards the threat of Turkish expansion into Central Europe became real for them.

Chroniclers and the birth of nations

Like political life, the stream of cultural evolution in Central Europe began after the fall of the Roman Empire in the West. At the end of the eighth and during the ninth century two different trends came into conflict in the area: on the one hand western Latin culture, deriving mainly from the Carolingian Renaissance in the Frankish Empire, and on the other the eastern Byzantine culture introduced mainly for political ends by the rulers of the Great Moravian Empire. The civilization of the early Middle Ages was of course closely bound up with the Church, which was also a political force. The Slav regions of Central Europe originally fell within the sphere of the western Church, but abuse of the goal of conversion of the heathen to Christianity to provide cover for Frankish expansionism led Moravia to seek a counterpoise in the Christianity of the East, supported by the political power of the Byzantine Empire. As a result, after the middle of the ninth century the Latin culture of Central Europe saw the emergence of another, western Slav culture, with a literature in the native tongue. The fall of the Great Moravian Empire at the outset of the tenth century, however, brought the evolution of this second culture to a standstill, and before long the territory of the Empire came once again and for good into the sphere of the Roman Church and Latin civilization.

It was under these conditions that historical literature began to develop, although still far from an objective scientific approach. It was literary writing, closely tied at first to the interests of religion and the Church. Among the literary forms which expressed the dawning interest in history shown by the upper ranks of feudal society were church legends and the lives of the saints, annals and chronicles. All this literature was in Latin (except for the Slav cultural episode under the Great Moravian Empire), while heroic epic poetry was the domain of the native languages and of oral tradition (e.g. in the German sphere the *Song of Hildebrand* – early ninth century – and the *Song of the Nibelungs*, written down about the year 1200 but reflecting historical events of the fifth and sixth centuries). Records of such epics have not survived for the Slav sphere. The oral tradition found its way into chronicles in the form of historical legends.

Early in the Middle Ages historical literature began to reflect the interests of national states. The legends and lives of native saints sometimes attempted to depict the distant past of the 'nation' as it was then understood, a linguistic community of free men, particularly men of social standing. An interesting and somewhat unusual case is that of the Czech legend *Vita et Passio Sancti Wenceslai*, written down in the late tenth century by the monk Christianus, who seems to have belonged to the ruling family. It is not a legend in the usual sense of the term, but an attempt to present the early history of Christianity in Bohemia and Moravia, written with definite secular aims in mind. It gives a brief account of the earliest history of the Czech people, based on semi-mythical traditions, and naturally reflects the contempt of the Church dignitaries for the heathen, who 'worshipping idols, lived like a horse without a bridle, having no laws, no princes or rulers, no towns, but wandered about, scattered like senseless animals'.

Treating the legend in this way, Christianus came close to real historical writing – annals and chronicles. While the annals, mostly recorded in monasteries, usually dealt with contemporary events, the literary chronicle or 'history' offered much greater scope for the treatment of events in the past and for observations on the early history of the country and the people. The authors faced a difficult task in their introductory passages, because of the lack of source material, and so they fell back on the Bible (it was the ambition of the historian, particularly in the later Middle Ages, to trace the origin of his people or the ruling family back to the Deluge, the Tower of Babel, Noah or Japhet as the case might be), and on local myths and legends or on heroic epics, which sometimes had a core of historical fact. The better educated among these writers soon revealed, too, some acquaintance with the mythology and history of classical antiquity. There was even scope for the writer's fantasy in filling in the gaps left by lack of knowledge.

It is interesting to note that the national chronicle, as a form, found little ground in Germany, where it was rather individual branches of the still unformed nation that found a chronicler. The first was in the west of the country, with the sixth-century Gregory of Tours for the Franks, and later in Central Europe, where the monk Widukind recorded the history of the Saxons from the earliest legends up to the second half of the tenth century, in his *Rerum Gestarum Saxonicarum Libri Tres*. There were attempts to write the history of the world, based of course on the Biblical account (like that of Rudolph von Ems, in the mid-thirteenth century), narrowly specialized town chronicles (from the middle of the fourteenth century), and various invented chronicles like that of the Dukes of Austria, by the Viennese university professor T. Ebendorfer von Haselbach (d. 1464); but the first real attempt to write a history of Germany had to wait for early sixteenth-century humanism, in the work *Germania* by the Alsatian historian Jacob Wimpfeling.

We find such national chronicles earlier among the smaller nations of Central Europe. The earliest real chronicle in Bohemia, following the outline of early history given by Christianus, was the *Chronica Boëmorum*, by the canon of Prague, Cosmas. The first book of this chronicle, written around the year 1120, was said by Cosmas to be based on the 'legendary tales of old men', and seems to be a record (and expansion) of the Czech legends handed down by word of mouth and basically already used by Christianus. The legends form a systematic cycle beginning with the arrival of the mythical father of the nation, Czech (Čech) and going up to the conversion of the Czechs to Christianity after the middle of the ninth century. It is difficult to trace the core of historical fact in this narrative, however, in part because the writer was a man of literary culture who enriched his story with more general motifs taken from classical and contemporary literary sources. Cosmas' record of the earliest Czech history became the basis for all later historians of the period.

The first Polish chronicle also dates from the early twelfth century; it was the work of one Gallus Anonymus, a priest of Poznań (Posen), who seems to have been a Frenchman. There is much more about the ancient history of Poland, naturally from legendary sources, in the chronicle of the bishop of Cracow, Vincent Kadłubek (d. 1223). The fundamental work of early Polish history is the chronicle of John Długosz-Longinus, episcopal secretary in Cracow, in the fifteenth century.

The earliest chronicle which has survived in Hungary is the *Gesta Hungarorum*, recorded about the year 1200 by an anonymous writer at the court of Béla III, probably Peter, the bishop of Györ. It presents mythical and semi-historical events in the history of the Magyar tribes from the days when they left their original homeland somewhere in Scythia, up to the formation of the Magyar state, and describes their struggles particularly against the Slavs. Here the national bias is even more noticeable than in the Czech or Polish chronicles, a defensive bias which also explains the stress on what was thought to be the relationship of the Magyars to the Huns in the late thirteenth-century chronicle of Simon Kézai.

This brings us to the interesting question of nationalism, which was one of the ideological factors that brought archaeology into being. The national question which was so burning a cause in nineteenth-century archaeology was not as a rule in the forefront of medieval writers' interests – for one thing, the Middle Ages and modern times had different conceptions of nationhood. Yet it would be wrong to underestimate the significance of the roots of this phenomenon in a region so fraught with these problems as Central Europe. There often appears here a sense of kindred, looking back into the past and usually based on linguistic affinity. This brief outline of the works of the chroniclers has shown this trait particularly among the smaller ethnic units, where it served primarily a protective purpose.

The Germans were not too much in need of this defensive sense of kindred, although signs of an awareness of the issue can be traced in the eastern Frankish Empire as soon as it broke away, in the mid-ninth century. On the whole, however, the Germans tended to identify more with the political entity of the Holy Roman Empire, and it was left for the humanists of the sixteenth century to establish the idea that the Germans were a nation in themselves, distinct from that traditional model.

The first signs of a national consciousness among the Czechs can be seen as early as the tenth century, and the earliest chronicles reveal the first traces of nationalism; the same phenomenon appears a little later among the Poles. These tendencies, springing from the need to struggle for independence from their German neighbours, increased during the Middle Ages. An awareness of a wider kinship of the Slav peoples emerged, and in the eleventh and twelfth centuries some Russian chroniclers supposed the Slav-speaking peoples to have come from a common homeland somewhere in the lower Danube basin, among the ancient Illyrians, on territory that was later predominantly Croatian. A sense of Slav kinship can also be felt in the first Czech, Polish and Croatian (Dalmatian) chronicles. The Hungarian chroniclers made similar efforts to link their nation, isolated as it was in Central Europe, with Turco-Tartar nomads from Asia and particularly with the dreaded Huns; the cause of the disdain shown them by the earlier peoples of Central Europe was thus turned into a source of national pride. The anomalous position of the Hungarians in the region gave rise to a relatively early and powerful sense of nationhood.

The chronicles mentioned here, along with many more of a later date, represent the earliest and indeed the only medieval 'historical' writing. It was of course predominantly literary in character, and treated historical fact accordingly. In addition, history proper was of interest only to a few educated upper-class readers, and had no wide public. The only scientific institutions of the time were the universities, established from the mid-fourteenth century onwards in Central Europe. The first university north of the Alps was founded in Prague in 1348 by Charles IV, King of Bohemia and Holy Roman Emperor, to serve the needs of the Czech kingdom and the neighbouring German territories of Saxony and Bavaria. The first university in Poland soon followed (Cracow, 1364), in Austria the university of Vienna in 1365 and two in Hungary (Pécs, 1367, and Buda, 1389). University history in Germany began in the west with the foundation of Heidelberg in 1386, while Saxony to the east had its first university in Erfurt in 1392, followed by Leipzig in 1409.

These medieval centres of learning, however, were of no significance for the formation of a scientific approach to history, and still less for the study of archaeology. On the contrary, the narrow scholasticism which reigned there impeded the search for new ways to find out about the past.

Fact and superstition in medieval 'archaeology'
By the end of the Middle Ages, then, almost all the peoples of Central Europe had acquired a colourful picture of their distant past, enshrined in their chronicles. Nobody minded the utter lack of historical proof; legends and traditions were as prized as written documents – and the latter were often invented to meet the case. The possibility of using material sources, archaeological finds, was something outside the medieval historian's approach to his task.

The entire spiritual climate of the Middle Ages prevented such an attitude, for the writer on ancient history was bound to respect the teachings of the Christian Church, which were content with a simple and unequivocal interpretation of the Scriptures. Local history only began with the conversion of the land or its people to Christianity, and what went before was not worthy of interest. The ancient world was pagan, and every good Christian regarded it with scorn. The Roman statue of

Venus discovered at Trier on the Mosel was set up by the church door for the faithful to throw stones at. Even then, however, there were Popes and other dignitaries in Italy who were not prevented by fear of pagan contagion from collecting classical works of art.

Nevertheless it was still a long way from classical statues to prehistoric vessels, from the artistic to the archaeological approach. Nobody as yet was interested in the historical evidence offered by archaeological remains, and they had to come to man's notice by devious ways. The only monuments in which scholars were interested were large and striking structures interpreted in terms of Biblical history or literary traditions; when ordinary people turned up various objects in the course of their daily labours, lacking the education of the monks, they invented superstitions to account for their finds.

We know very little about the reaction of people to archaeological finds in the Middle Ages, partly because the megalithic structures which stimulated antiquarian interests in the northern and western regions of Europe were lacking in Central Europe, except for the most northerly belt. Their place was taken by barrows (tumuli); these were much less noticeable in the landscape, but very often were already given their correct interpretation. Barrows often served as landmarks when boundaries were being marked out, and it is in this role that they appear in early medieval documents and title-deeds. (We should not forget, however, that artificially raised barrows are also attested as landmarks during this period.) In Lower Austria, for example, we find 'duo tumuli' ('two barrows') in a document dated 808 A.D.; these were Roman tumuli near Niederndorf. In Bavarian Ising, in 1036, an estate was said to extend 'usque ad veteres tumulos' ('up to the ancient barrows'). Such references were particularly frequent in the Baltic region, in Mecklenburg and Pomerania, where there were large barrows over megalithic tombs, and where paganism and the Slav inhabitants were not crushed by their German rulers until the twelfth century, so that pagan burial rites were still in living memory. A deed from the Dargun monastery, for instance, refers in 1174 to a part of the boundary 'inde in quosdam tumulos, qui sclavice dicuntur trigorke, antiquorum videlicet sepulcra' ('from here to those barrows, which in Slavic are called *trigorke*, and which are graves of the ancients'), and elsewhere mentions 'in cumulum satis magnum qui sclavice vocatur mogela' ('up to a fairly large barrow which is called in Slavic *mogela*'. At the beginning of the twelfth century the Czech chronicler Cosmas used striking barrows to site the 'pagan' legends he recorded. Elsewhere the popular interpretation of barrows and megaliths as 'giants' graves' ('tumulus gigantis' in Pomerania, 1234) was the most usual.

As a rule those historical remains which differed little from what was customary in medieval life, such as protective earthworks and skeleton graves, passed unremarked. The same was true of moveable objects. If we disregard the finds of Roman antiquities on former Roman territory in the Rhine and Danube valley, and finds of Roman coins carried by traders or as booty even beyond the confines of the Empire, like those at Steyr in Austria (1297) or Plzeň (Pilsen) in Bohemia (1309), there are only two types of archaeological finds recorded in medieval texts: stone tools and pottery vessels.

The ancient superstition that stone axe-heads – 'thunderstones' – fell from the sky during thunderstorms, continued to figure in literature, following the writers of classical antiquity. We find it in 'scientific' works as well, and in the lyrics of the German poet, Wolfram von Eschenbach. There is even a German drawing, dating from 1491, showing thunderstones falling from the sky.

Prehistoric pottery did not arouse so much interest, because it differed little from the pottery of the Middle Ages, and the earliest records of finds of pottery date from the fifteenth century. A very popular superstition, although it does not seem to have originated earlier than the Middle Ages, was that these 'magic crocks' grew out of the earth. Up to the Renaissance these 'magic crocks' therefore attracted the interest of naturalists, geologists and mineralogists. It is sometimes thought that this superstition spread to Central Europe from Silesia and Greater Poland, which is the region where this pottery is most widely found in the 'urnfields'. It is from this region that the earliest 'magic crocks' are attested. John Długosz, archbishop of Lwow in Polish Galicia, writing his *Polish Chronicle* in the second half of the fifteenth century, speaks of 'magic crocks' resembling vessels made by human hands, found in the town of Śrem in Greater Poland, and elsewhere.

In 1416, Długosz writes, King Vladislaus of Poland met in Śrem with an envoy of the Austrian Duke Ernst der Eiserne, who had sent him to investigate in person the report that crocks grew out of the earth in Poland. Together the king and the envoy rode to the nearby village of Nochow and watched a number of vessels being dug out of the ground; the king then sent some of the finds to the Austrian Duke, as additional proof.

It is also true, of course, that there were writers who held a different and more correct view on the origin of these vessels – even in Austria, where T. Ebendorfer (d. 1464) described vessels found in Stockerau as artificial objects (*Chronicon Austriacum*). But for the most part, superstition reigned in the minds of scholars and simple men alike when faced with archaeological finds. It is rare to find more real, although undefined, human beings quoted as the authors of prehistoric monuments – precursors of contemporary man, 'the ancients' (*antiqui*) in documents from North Germany, for instance, or the more frequent 'pagans'. The latter term was originally an ecclesiastical one, which passed into general use. Thanks to the literary tradition, the Huns were sometimes credited in Germany with the authorship of archaeological finds – for example, in the popular words for megalithic graves: Hünengrab, Hünenbett; or in place-names in the older form Heune, as in the fortress of Heuneburg. Far more often, however, thunderstones and magic crocks were attributed to the elements or more precisely to an Act of God, while 'pagan' archaeological sites were regarded as probably invested with supernatural beings like giants, dwarfs, or even the Devil himself.

The earliest archaeological finds in Central Europe were almost exclusively the result of chance or unpremeditated surveying of the countryside, but occasionally we do hear of deliberate operations, even though scientific goals were not set, as yet. Sometimes the search was for ecclesiastical monuments, either for political motives or reasons of property, as when in 1390 Prince Louis of Brzeg in Silesia initiated

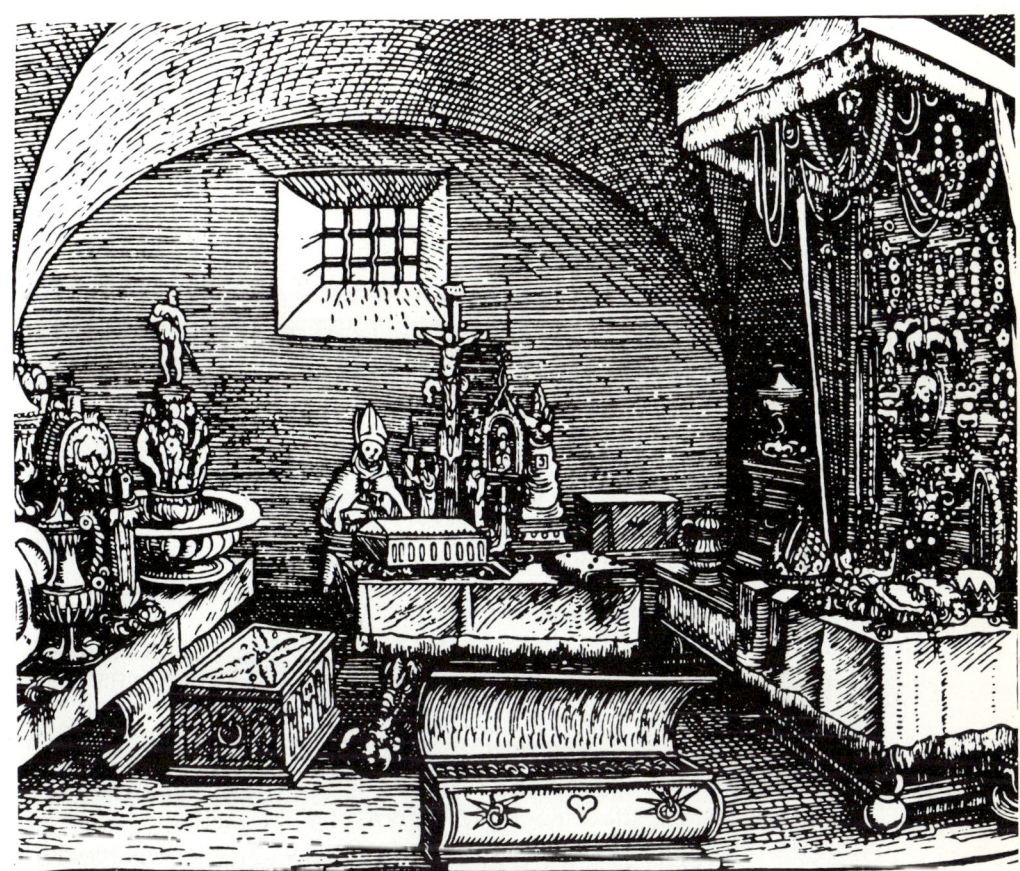

Den grösten schatz hat er allein
Von silber gold vnnd edelstein
Von perlein gut auch köstlich gwat
Als nie keim fürsten ward bekannt
Dauon zu gotes dienst vnnd eer
Vil geben hat vnd gibt noch mer

2. The first collections: the treasure chamber of the Hapsburg Emperor
Maximilian I (1515).

excavation of an ancient Slav fortress at Ryczyn on the Oder, in order to find the remains of the seat of the bishops of Wroclaw in the eleventh century. Elsewhere men sought the relics of saints, or were simply treasure-hunting, or looking for collectors' curiosities. The dig at Nochow in Poland, in 1416, comes under this heading; it was certainly located in a cremation cemetery, in one of the urnfields.

Collections such as that of Duke Ernst were certainly far from scientific in purpose, but they provided the most important stimulus for archaeological excavation in the Middle Ages. They also offered the first home for finds at a time when scientific institutions had not yet thought of the subject. Collections were formed much as they had been in ancient times, by ecclesiastical and secular dignitaries, and for ideological and material reasons. Two groups of collectors' items thus arose, of some significance for the archaeologists of the future: among items collected for their ideological value, such as the relics of saints and emblems of power, there were family heirlooms symbolizing the continuity of secular power; and among material treasures there were many examples of the old arts and crafts. A third category was gradually formed: curiosities, mostly natural objects ('unicorn's horns'), but also including prehistoric objects considered as the work of nature, like thunderstones and 'magic crocks'.

Still, these collections could not serve as source materials, partly because medieval man had no idea of the great possible age of such finds, nor indeed of how far back the past might stretch. This is well illustrated by medieval paintings of biblical themes, in which the costumes and the surrounding features are those of the painter's own time. This was equally true when the subject to be illustrated was ancient history; the *Augsburg Chronicle* of S. Meisterlin, dating from 1457, shows the ancient Germani in front of their cave – wearing the costumes of the illustrator's time and standing.

It is not possible to speak of archaeological chronology in the Middle Ages, particularly not of absolute chronology. The calculations of biblical chronologists, usually dating the Creation 5–7,000 years back, were practically useless. Yet relative chronology had taken its first steps; the first rough dividing line appeared, one which would play an important role right up to the nineteenth century: the division of monuments into 'pagan' and 'Christian'. The former included everything thought to date from between the Deluge and the conversion of various regions to Christianity; it covered everything that was 'ancient', that is to say not in human memory, and also everything that differed from Christian ritual and custom, such as cremation graves or skeleton graves where the dead lay in an unusual position, and with grave goods. The capitulary of Paderborn issued by Charlemagne in 780 already distinguished between 'cimiteria ecclesiae' (Christian cemeteries) are 'tumuli paganorum' (pagan burial mounds).

The established Christian rites were in fact the only satisfactory criterion by which to discern 'non-Christian' features and realize that they existed in the archaeological material. Ideas on the economic, social and cultural life of pagan times were derived essentially from the Bible or unconsciously modelled on medieval forms. There were two different approaches to relics of pagan times, deriving from the two approaches of the scholarly world, i.e. the Church, and reflecting the two tendencies seen in classical antiquity. Some writers, like the Czech chronicler Cosmas in the early twelfth century, thought in terms of a literary and mythological Golden Age followed by the decadence of human life. Yet elsewhere the same writer adopts the view of most medieval thinkers, that before the arrival of Christianity men were primitive barbarians, unworthy of notice. It was this generally accepted and very simple attitude, corresponding to the religious ideas of the time, which was one of the main reasons for (and consequences of) the complete lack of realistic ideas about prehistoric times and prehistory so characteristic of the whole of the Middle Ages.

The historical background II: Renaissance and Baroque – feudal Central Europe up to the middle of the eighteenth century
We left the history of Central Europe at the end of the fifteenth century, traditionally considered to mark the end of the Middle Ages. The date of the discovery of America is certainly only a formal boundary in the history of Europe, yet one which is justified from some points of view. From the sixteenth century onwards the difference between the regions of Europe to the east and west of a line running roughly through the middle of Germany, from north to south, began to be apparent and to increase. While to the west of that line economic and social progress was moving towards capitalism, with a growing role falling to the citizen class, in Central Europe after a few moves towards progress feudalism strengthened its positions and economic development was slowed down. In the west national states emerged, taking the form of absolute monarchy; in Central Europe either the states represented only part of the nation (like the numerous German states formally embraced by the 'Holy Roman Empire'), or super-national conglomerations like the Hapsburg Empire evolved. These forms of state differed, of course, in character and in their degree of inner consistency.

The feudal fragmentation of Germany was further heightened by the Reformation (Martin Luther made his declaration in Saxony in 1517), which split the feudal rulers into two hostile camps. Bavaria (and of course Hapsburg Austria) led the Catholic states, while the Lutherans dominated the north (Saxony and Brandenburg) and the Calvinists the south-west. It is not possible to name here all the German states and statelets; there were over a thousand of them, more or less independent because the central power of the Holy Roman Empire was practically non-existent. This was fertile ground for absolute rule, for economic and cultural stagnation and isolation. The Rhine remained the most forward-looking region.

To the east of Germany the Hapsburg Empire developed from the first half of the sixteenth century into a complex union of more or less independent states under a single ruler. The Hapsburgs ruled the Alpine territory of present-day Austria, gaining greater power in 1526 when the Austrian Archduke Ferdinand was elected King of Bohemia and then King of Hungary. The most advanced region of the Hapsburg Empire was Bohemia and Moravia, where the Reformation was predominant, but gradually Hapsburg Catholic centralism became victorious, breaking the power first of the burghers and then the nobles. This policy was less successful in Hungary, where the situation was further complicated by the threat of Turkish expansion. The Osman Empire gradually spread over most of Hungary, and by the middle of the sixteenth century reached almost to Vienna itself. War against the Turks was a constant drain on Hapsburg finances, although the Empire managed to recover considerable territory in the second half of the seventeenth century: most of Hungary proper, Transylvania, Croatia and Slovenia.

In Poland, which formed a single state with Lithuania in 1569 and was constantly battling with the Swedes, the Russians and the Turks, the economic situation developed along similar lines, but politically things were very different. The royal power weakened and a 'republic of noblemen' evolved. There was, however, incessant conflict between the nobles, leading to such internal strife that Poland's neighbours had ever more frequent excuse for intervention until in the eighteenth century they began to dismember the weakened state.

The Thirty Years' War contributed in decisive measure to the decline of the states of Central Europe, for it was largely fought out on their territory, beginning in Prague in 1618 with a Czech rising against the Hapsburgs; military operations ended there in 1648. This prolonged struggle between Catholicism and Protestantism ended in victory for the Hapsburg Emperor Ferdinand III and the consolidation of the old way of life, a strengthening of feudalism and the Counter-Reformation. At the same time it did immense damage to life in the region, causing an undeniable drop in the population, the disruption of trade, the decline of the towns and of production. Under these conditions the decline which had set in before the war continued into the eighteenth century, moving in the opposite direction to developments in western Europe. There the political tendency led to constitutional monarchy, in which the bourgeoisie acquired a growing influence, while in eighteenth-century Central Europe feudalism, absolutism and centralism became firmly entrenched. A typical feature of the time was the incessant wars of succession, in the course of which a new factor emerged in Central Europe: Prussia.

Prussia grew out of what had been Brandenburg. This Electorate became powerful in the second half of the seventeenth century, when East Prussia came under its rule. In 1701 the Emperor elevated the Elector of Brandenburg to royal status, making him King of Prussia, formally within the Holy Roman Empire. It was as a militaristic absolute monarchy that Prussia appeared on the scene, to go on to expand at the expense of the enfeebled Hapsburg Empire which was forced after several defeats to cede Silesia to Prussia. Silesia was one of the few relatively industrialized regions of Central Europe, along with parts of Bohemia and Moravia, and Saxony.

The Renaissance north of the Alps
In the fourteenth and fifteenth centuries Italy gave civilization new ideas that marked the end of the Middle Ages in the life of the soul and of the mind. 'Humanism' itself suggests a turning away from religious to secular themes, to human life and to nature, from the narrow scholastic approach to free empiricism. The humanists renewed the links with classical civilization which had all but disappeared – a renewal which is expressed in the term 'renaissance'. They revived the interest of the scholarly world in the historical relics of that civilization, first in the written word and then in material relics – the graphic and visual arts,

inscriptions, coins, urns; for the most part, objects dug out of the earth. In Renaissance Italy modern archaeology was slowly born, in the shape of scientific curiosity about antiquities, part of a broad tendency towards a new system of ideas for Europe, where feudalism was gradually being replaced in the more advanced areas by more progressive forms of economic and social relationships – a tendency which embraced both the humanist Renaissance and the religious Reformation.

Soon after it was born the Renaissance spirit penetrated north of the Alps, at first in isolated cases as an alien influence, like the relations between Petrarch and other Italian humanists and the court of Charles IV in Prague in the middle of the fourteenth century. A century later the Italian Renaissance had already taken root there, especially among the upper classes of the city including the representatives of secular scholarship, university professors, school teachers, doctors and the like.

Map 3. Central Europe after the Thirty Years' War (1648).

Collections mentioned in this chapter:		*Localities:*	
	5 Dresden		14 Helmstedt
	6 Munich	9 Mužaków/	15 Vineta
	7 Salzburg	Muskau	16 Závist
1 Szombathely	8 Berlin	10 Marzahna	17 Staré
2 Vienna		11 Gdańsk	Hradisko
3 Ambras		12 Maslow	18 Sitzenroda
4 Prague		13 Gryżyce	19 Altenburg

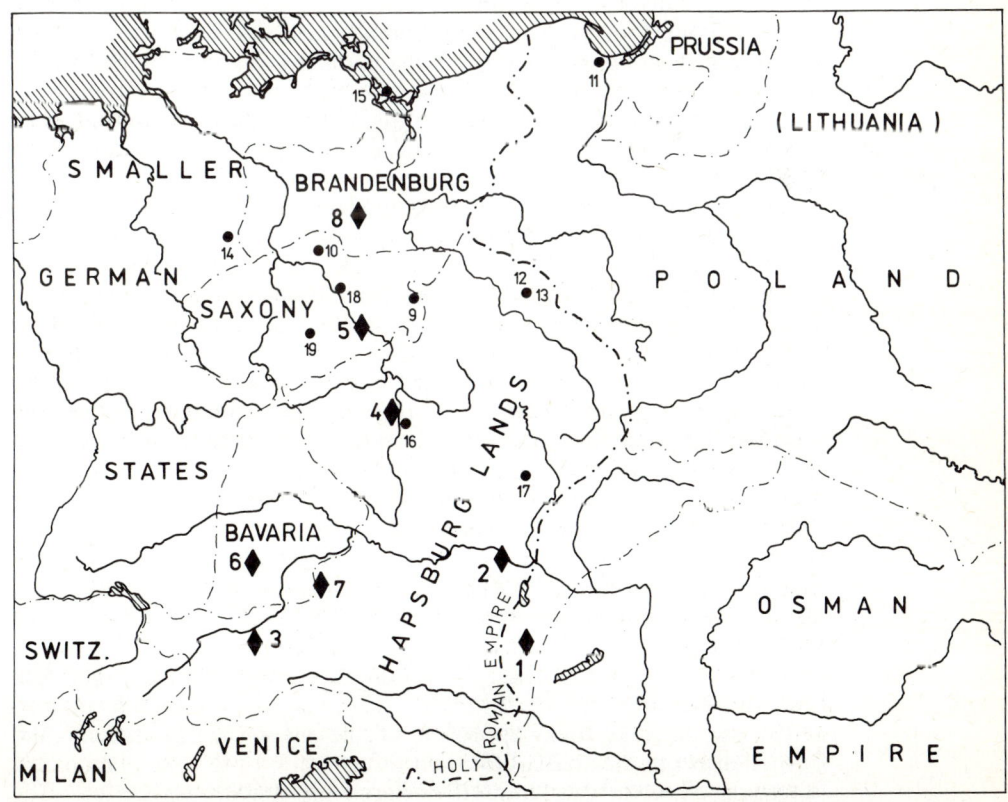

The first humanist circles were formed, on the Italian model. In Germany, where the earliest centres of the Renaissance were formed in the Rhineland, humanism was predominantly a feature of burgher life, affecting secular scholars, and the same was true elsewhere north of the Alps. The first circle formed further east was probably the Societas Vistulana, founded in Cracow in 1489 by the German humanist K. Celtis with the ulterior motive of spreading German culture eastwards, something which naturally met with Polish opposition. There was an even earlier humanist tradition in Poland, however, linked with the name of the Italian historian Philip Buonaccorsi (d. 1496), a member of the Antiquarian Academy of Rome; he was the protégé of the archbishop of Lwow, Gregory of Sanok, who is said to have lectured on Virgil at Cracow University as early as 1430.

Another Italian humanist with historical interests was active in Hungary – Antonio Bonfini; Latin humanism developed relatively early at the court of Matthias Corvinus, in the second half of the fifteenth century, cultivated by Italian, Czech and native writers. In Bohemia it was mainly Catholic scholars who cultivated Renaissance ideas; the foremost were members of a literary group at the Czech-Hungarian royal court of Buda (now part of Budapest). There were other circles in Vienna (where Virgil and other Roman authors were read at the University in 1454), in Prague and in Olomouc. Humanist lectures appeared in the Charles University of Prague in the second half of the fifteenth century, but since the Protestant influence was paramount there, the university was little affected. E. S. Piccolomini, later to become Pope Pius II, had some contact with Czech politics, and his *Historia Bohemica* (1458) was the first humanist treatment of the history of a transalpine country, adding the earliest information drawn from newly discovered classical works to the facts incorporated in medieval Czech chronicles.

In some respects the Renaissance period led to national differentiation in culture, for instance in literature, where a number of languages took on literary form. The sixteenth century was the 'golden age' of Polish and of Czech literature; Hungarian literature took shape, and in Germany Luther's Bible became the foundation of literary German. At the other extreme, Latin was the common language of all humanists, the heritage of the revered classical world; gradually, however, it became the dead language of dry scholarship. The study of the classics did not have the same significance for Central Europe as for Italy, and was to some extent pursued for its own sake. The divergence between universal Latinizing tendences and the use of the national tongue was reflected in the historical literature, called into being by a new wave of interest in historiography. Books for learned readers were still written in the traditional Latin, while the native languages were used for the broader public. An important milestone in the distribution of this literature, and the extent to which it could affect the public, was the invention of printing in Germany in the middle of the fifteenth century.

This literature was marked by yet another divergence, that between the purpose and the performance. Many writers did their best to overcome the uncritical approach of the medieval chroniclers, and turned direct to the sources for their information – the famous humanist Erasmus of Rotterdam himself declared his slogan: 'ad fontes!' The

The first scholarly debate on the origin and early history of the Slavs, which was carried on in the Charles University of Prague during 1614–16, concerned these theories. At this university the humanist Daniel Adam of Veleslavín was already lecturing on ancient history at the end of the sixteenth century, and in 1603 the professor of history, Jan Campanus, inaugurated regular lectures on Czech history; it was here that the professor of law, Jan Matyáš a Sudetis, came forward with the idea that the cradle of the Slavs was in Eastern Europe, in Russia. His printed treatise *De Origine Bohemorum et Slavorum* (1615) is devoted to the theory.

It is an interesting point that not only among the Slavs, but elsewhere in Europe as well, suggestions that our ancestors were nomads from Asia appeared during this period. G. W. Leibniz and Eccard put this theory forward for the Germani, while about 1730 it was suggested that the Celts might have been of Tunguz origin. The search for the cradle of the peoples of Europe somewhere in Asia was not without influence on the emergence, later, of the Indo-European idea.

These theoretical considerations had of course little to do with archaeological practice. Consciousness of Slav identity was still a philological and literary matter. One retarding factor was the lack of clear references in the works of classical writers – there was no Tacitus for the Slavs and the lands they inhabited. Historical evidence of the Slavs was most abundant for the early Middle Ages, for the Elbe basin and the coastal region of Germany, and here their presence was assumed by archaeologists as yet free from nationalist bias. The first modern, thorough studies of early Slav history came from this mixed Slav-German border region (e.g. J. C. von Jordan, a scholar of Slav origin from Lusatia, in his *De originibus slavicis*, 1745).

In this area archaeologists were forced in time to decide the ever more urgent question of what to attribute to the Slavs and what to the Germans, not only because ethnic relationships in the region had changed, but also because the political aspect of the question was coming on the archaeological horizon in the shape of claims to 'historical' rights over given territories. At first the attempts at classification were simple. Writing at the beginning of the sixteenth century, Marschalk attributed megaliths to the German tribe of the Heruli and barrows to the Slav Obodrites in Mecklenburg. Even around the year 1700 G. W. Leibniz was motivated purely by scholarly considerations of where the original boundaries between Germanic and Slav element lay. But the question of ethnic attribution of archaeological finds, voiced as a matter of principle in the seventeenth century by the German G. Hecht in his *Bustum Lusatiae*, was slowly becoming acute. Up to the eighteenth century practically no account was taken of the role of the Celts in the archaeology of Central Europe, although several humanist writers had noted their presence in the area (M. Kuthen in Bohemia in 1539, as mentioned above, and in Germany Aventinus in his *Annales Boiorum*, ed. 1554). There was no ethnic group in Central Europe, apart from the Slavs and the Germans, who had any interest in claiming for themselves the heritage of the Celts. We have seen that the birth of nationalism occurred at roughly the same time among the Slavs and among the Germans, and that its traces are discernible in archaeology. At this time, however, these were simply majority of Renaissance historical writings, however, were committed to the spirit of the age and fell into another trap: it was thought more important to produce readable works of good literary standard, rather than works of strict scientific reliability. Many chronicles were written primarily to entertain, and in the absence of sufficient facts their authors drew on their own fantasy to embellish the accounts given in earlier works.

A good example of this sort of writing was the *Czech Chronicle* of Václav Hájek of Libočany (1541), which offered particularly detailed 'information' about the earliest history of Bohemia. Less popular, but more reliable, was Martin Kuthen's *Chronicle of the Founding of the Land of Bohemia, and of its First Inhabitants* (1539). This was the first work to state that at the time the Slavs arrived in Bohemia it was not uninhabited, but that Celts and later on the Germani had lived there. These and similar publications shows how fashionable it was at this time to write popular didactic works in the native language, particularly in Germany and in Bohemia, where the Reformation was influential. In Czech literature the Latin trend was represented by the Bishop of Olomouc, John Skála of Doubravka (Joannes Dubravius), with his *Historiae Regni Boiemiae* (1552), and by Comenius with his lost work on the 'antiquities' of Moravia, written at the beginning of the seventeenth century.

The foundation stone of Polish historiography on the threshold of the humanist age was a work by Jan Długosz-Longinus, *Annales seu Chronicae inclyti Regni Poloniae*, finished after 1470. Other works, already in printed form, and equally biassed against the Reformation, were the *Chronica Polonorum*, by the Cracow professor of medicine, Maciej of Miechow (Miechowius) (1519), and two works by Marcin Kromer (Cromerus), *De Origine et Rebus Gestis Polonorum* (1555) and *Polonia* (1577).

Some of the sixteenth-century chronicles in Germany, particularly in northern Germany, also show this combination of humanism with the traditional medieval religious line. It was not long, however, before the Reformation rejected purely Renaissance writing, and thus smothered interest in the country's earliest history. Among the outstanding humanist historiographers in the eastern part of 'Germania' in the sixteenth century were Johann Spiesshaym-Cuspinianus, a writer at the court of Maximilian I of Hapsburg, and Johann Thurmayr-Aventinus, historian of the dukes of Bavaria, who published not only Latin works but German as well (*Bayrische Chronik*, 1566). In the sixteenth century regional chronicles also appeared in Mecklenburg (N. Marschalk-Thurius), Pomerania (T. Kantzow) and Prussia (L. David).

There were no outstanding histories written in Hungary during the Renaissance. At the end of the fifteenth century Antonio Bonfini wrote a chronicle of Hungary from the earliest days (*Rerum Hungaricum Decades Quattuor*, not published until 1568) which relied entirely on ancient native chronicles. The later chronicles in Latin (*Chronicon Budense*, 1473; *Chronica Hungarica*, J. Thuroczy, 1488), as well as the first chronicles written in Hungarian (K. Heltai, d. 1575), were in turn entirely drawn from Bonfini. The Slav element in Hungary, the Slovaks, who were relatively slow in evolving as a nation, produced the first history of Hungary as late as 1733 (S. Timon, *Imago Antiquae Hungariae*).

The Renaissance tradition of historical literature was carried forward into the 'baroque' seventeenth century, but in Central Europe it was not a favourable time for historical studies. The Thirty Years' War and its consequences drove thoughts of ancient history into the background. This was also partly the influence of the Counter-Reformation, which had already suppressed interest in classical civilization in Italy after the Council of Trent in the mid-sixteenth century. In Central Europe the Counter-Reformation was centred in the Hapsburg monarchy. From this time up to the middle of the eighteenth century, works written by historians here were no improvement on those of Renaissance authors, either in form or in content.

We have, of course, quoted here only the more important historical works written in Central Europe and covering the earliest history of these countries and their peoples. For the contemporary Central European reader this was decidedly not as interesting a period as their own day or fairly recent history. Nevertheless these works touched on a problem which was to become increasingly important in political life: the origin of various ethnic groups and the validity of their possible claims to the territory they inhabited. The problem of ethnicity in the distant past, only superficially touched on during the Middle Ages, and assuming greater importance during the Renaissance, was not of prime significance even in the eighteenth century. This development was due in part to the need to attribute every find and every archaeological site to a specific 'nation', known by name from history; and in part to the emergence of the phenomenon of nationalism, enhanced by the birth of modern nations where the middle classes, the progressive element, played an ever increasing part in a society whose feudal structure was falling apart.

Classical antiquity could not mean as much to the humanists of Central Europe as it did for the national tradition of its direct heirs, the Italians. To prove themselves at least its equals, the historians of Central Europe felt bound to prove the glorious past of their own peoples. This motive can already be discerned in Renaissance historiography.

Nationalism was most pronounced in German scholarship, where in archaeology and ancient history the Germanic element traditionally opposed the Slav, while on the other hand it was overshadowed by the heritage of the Roman provinces. As early as the sixteenth century a number of more critical minds among the humanists rejected the ancient historical legends and replaced them with reports by classical writers, and particularly by Tacitus. His *Germania* was discovered in an early medieval manuscript in the monastery of Hersfeld in 1451, printed in Venice in 1470 and then in Nuremberg in 1473, edited by K. Celtis. In 1526 J. Eberlin published a German translation of another *Germania* – the work of the Italian humanist E. S. Piccolomini (1458), which formed a commentary of sorts on Tacitus. A more serious commentary had been published in 1519 by B. Rhenanus.

The works of Tacitus became the bible of German archaeologists and ancient history scholars, not only for factual information on the Germanic tribes, but principally because of his praise for the ancient Germanic virtues. (It was not understood at the time that Tacitus exaggerated those virtues and ignored the Germanic vices, endeavour-

ing as a moralist to put before his fellow Romans under t[h]
model of untainted moral life.) Not all humanists were sat[isfied with the]
picture painted by Tacitus, however, and some foun[d]
exalted. Voices rose in protest against underestimation [of]
the Germani, and the attribution of important finds to th[e]
first wave of antiquarian nationalism in Germany not on[ly]
number of tendentious works of scholarship, beginnin[g with]
feling's *Epitome Rerum Germanicarum* (1505), but p[roduced]
forgeries. One, attributed to the ancient historian Be[rosus, 'dis-]
covered' in 1498, confirmed that the Germani were d[escended]
from Noah; the work known as *Hunibald's Chron[icle' traced the]
descent of the Franks from ancient Troy (1514).

Real scholarship was of course of greater significa[nce. For the most]
part the writers were humanists of the Rhineland. [...]
published the first compilation of classical referen[ces to the]
history of the Germani in 1531, while P. Melanchtho[n sought]
to localize the tribes mentioned by Tacitus. The firs[t serious]
work on ancient Germany is considered to be th[e work of P.]
Cluverius, *Germaniae Antiquae Libri Tres* (1616). [In the second]
wave of interest in the subject, eighteenth-centur[y scholars]
have reversed the trend in favour of the high[er developed]
classical world, developing research into the Rom[an]
provinces.

Archaeology was thus one of the spheres i[n which nations]
gradually became aware of their national ide[ntity and of]
political fragmentation. This was particularly tru[e of German]
scholars (Major, Arnkiel, Rhode, Keyssler a[nd others) who were]
already quite convinced by the end of the seve[nteenth century that]
archaeological remains found in non-Roman 'f[ields' had been]
left by the ancient Germani. To try to attribut[e finds to particular]
German tribes, according to the geographical [...]
records in classical writers, then became the [...]

The Slavs passed through a similar stage o[f development. Those]
most closely in touch with the Renaissance [and with]
classical antiquity in Dalmatia, settled by [...] the]
humanists evolved the concept of Illyrian [... the]
traditions of the southern Slavs from the I[llyrian inhabi-]
tants of the northern part of the Balkan pe[ninsula. Typical of]
this school of thought was the *Oratio [de Origine Successibusque]
Slavorum* (1532) of V. Priboević-Priboevi[... that Dalmatia]
was the cradle of the Slavs goes further [... for]
example, in the work of the earliest Czec[h ...]

Another important theory identified th[e Slavs with one of]
the ancient world, Black Sea nomads rela[ted to ...] Appear-]
ing in the thirteenth century, this idea ga[ined currency in the]
Renaissance, when it can be found in Po[lish works such as]
his *Tractatus de Duabus Sarmatiis*, 1518 [... (died]
1552) and German and Italian humani[sts ...]
When Central European archaeologist[s ...]
(like J. von Mellen in his *Historia Urna[rum ...*]
the first book on archaeological finds [in ...]
fact attributing them to the Slavs.

expressions of national pride; militant nationalism going so far as chauvinism did not appear in archaeology until the Romantic Age.

Antiquarians and collectors
In southern Europe, to some extent, material vestiges of ancient cultures as well as written sources contributed to knowledge of the ancient world, and this circumstance led to the revival of some classical terms, with a new meaning. After disappearing during the Middle Ages, the word 'archaeology' reappeared, as well as 'antiquarian', designating one who was concerned with the subject. 'Antiquities' were understood by the humanists of Italy in the broadest sense, including material and written sources, articles of daily use and works of art, inscriptions, coins, etc.

Humanists north of the Alps were at a decided disadvantage compared with their Italian contemporaries. They, too, were enthusiastic admirers of classical Rome, but Rome had left far fewer relics of its glory beyond the Alps, and beyond the former Roman frontiers, that is to say north of the Danube and east of the Rhine, there were practically none. The humanists of southern Germany, Austria and Hungary could make a certain contribution to the efforts of the Italian antiquarians. The ruins of the ancient town of Carnuntum were already known in Austria in the fifteenth century. Wolfgang Lazius, in his *Vindobona Austriae* (1546), described Roman antiquities in the vicinity of Vienna, while in Hungary King Matthias, influenced by humanist ideas, initiated the collection of Roman antiquities in the second half of the fifteenth century, and assembled them in the castle of Szombathely.

These were the beginnings of serious scholarly interest in the Limes Romanus, the fortified boundary belt of the Roman Empire running through the provinces of Rhaetia, Noricum and Pannonia and protecting the Empire against the barbarians of the North. It was not only the antiquities of the Limes that aroused interest, but the significance of the area for historians, enabling them to settle the vexed question of how far, in fact, the power of Rome had penetrated into Germany. In 1748 the Prussian Academy of Science offered a prize for the best treatise on the subject. In 1741 Count L. F. Marsigli summed up what was known about the Danube Limes during the age of antiquarianism, in his *La Hongrie et la Danube*.

Archaeological research into classical antiquity was of importance, too, for the archaeology of prehistoric times and the early Middle Ages, a theme which occurred here and there, incidental to that research. Historical research also played a role here, for the classical writers such as Tacitus testified to the existence at least in name of a number of Celtic and Germanic tribes in Germania and neighbouring regions, and archaeologists began to wonder whether there were not relics of these 'barbarians' hidden in the earth, waiting to be discovered. It is true that throughout the Renaissance and the period of baroque which followed, the question of indigenous tribes was treated on the level of primitive etymologies, and we can see the characteristic lack of interest displayed by 'pure' historians in the evidence of material culture, even then. There were of course exceptions, like the German humanist J. Aventinus (d. 1534) who considered archaeological relics as a source for history, and the Hamburg archaeologist A. A. Rhode who two centuries later declared such relics to be the only reliable evidence, capable of yielding more information about the country than the *Germania* of Tacitus – but in practice this was not the general approach. Up to the end of the eighteenth century archaeological finds were relegated to the role of passive additional evidence, illustrations taken from cultural history to supplement the evidence of the written sources.

'Local' archaeology, once it had achieved results, had to overcome the odium of being 'collectors' curiosities' that still clung to prehistoric finds, and integrate prehistory into history proper. The latter task was first explicitly deal with in Central Europe by J. G. von Eccard in his *Introductio ad Historiam Germaniae* (1712, republished up to 1750). Inspired by the philosopher and historian Leibniz, Eccard divided the history of the world into six sections, the first of which he called 'historia obscura' and defined as from the creation of the world up to the reign of Julius Caesar.

The first homes of antiquities were the private collections of notable political figures, churchmen and scholars, called in the fashion of the time 'cabinets of rarities and curious objects'. Archaeological finds relating to prehistoric and to classical times had already found their place in these collections during the Middle Ages, but the trend towards scholarly discrimination in the choice of 'curiosities' was the result of Italian Renaissance influences in the sixteenth century. The dominant features of these collections, at first, were classical finds from Italy and the Roman provinces, often brought from great distances. In 1508, for instance, finds from the Roman *castellum* of Roomburg near Leiden in Holland were brought to enrich the collection of the Hapsburg emperor Maximilian I.

The Hapsburgs were the most insatiable collectors in Renaissance and baroque Europe. The collections of Archduke Ferdinand of Tyrol, in his castle in Ambras, and the cabinet of the Emperor Ferdinand I were famous in their time. The latter found its way later into the remarkable collections of the Emperor Rudolph II in Prague Castle; they were unique both in extent and variety, and included many archaeological finds, some deliberately sought by the Emperor in Silesia, others discovered in Bohemia, and of course archaeological material from classical Italy. Alas, soon after the Emperor's death in 1612, this priceless material fell victim to the Thirty Years' War.

There were of course innumerable smaller collections in existence, and some of them housed classical finds from the former Roman provinces. About the year 1520 a collection of Roman inscriptions was assembled in Salzburg by J. Thurmayer-Aventinus, while in Germany the 'Antiquarium' of Albert V, Duke of Bavaria, was noteworthy. In the second half of the sixteenth century a special home was built for them in Munich, and even Egyptian antiquities were included. North of the Danube, lacking the impulse of classical finds, collectors were slower to emerge, but here, on the other hand, native prehistoric finds were all the more important. From this point of view the collection of the Saxon Electors, in Dresden, was one of the most important, together with that of Rudolph II; the Saxon collection fared better than that of Rudolph, and today still contains items found in the sixteenth and seventeenth centuries. The Electors of Brandenburg were also collectors, attested from the year 1603. In the seventeenth century there

3. The first collectors: an early eighteenth-century German learned gentleman in his cabinet.

were also scholars with considerable private collections in Germany, among them J. C. Olearius in Arnstadt and J. von Mellen, and in the early eighteenth century L. D. Hermann in Silesia and Count Brühl in Lower Lusatia.

We can form some idea of the contents of these collections from the catalogues and inventories, often printed from the seventeenth century onwards. The earliest manuscript catalogue in Germany is that of the Dresden collection (1587); that of Berlin dates from 1605; and there are several early seventeenth-century inventories of the collections of Rudolph II in Prague. We know from these records that the royal collections were added to by purchase, by command, and sometimes by the results of royally commissioned research, as in the case of Rudolph's finds from Silesia. Purchases were very expensive, as we can see from the accounts of the Saxon court from the second half of the sixteenth

4. Private museums: the decorated pyramidal 'showcase' designed by L. D. Hermann as the shrine for his collection of Silesian urns and antiquities (1704).

century onwards. In 1797 Frederick I of Prussia spent 100 thaler for a vessel discovered in Anhalt – an exceptionally large sum at that time. The price of prehistoric vessels was also artificially raised by such devices as setting them in silver or pewter. There is an amphora of the Lusatian culture, from the urnfield region, in the museum of Frankfurt-on-Main which has been treated in this manner (see fig. 5). The words 'Lusatian vessel' or 'Silesian vessel' signified an object of exceptional value on the market for curiosities at that time.

These aristocratic collections were shown only to the owner's guests, and were arranged to show off the rarity of individual items as well as the extent of the collection, according to the degree of taste of the owner. Only a few scholars' collections were arranged according to some system, or at least classified under the headings 'naturalia' and 'artificialia'. Even scholars, of course, collected as they could, assembling natural and historical items with no specialized aim in mind. Up to the eighteenth century specifically archaeological collections were practically non-existent.

5. Archaeological finds in the Age of Antiquarianism: a Bronze Age urn from Lusatia set in pewter in Germany (c.1560).

In the course of time, as the number of collectors increased and institutions began to take an interest in archaeology, the idea of protecting historical monuments and relics still in the ground was born. This protection took four principal forms.

The first and most ancient was the application of the monarch's claim to all finds of precious metals. With various modifications some of these medieval laws are still valid today (in England and Denmark, for example); in Central Europe, however, the principles were never so clearly formulated, and varied from country to country. In the Polish-Lithuanian kingdom, for example, where the rights of the monarch were limited, it was accepted from 1529 onwards that anything found on his estate was the property of the landowner, while finds on other people's ground were divided equally between the finder and the government. These regulations only referred, of course, to finds of considerable value, not to common archaeological items.

The second form of protection consisted of orders issued by the authorities and commanding the protection or collection of archaeological material. In 1595 and 1605, for instance, Rudolph II ordered the governor of Muskau in Lusatia to send any vessels found there to his collections in Prague. The third form of protection was of later date: the cataloguing of monuments with regard to their numbers and state of preservation. As a rule this applied only to regions where there were large numbers of standing monuments; one such venture was the inclusion of questions of an archaeological nature in the questionnaire drawn up to provide material for a history of Brandenburg, in 1712. The fourth method was to appoint officials – royal antiquaries – whose duty was to supervise monuments. These last were rare personal appointments, however, except in Sweden, and usually of short duration.

In Central Europe the Hapsburg monarchs appointed their personal antiquaries. Thus in 1556 Maximilian II invited Jacopo Strada-Mantuanus to Vienna; this Italian humanist, connoisseur of antiquities, numismatist and collector, had already helped the Fuggers of Augsburg to establish their collection, and also the dukes of Bavaria in Munich. In Vienna Strada used the existing collections to form the Emperor's 'Kunstkammer', for which he was nominated Court Antiquarian in 1566. About this time he published Caesar's *Gallic Wars* (1575). In 1577 the new Emperor, Rudolph II, called Strada to Prague, where he established and supervised the famous collections which, as we know, already included archaeological finds. His son Ottavio Strada continued his work, filling the post of Court Antiquarian up to the year 1607. By then, however, the glorious era of Renaissance Hapsburg collectors was drawing to a close.

All this was but the modest beginning to organized care of historical relics, and had no effect on the destruction or disappearance of object, especially those found in the field. Indeed, even finds which were incorporated into collections disappeared, in fact, from the sight of the few qualified observers, and after the owner's death they often disappeared altogether. Soon after archaeology became a matter for serious study, therefore, scholars realized that their work must be completed by publication of their finds and their collections, in book form or in the ever-increasing number of periodicals. The first publications on archaeology appeared in the sixteenth century; dozens were majority of Renaissance historical writings, however, were committed to the spirit of the age and fell into another trap: it was thought more important to produce readable works of good literary standard, rather than works of strict scientific reliability. Many chronicles were written primarily to entertain, and in the absence of sufficient facts their authors drew on their own fantasy to embellish the accounts given in earlier works.

A good example of this sort of writing was the *Czech Chronicle* of Václav Hájek of Libočany (1541), which offered particularly detailed 'information' about the earliest history of Bohemia. Less popular, but more reliable, was Martin Kuthen's *Chronicle of the Founding of the Land of Bohemia, and of its First Inhabitants* (1539). This was the first work to state that at the time the Slavs arrived in Bohemia it was not uninhabited, but that Celts and later on the Germani had lived there. These and similar publications shows how fashionable it was at this time to write popular didactic works in the native language, particularly in Germany and in Bohemia, where the Reformation was influential. In Czech literature the Latin trend was represented by the Bishop of Olomouc, John Skála of Doubravka (Joannes Dubravius), with his *Historiae Regni Boiemiae* (1552), and by Comenius with his lost work on the 'antiquities' of Moravia, written at the beginning of the seventeenth century.

The foundation stone of Polish historiography on the threshold of the humanist age was a work by Jan Długosz-Longinus, *Annales seu Chronicae inclyti Regni Poloniae*, finished after 1470. Other works, already in printed form, and equally biassed against the Reformation, were the *Chronica Polonorum*, by the Cracow professor of medicine, Maciej of Miechow (Miechowius) (1519), and two works by Marcin Kromer (Cromerus), *De Origine et Rebus Gestis Polonorum* (1555) and *Polonia* (1577).

Some of the sixteenth-century chronicles in Germany, particularly in northern Germany, also show this combination of humanism with the traditional medieval religious line. It was not long, however, before the Reformation rejected purely Renaissance writing, and thus smothered interest in the country's earliest history. Among the outstanding humanist historiographers in the eastern part of 'Germania' in the sixteenth century were Johann Spiesshaym-Cuspinianus, a writer at the court of Maximilian I of Hapsburg, and Johann Thurmayr-Aventinus, historian of the dukes of Bavaria, who published not only Latin works but German as well (*Bayrische Chronik*, 1566). In the sixteenth century regional chronicles also appeared in Mecklenburg (N. Marschalk-Thurius), Pomerania (T. Kantzow) and Prussia (L. David).

There were no outstanding histories written in Hungary during the Renaissance. At the end of the fifteenth century Antonio Bonfini wrote a chronicle of Hungary from the earliest days (*Rerum Hungaricum Decades Quattuor*, not published until 1568) which relied entirely on ancient native chronicles. The later chronicles in Latin (*Chronicon Budense*, 1473; *Chronica Hungarica*, J. Thuroczy, 1488), as well as the first chronicles written in Hungarian (K. Heltai, d. 1575), were in turn entirely drawn from Bonfini. The Slav element in Hungary, the Slovaks, who were relatively slow in evolving as a nation, produced the first history of Hungary as late as 1733 (S. Timon, *Imago Antiquae Hungariae*).

The Renaissance tradition of historical literature was carried forward into the 'baroque' seventeenth century, but in Central Europe it was not a favourable time for historical studies. The Thirty Years' War and its consequences drove thoughts of ancient history into the background. This was also partly the influence of the Counter-Reformation, which had already suppressed interest in classical civilization in Italy after the Council of Trent in the mid-sixteenth century. In Central Europe the Counter-Reformation was centred in the Hapsburg monarchy. From this time up to the middle of the eighteenth century, works written by historians here were no improvement on those of Renaissance authors, either in form or in content.

We have, of course, quoted here only the more important historical works written in Central Europe and covering the earliest history of these countries and their peoples. For the contemporary Central European reader this was decidedly not as interesting a period as their own day or fairly recent history. Nevertheless these works touched on a problem which was to become increasingly important in political life: the origin of various ethnic groups and the validity of their possible claims to the territory they inhabited. The problem of ethnicity in the distant past, only superficially touched on during the Middle Ages, and assuming greater importance during the Renaissance, was not of prime significance even in the eighteenth century. This development was due in part to the need to attribute every find and every archaeological site to a specific 'nation', known by name from history; and in part to the emergence of the phenomenon of nationalism, enhanced by the birth of modern nations where the middle classes, the progressive element, played an ever increasing part in a society whose feudal structure was falling apart.

Classical antiquity could not mean as much to the humanists of Central Europe as it did for the national tradition of its direct heirs, the Italians. To prove themselves at least its equals, the historians of Central Europe felt bound to prove the glorious past of their own peoples. This motive can already be discerned in Renaissance historiography.

Nationalism was most pronounced in German scholarship, where in archaeology and ancient history the Germanic element traditionally opposed the Slav, while on the other hand it was overshadowed by the heritage of the Roman provinces. As early as the sixteenth century a number of more critical minds among the humanists rejected the ancient historical legends and replaced them with reports by classical writers, and particularly by Tacitus. His *Germania* was discovered in an early medieval manuscript in the monastery of Hersfeld in 1451, printed in Venice in 1470 and then in Nuremberg in 1473, edited by K. Celtis. In 1526 J. Eberlin published a German translation of another *Germania* – the work of the Italian humanist E. S. Piccolomini (1458), which formed a commentary of sorts on Tacitus. A more serious commentary had been published in 1519 by B. Rhenanus.

The works of Tacitus became the bible of German archaeologists and ancient history scholars, not only for factual information on the Germanic tribes, but principally because of his praise for the ancient Germanic virtues. (It was not understood at the time that Tacitus exaggerated those virtues and ignored the Germanic vices, endeavouring as a moralist to put before his fellow Romans under the emperors a model of untainted moral life.) Not all humanists were satisfied with the picture painted by Tacitus, however, and some found it too little exalted. Voices rose in protest against underestimation of the legacy of the Germani, and the attribution of important finds to the Romans. This first wave of antiquarian nationalism in Germany not only gave rise to a number of tendentious works of scholarship, beginning with J. Wimpfeling's *Epitome Rerum Germanicarum* (1505), but prompted literary forgeries. One, attributed to the ancient historian Berossos, and 'discovered' in 1498, confirmed that the Germani were directly descended from Noah; the work known as *Hunibald's Chronicle* 'proved' the descent of the Franks from ancient Troy (1514).

Real scholarship was of course of greater significance. For the most part the writers were humanists of the Rhineland. Beatus Rhenanus published the first compilation of classical references to the ancient history of the Germani in 1531, while P. Melanchthon attempted in 1557 to localize the tribes mentioned by Tacitus. The first all-round historical work on ancient Germany is considered to be that of Philip Klüver-Cluverius, *Germaniae Antiquae Libri Tres* (1616). Compared with this wave of interest in the subject, eighteenth-century Germany seems to have reversed the trend in favour of the higher civilization of the classical world, developing research into the monuments of the Roman provinces.

Archaeology was thus one of the spheres in which the Germans gradually became aware of their national identity in spite of their political fragmentation. This was particularly true of the North German scholars (Major, Arnkiel, Rhode, Keyssler and others), who were already quite convinced by the end of the seventeenth century that the archaeological remains found in non-Roman 'free Germania' had been left by the ancient Germani. To try to attribute specific finds to specific German tribes, according to the geographical possibilities suggested by records in classical writers, then became the goal of local patriots.

The Slavs passed through a similar stage of development. They were most closely in touch with the Renaissance world and the heritage of classical antiquity in Dalmatia, settled by the Croatians; here the humanists evolved the concept of Illyrianism, deriving the historic traditions of the southern Slavs from the Illyrians, the ancient inhabitants of the northern part of the Balkan peninsula. The classic work of this school of thought was the *Oratio de Origine Successibusque Slavorum* (1532) of V. Priboević-Priboevius; but the idea that Croatia was the cradle of the Slavs goes further back, and can be traced, for example, in the work of the earliest Czech and Polish chroniclers.

Another important theory identified the Slavs with the Sarmatians of the ancient world, Black Sea nomads related to the Scythians. Appearing in the thirteenth century, this idea gained wider credence during the Renaissance, when it can be found in Polish writers (M. Miechowius in his *Tractatus de Duabus Sarmatiis*, 1518), Czech writers (J. Dubravius, 1552) and German and Italian humanists (B. Rhenanus, F. Blondus). When Central European archaeologists described finds as 'Sarmatian' (like J. von Mellen in his *Historia Urnae Sepulchralis Sarmaticae*, 1679 – the first book on archaeological finds on Polish territory), they were in fact attributing them to the Slavs.

The first scholarly debate on the origin and early history of the Slavs, which was carried on in the Charles University of Prague during 1614–16, concerned these theories. At this university the humanist Daniel Adam of Veleslavín was already lecturing on ancient history at the end of the sixteenth century, and in 1603 the professor of history, Jan Campanus, inaugurated regular lectures on Czech history; it was here that the professor of law, Jan Matyáš a Sudetis, came forward with the idea that the cradle of the Slavs was in Eastern Europe, in Russia. His printed treatise *De Origine Bohemorum et Slavorum* (1615) is devoted to the theory.

It is an interesting point that not only among the Slavs, but elsewhere in Europe as well, suggestions that our ancestors were nomads from Asia appeared during this period. G. W. Leibniz and Eccard put this theory forward for the Germani, while about 1730 it was suggested that the Celts might have been of Tunguz origin. The search for the cradle of the peoples of Europe somewhere in Asia was not without influence on the emergence, later, of the Indo-European idea.

These theoretical considerations had of course little to do with archaeological practice. Consciousness of Slav identity was still a philological and literary matter. One retarding factor was the lack of clear references in the works of classical writers – there was no Tacitus for the Slavs and the lands they inhabited. Historical evidence of the Slavs was most abundant for the early Middle Ages, for the Elbe basin and the coastal region of Germany, and here their presence was assumed by archaeologists as yet free from nationalist bias. The first modern, thorough studies of early Slav history came from this mixed Slav-German border region (e.g. J. C. von Jordan, a scholar of Slav origin from Lusatia, in his *De originibus slavicis*, 1745).

In this area archaeologists were forced in time to decide the ever more urgent question of what to attribute to the Slavs and what to the Germans, not only because ethnic relationships in the region had changed, but also because the political aspect of the question was looming on the archaeological horizon in the shape of claims to 'historical' rights over given territories. At first the attempts at classification were simple. Writing at the beginning of the sixteenth century, N. Marschalk attributed megaliths to the German tribe of the Heruli and barrows to the Slav Obodrites in Mecklenburg. Even around the year 1700 G. W. Leibniz was motivated purely by scholarly considerations of where the original boundaries between Germanic and Slav settlement lay. But the question of ethnic attribution of archaeological finds, voiced as a matter of principle in the seventeenth century by the German G. Hecht in his *Bustum Lusatiae*, was slowly becoming acute.

Up to the eighteenth century practically no account was taken of the place of the Celts in the archaeology of Central Europe, although several humanist writers had noted their presence in the area (M. Kuthen in Bohemia in 1539, as mentioned above, and in Germany J. Aventinus in his *Annales Boiorum*, ed. 1554). There was no ethnic group in Central Europe, apart from the Slavs and the Germans, who had any interest in claiming for themselves the heritage of the Celts.

We have seen that the birth of nationalism occurred at roughly the same time among the Slavs and among the Germans, and that its traces are discernible in archaeology. At this time, however, these were simply expressions of national pride; militant nationalism going so far as chauvinism did not appear in archaeology until the Romantic Age.

Antiquarians and collectors

In southern Europe, to some extent, material vestiges of ancient cultures as well as written sources contributed to knowledge of the ancient world, and this circumstance led to the revival of some classical terms, with a new meaning. After disappearing during the Middle Ages, the word 'archaeology' reappeared, as well as 'antiquarian', designating one who was concerned with the subject. 'Antiquities' were understood by the humanists of Italy in the broadest sense, including material and written sources, articles of daily use and works of art, inscriptions, coins, etc.

Humanists north of the Alps were at a decided disadvantage compared with their Italian contemporaries. They, too, were enthusiastic admirers of classical Rome, but Rome had left far fewer relics of its glory beyond the Alps, and beyond the former Roman frontiers, that is to say north of the Danube and east of the Rhine, there were practically none. The humanists of southern Germany, Austria and Hungary could make a certain contribution to the efforts of the Italian antiquarians. The ruins of the ancient town of Carnuntum were already known in Austria in the fifteenth century. Wolfgang Lazius, in his *Vindobona Austriae* (1546), described Roman antiquities in the vicinity of Vienna, while in Hungary King Matthias, influenced by humanist ideas, initiated the collection of Roman antiquities in the second half of the fifteenth century, and assembled them in the castle of Szombathely.

These were the beginnings of serious scholarly interest in the Limes Romanus, the fortified boundary belt of the Roman Empire running through the provinces of Rhaetia, Noricum and Pannonia and protecting the Empire against the barbarians of the North. It was not only the antiquities of the Limes that aroused interest, but the significance of the area for historians, enabling them to settle the vexed question of how far, in fact, the power of Rome had penetrated into Germany. In 1748 the Prussian Academy of Science offered a prize for the best treatise on the subject. In 1741 Count L. F. Marsigli summed up what was known about the Danube Limes during the age of antiquarianism, in his *La Hongrie et la Danube*.

Archaeological research into classical antiquity was of importance, too, for the archaeology of prehistoric times and the early Middle Ages, a theme which occurred here and there, incidental to that research. Historical research also played a role here, for the classical writers such as Tacitus testified to the existence at least in name of a number of Celtic and Germanic tribes in Germania and neighbouring regions, and archaeologists began to wonder whether there were not relics of these 'barbarians' hidden in the earth, waiting to be discovered. It is true that throughout the Renaissance and the period of baroque which followed, the question of indigenous tribes was treated on the level of primitive etymologies, and we can see the characteristic lack of interest displayed by 'pure' historians in the evidence of material culture, even then. There were of course exceptions, like the German humanist J. Aventinus (d. 1534) who considered archaeological relics as a source for history, and the Hamburg archaeologist A. A. Rhode who two centuries later declared such relics to be the only reliable evidence, capable of yielding more information about the country than the *Germania* of Tacitus – but in practice this was not the general approach. Up to the end of the eighteenth century archaeological finds were relegated to the role of passive additional evidence, illustrations taken from cultural history to supplement the evidence of the written sources.

'Local' archaeology, once it had achieved results, had to overcome the odium of being 'collectors' curiosities' that still clung to prehistoric finds, and integrate prehistory into history proper. The latter task was first explicitly deal with in Central Europe by J. G. von Eccard in his *Introductio ad Historiam Germaniae* (1712, republished up to 1750). Inspired by the philosopher and historian Leibniz, Eccard divided the history of the world into six sections, the first of which he called 'historia obscura' and defined as from the creation of the world up to the reign of Julius Caesar.

The first homes of antiquities were the private collections of notable political figures, churchmen and scholars, called in the fashion of the time 'cabinets of rarities and curious objects'. Archaeological finds relating to prehistoric and to classical times had already found their place in these collections during the Middle Ages, but the trend towards scholarly discrimination in the choice of 'curiosities' was the result of Italian Renaissance influences in the sixteenth century. The dominant features of these collections, at first, were classical finds from Italy and the Roman provinces, often brought from great distances. In 1508, for instance, finds from the Roman *castellum* of Roomburg near Leiden in Holland were brought to enrich the collection of the Hapsburg emperor Maximilian I.

The Hapsburgs were the most insatiable collectors in Renaissance and baroque Europe. The collections of Archduke Ferdinand of Tyrol, in his castle in Ambras, and the cabinet of the Emperor Ferdinand I were famous in their time. The latter found its way later into the remarkable collections of the Emperor Rudolph II in Prague Castle; they were unique both in extent and variety, and included many archaeological finds, some deliberately sought by the Emperor in Silesia, others discovered in Bohemia, and of course archaeological material from classical Italy. Alas, soon after the Emperor's death in 1612, this priceless material fell victim to the Thirty Years' War.

There were of course innumerable smaller collections in existence, and some of them housed classical finds from the former Roman provinces. About the year 1520 a collection of Roman inscriptions was assembled in Salzburg by J. Thurmayer-Aventinus, while in Germany the 'Antiquarium' of Albert V, Duke of Bavaria, was noteworthy. In the second half of the sixteenth century a special home was built for them in Munich, and even Egyptian antiquities were included. North of the Danube, lacking the impulse of classical finds, collectors were slower to emerge, but here, on the other hand, native prehistoric finds were all the more important. From this point of view the collection of the Saxon Electors, in Dresden, was one of the most important, together with that of Rudolph II; the Saxon collection fared better than that of Rudolph, and today still contains items found in the sixteenth and seventeenth centuries. The Electors of Brandenburg were also collectors, attested from the year 1603. In the seventeenth century there

3. The first collectors: an early eighteenth-century German learned gentleman in his cabinet.

were also scholars with considerable private collections in Germany,
among them J. C. Olearius in Arnstadt and J. von Mellen, and in the
early eighteenth century L. D. Hermann in Silesia and Count Brühl in
Lower Lusatia.

We can form some idea of the contents of these collections from the
catalogues and inventories, often printed from the seventeenth century
onwards. The earliest manuscript catalogue in Germany is that of the
Dresden collection (1587); that of Berlin dates from 1605; and there are
several early seventeenth-century inventories of the collections of
Rudolph II in Prague. We know from these records that the royal
collections were added to by purchase, by command, and sometimes by
the results of royally commissioned research, as in the case of Rudolph's
finds from Silesia. Purchases were very expensive, as we can see from
the accounts of the Saxon court from the second half of the sixteenth

4. Private museums: the decorated pyramidal 'showcase' designed by L. D.
Hermann as the shrine for his collection of Silesian urns and antiquities (1704).

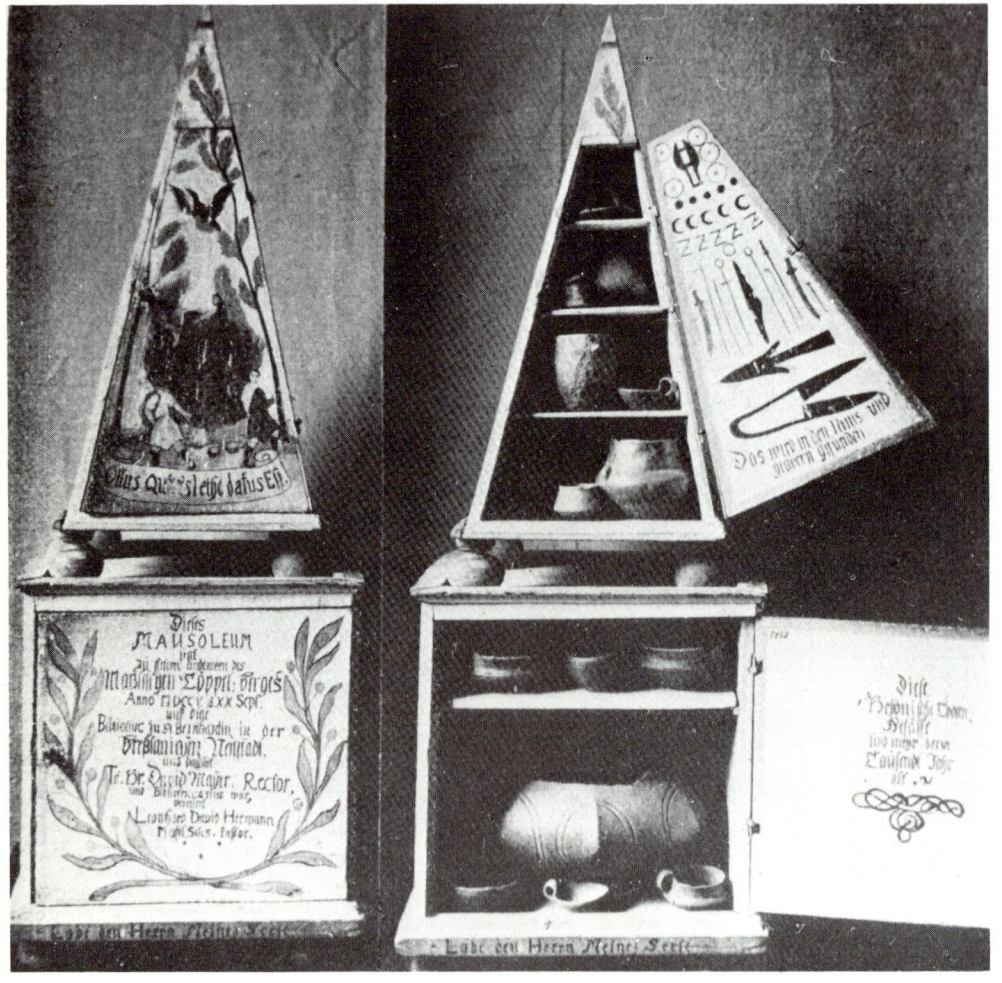

century onwards. In 1797 Frederick I of Prussia spent 100 thaler for a vessel discovered in Anhalt – an exceptionally large sum at that time. The price of prehistoric vessels was also artificially raised by such devices as setting them in silver or pewter. There is an amphora of the Lusatian culture, from the urnfield region, in the museum of Frankfurt-on-Main which has been treated in this manner (see fig. 5). The words 'Lusatian vessel' or 'Silesian vessel' signified an object of exceptional value on the market for curiosities at that time.

These aristocratic collections were shown only to the owner's guests, and were arranged to show off the rarity of individual items as well as the extent of the collection, according to the degree of taste of the owner. Only a few scholars' collections were arranged according to some system, or at least classified under the headings 'naturalia' and 'artificialia'. Even scholars, of course, collected as they could, assembling natural and historical items with no specialized aim in mind. Up to the eighteenth century specifically archaeological collections were practically non-existent.

5. Archaeological finds in the Age of Antiquarianism: a Bronze Age urn from Lusatia set in pewter in Germany (c.1560).

In the course of time, as the number of collectors increased and institutions began to take an interest in archaeology, the idea of protecting historical monuments and relics still in the ground was born. This protection took four principal forms.

The first and most ancient was the application of the monarch's claim to all finds of precious metals. With various modifications some of these medieval laws are still valid today (in England and Denmark, for example); in Central Europe, however, the principles were never so clearly formulated, and varied from country to country. In the Polish-Lithuanian kingdom, for example, where the rights of the monarch were limited, it was accepted from 1529 onwards that anything found on his estate was the property of the landowner, while finds on other people's ground were divided equally between the finder and the government. These regulations only referred, of course, to finds of considerable value, not to common archaeological items.

The second form of protection consisted of orders issued by the authorities and commanding the protection or collection of archaeological material. In 1595 and 1605, for instance, Rudolph II ordered the governor of Muskau in Lusatia to send any vessels found there to his collections in Prague. The third form of protection was of later date: the cataloguing of monuments with regard to their numbers and state of preservation. As a rule this applied only to regions where there were large numbers of standing monuments; one such venture was the inclusion of questions of an archaeological nature in the questionnaire drawn up to provide material for a history of Brandenburg, in 1712. The fourth method was to appoint officials – royal antiquaries – whose duty was to supervise monuments. These last were rare personal appointments, however, except in Sweden, and usually of short duration.

In Central Europe the Hapsburg monarchs appointed their personal antiquaries. Thus in 1556 Maximilian II invited Jacopo Strada-Mantuanus to Vienna; this Italian humanist, connoisseur of antiquities, numismatist and collector, had already helped the Fuggers of Augsburg to establish their collection, and also the dukes of Bavaria in Munich. In Vienna Strada used the existing collections to form the Emperor's 'Kunstkammer', for which he was nominated Court Antiquarian in 1566. About this time he published Caesar's *Gallic Wars* (1575). In 1577 the new Emperor, Rudolph II, called Strada to Prague, where he established and supervised the famous collections which, as we know, already included archaeological finds. His son Ottavio Strada continued his work, filling the post of Court Antiquarian up to the year 1607. By then, however, the glorious era of Renaissance Hapsburg collectors was drawing to a close.

All this was but the modest beginning to organized care of historical relics, and had no effect on the destruction or disappearance of object, especially those found in the field. Indeed, even finds which were incorporated into collections disappeared, in fact, from the sight of the few qualified observers, and after the owner's death they often disappeared altogether. Soon after archaeology became a matter for serious study, therefore, scholars realized that their work must be completed by publication of their finds and their collections, in book form or in the ever-increasing number of periodicals. The first publications on archaeology appeared in the sixteenth century; dozens were published during the seventeenth and hundreds during the eighteenth century; by the end of the century there were already thousands. Writers in Saxony-Silesia-Lusatia contributed the lion's share, and indeed scholars in northern Germany generally. By the end of the antiquarian period German archaeological publications alone had reached a figure over 2,000. (The quality did not improve with the increase in quantity, however, and much was repetition and plagiarism.) It was already essential to draw up a bibliography, and some writers attempted to include this in the scope of their works (e.g. D. S. Büttner, *Description of a Cremation Grave*, 1695; J. C. Olearius, *Mausoleum in Museo*, 1701; and J. G. von Eccard, in his *Introductio ad historiam Germaniae* already cited).

This early archaeological literature is of a double significance for us today. Not only does it contain a record of objects which have long since disappeared, but it also provides a picture of archaeology itself at that time, of archaeological theory and methods. It becomes clear that although the urge to study their finds emerged early on, archaeologists lacked suitable methods. The basic rules for the description of finds had not yet been drawn up; each object was treated singly, and the concept of the archaeological context in which it was found did not yet exist. The earliest method of classification employed was that of comparison, a simple comparison of the external appearance of relevant objects. The method was of course severely limited by the scarcity of 'pagan' items as yet discovered, and by the fact that very little of this material was actually available to the author in the form of notes made from personal observation or in the embryonic scientific literature. Little had been published as yet, and of the items published few had been illustrated, and even then rarely so well as to give the principal features of the object. The foundation of any archaeologist's treatment of his material was thus formed by his personal knowledge, his contacts with other collectors, and his acquaintance with the archaeological literature and also with classical literature, so frequently quoted.

The first extensive attempt at comparative study seems to have been made by J. C. Olearius in 1701, when he compared his own finds of grave pottery from Thuringia with those of Major from Holstein. Since Major attributed his finds to the Germanic tribe of the Cimbri, according to the accepted local tradition, Olearius was bound to regard his Thuringian 'analogy' as archaeological proof of historical reports that the Cimbri were present in Central Europe at the end of the second century B.C. These conclusions had of course very little to do with real archaeological facts.

Rare indeed were the authors who went from broader comparison of their material to the elaboration of the first morphological systems. As early as 1500 N. Marschalk had tried to classify the megaliths of Mecklenburg according to their shapes. As far as movable objects are concerned, a notable attempt was made in 1688 by G. Treuer, distinguishing urns (subdivided into large, small, ossuaria and lids) and funerary vessels for food for the dead (one- and two-handled jars, pots, pitchers, bowls, dishes and plates), in his Brandenburg material. Although his classification actually only recorded and arranged in terms which were in common use at the time, based on similarity in shape between the prehistoric and contemporary pottery, it was nevertheless one of the first important steps towards systemization of archaeology and the establishment of a terminology. It is an interesting fact that during the age of antiquarianism discussion of pottery ignored the question of ornament, which was thought to be an individual feature in the case of each vessel. Nor did any writer distinguish between vessels made by hand and those turned on the wheel.

The first attempts at classification did not, as a rule, try to establish a chronology, and indeed the idea of relative chronology had not yet emerged in archaeology. All 'pagan' objects were compared on the same basis. This is of interest because an awareness was already forming that prehistory, still defined by the Deluge at one end and Christianity at the other, was not a single unified period. During the Renaissance Lucretius had been rediscovered, and his poem *De Natura* published about the year 1500; and so had the even earlier work by Hesiod, *Work and Days*. Readers could not fail to note, especially in Lucretius, a clear assumption that there had been three successive ages in human history, characterized by the use of stone, bronze and iron, respectively. The application of this idea to archaeological chronology was slow in coming, and was pure speculation; undoubtedly reports by explorers that they had found primitive human societies which knew nothing of metals, contributed to establish the new approach. The first relative chronological line to be drawn – whether stone was used, rather than metal – appeared in the sixteenth century, to become clearer during the seventeenth and fairly widely accepted during the eighteenth century. Thus the way was being prepared for the Three Age System.

Relics above ground and below
It is certainly striking, from the geographical point of view, to note the concentration of important finds and antiquarian collections in the northern parts of Central Europe, between the Elbe and the Oder, in Silesia, Lusatia, Brandenburg and Saxony. It was here that non-classical archaeology first took shape in Central Europe, in what was as it were the 'promised land' of the antiquarians. The urnfields found there, and especially the cremation cemeteries of the Lusatian culture (in the broad sense, from the Middle Bronze Age to the Late Iron Age), sometimes comprised over a thousand graves, relatively near the surface in light sandy soil; in many of these graves there were two or three dozen vessels. From the end of the Middle Ages the urnfields were the chief source of supply for Central European collectors, and played the same role in arousing general interest in archaeology as that of the megaliths in northern and western Europe.

It is worthy of note that it was in northern Germany, the only area where the region of megaliths is in close contact with Central Europe, that one of the earliest writers to present a correct interpretation of these monuments appeared. In his *Pomeranian Chronicle*, written in the first third of the sixteenth century, T. Kantzow described the structure of megalithic tombs and the way the dead were buried in them, together with the arrangement of votive objects. On the other hand, as late as 1665 another north German antiquarian, Conring, wrote of megaliths near Helmstedt as the work of antediluvian giants! The megaliths were sometimes attributed to the Romans, sometimes to the barbarians after the decline of Rome, and even to the Slavs. In his *Methodus Apodemica* the Danish author H. Rantzau (d. 1598) included in the notable features of Mecklenburg 'gigantum strata seu lectisternia quae . . . Vandalorum coemeteria appellantur' ('giants' beds or pulpits which . . . are called cemeteries of the Vandals'). This passage attests the ancient popular words 'Riesenbett', 'Hünenbett' for the 'giant's bed', the contemporary scholarly view of the megaliths as the pulpits of pagan priests; and the existence of a popular term which can hardly have originated as a folk term, 'Slav cemetery' (German: Wendenkirchhof), later used to designate the urnfields. (The name of the Germanic tribe of the Vandals was considered at this time to be the ancient word for the Slavs, by analogy with the east German name for them, Wende; hence 'Vandalorum coemeteria').

In Central Europe itself the most striking archaeological monuments in the field were barrows, but they did not attract so much attention as megaliths. The plough soon laid them low in the cultivated fields, and in the woods they looked so natural that they passed unnoticed. The same was true of the earthworks of ancient forts – at first sight they looked like those of a much later date. Here and there an antiquarian noticed them, however, and as early as the first half of the sixteenth century we find J. Bugenhagen, in his *Pomerania*, describing Slav forts on the German-Polish Baltic coast; in particular he discussed the site of the once famous sea-port fortress of Vineta, at the mouth of the Oder. The Czech chronicler V. Hájek of Libočany (1541) referred to the Celtic oppidum of Závist, near Prague, as the seat of the ancient Germanic chief Marobud. Many other hill-forts, however, were regarded as sacrificial and burial mounds of the pagan world, right up to the middle of the nineteenth century, while other types of settlement were simply not recognized at all.

The most important relics below ground were of course graves. It is interesting that skeleton graves aroused little attention, perhaps because they seemed to resemble the Christian burial customs. They were frequently uncovered, but rarely described. Cremation graves were more popular, the antiquarians of the Renaissance having learned of them from references in classical authors to the custom of cremating the dead, practised by many ancient peoples. A. Ortelius, for instance, drew on Roman writers for his interpretation of cremation graves, in his *Aurei Saeculi Imago* (1546), but we can already find the correct interpretation in the Mecklenburg Chronicle of N. Marschalk-Thurius (1513). In 1529 a learned commission summoned to view finds at Sitzenroda in Saxony pronounced them as coming from cremation graves. The custom of using the word 'urn' for all vessels from real and supposed cremation graves persisted for almost 300 years from the sixteenth century onwards, in spite of the fact that the Brandenburg antiquarian G. Treuer, in his *Brief Description of Pagan Grave-Vessels* (1688), was already clearly distinguishing real cremation urns from other vessels placed in the grave with the dead.

In practice, of course, it was no simple matter to classify finds correctly; many cremation graves (especially when no urns were present) escaped notice, while a large proportion of the so-called 'cremation graves' excavated up to the middle of the nineteenth century were actually ancient pit dwellings or refuse pits. Thus the concepts of the cremation grave and the urn were theoretically known from the literature before the phenomena had been reliably determined among excavated material, and indeed before belief in 'magic crocks' had been eradicated from the popular imagination; this state of affairs was sustained by the vast number of cremation graves found in the urnfields between the Oder and the Elbe.

It was neither a simple nor a short-term matter to overcome this medieval superstition. Although pottery was the most frequent among archaeological finds from the sixteenth century onwards, 'ollae naturales' still survived in the minds of scholars, perpetuated by more than one chronicler (Miechowski in Poland, 1521; Kromer, 1577). In the middle of the seventeenth century a German theologian, J. H. Ursinus, even tried to find biblical evidence for the belief, while a century earlier the Lutheran pastor J. Mathesius (in a volume of sermons, *Sarepta oder Bergpostill*, 1562) put forward the 'magic crocks dug up from the earth in Bohemia' as proof of the omnipotence of the Almighty:

It is indeed remarkable that these vessels are so varied in shape that no one is like the other, and that in the earth they are as soft as coral in water, hardening only in the air. . . . It is said that there was once a grave on the spot, with the ashes of the dead, as in an ancient urn. . . . But since the vessels are only dug up in May, when they reveal their position by forming mounds as though the earth were pregnant (which guides those who seek them), I consider them to be natural growths, not manufactured, but created by God and Nature.

In the popular *Cosmographia* of Sebastian Münster, frequently published from 1544 (1541?) onwards, and often translated from the German, 'magic crocks' could be seen illustrated, but apparently according to the draughtsman's imagination. The idea persisted in a number of literary works into the seventeenth and even into the eighteenth century, while some scholars connected it with Aristotle's 'vis plastica'. Nor was this the only superstition surrounding this pottery: in the mining districts of Saxony gnomes were thought to make the vessels underground; we find them in the Meissen chronicles of G. Fabricius (1569) and P. Albinus (1589). According to L. Thurneysser, physician to the Elector of Brandenburg (1572), fragments of this pottery were recommended in the treatment of wounds.

The persistence of superstition surrounding prehistoric pottery is all the more remarkable since the true origin was already known in the middle of the fifteenth century (T. Ebendorfer in Austria, see p. 16) and its acceptance was not uncommon in the sixteenth century. As mentioned above, it can be found in the work of the Mecklenburg chronicler N. Marschalk-Thurius (1513), and in a letter from the Wroclaw (Breslau) humanist G. Uber to his friend A. Aurifaber in 1544. In his widely read treatise *Tractatus de Natura Fossilium* (1546), the famous natural scientist G. Bauer-Agricola explained vessels found in Saxony, Thuringia and Lusatia as urns to hold the ashes of the ancient Germani; the same view was held by P. Albinus, writing of finds from Marzahna in Saxony in 1589, by C. Schütz dealing with grave pottery from Pagan Hill in Gdańsk (*Historia Rerum Prussicarum*, 1592), by the Polish naturalist of Scottish extraction, J. Jonstonus, in his *Thaumatographia Naturalis* (1632), and later (perhaps influenced by Jonstonus) by Comenius in his *Orbis Sensualium Pictus* (1658), and by many others. It is worthy of note that the oldest illustration known to us of archaeological finds of pottery is a vessel reproduced in a collection of Roman inscriptions published at Erfurt in Saxony in 1502.

There were many medieval superstitions surrounding another widely distributed type of relic, stone axes and adzes; these superstitions persisted into the eighteenth century and survived in folk tradition right into the nineteenth century. At first scholars thought these stone implements were the work of Nature – for instance, the Saxonian physician and naturalist J. Kentmann in his *Nomenclatura Rerum Fossilium* (1565), which also contains the first illustration of these finds. However, G. Agricola had already declared in 1546 that 'thunderstones' did not come from the skies. The physician to Rudolph II, A. de Boodt-Boëtius, in his book *Gemmarum et Lapidum Historia* (1609), believed the stone implements were prehistoric iron tools which had turned to stone with age. That ground stone tools were artifacts was accepted in principle by the early eighteenth century; we may quote the contemporary author J. Oesterling, who cited Tacitus and the North American Indians in support of his view that they were the weapons of the ancient Germani (*Dissertatio Historica de Urnis et Armis Lapideis Veterum Cattorum*, 1714).

Other finds which must be considered are bronze articles. The word bronze did not exist before the chemical basis of the alloy of copper and tin was known, and various terms were used to describe it (copper, brass, metal). The function of these objects was usually explained in terms of classical literature. Knives and axes were explained as implements for preparing animals for sacrifice, as early as 1596, in the inventory of the Ambras collections. A. A. Rhode (1719) was the first writer to use the classical term 'framea', usually taken to mean a spear, for flanged and winged axes. Bronze pins were usually thought to be styles for writing on wax tablets. Some writers believed fibulae were badges of orders of chivalry, but Rhode compared them to Roman fibulae, and the term became generally accepted.

There were also coins among the archaeological finds to be classified. Those dating from classical antiquity presented no difficulty, but Celtic coins were also found, and their function and age remained unclear for a long time. Celtic coins entered archaeology shrouded in folk legends of 'rainbow gold' – discs or platelets of gold said to be found at the rainbow's end after rain; the superstition first appeared in the sixteenth century. During the seventeenth century it was in Bohemia that these coins were most frequently discovered, and here they were distinguished from classical coins and called 'barbarian'.

The many reports of finds in the urnfields and elsewhere in Central Europe should not be allowed to disguise the fact that altogether there were as yet very few finds. What was buried in the ground remained practically untouched during the antiquarian period, since the terrain was disturbed only to a small extent for the foundations of buildings or road-laying. There were a few exceptions: in 1688 G. Treuer wrote of thousands of urns being destroyed when the Frederick William Canal was built in northern Germany. But the buried archaeological treasures suffered more damage from treasure-hunters, people looking for building materials (in the case of megaliths), and occasionally from the elements – in 1573 floods uncovered and partly destroyed a cremation burial ground at Altenburg in Saxony. Such chance discoveries were not infrequent.

Of greater significance for the advance of scientific knowledge, however, were the systematic investigations in the field which became more and more important from the sixteenth century onwards, thanks to research into Roman sites. It would appear that the Mecklenburg humanist scholar, Marschalk-Thurius, who was a professor in Rostock, had already excavated the local megalithic tombs at the very beginning of the sixteenth century, but the classical field for Central European archaeology was of course the region of the urnfields. Two of the best-known localities were in Silesia: Masłów and Gryżyce. Georg Uber's letter mentioned above refers to finds from Maslow; on 1544, when belief in 'magic crocks' was at its height, he wrote: 'I have the impression that it is a pagan burial ground, where not having true urns, they placed in the ground vessels containing the ashes, the charred remnants of the funeral pyres, and the remains of implements not burned up, as signs of respect for the dead'.

It may have been hither that the knight, Otto von Neydeck, hastened in 1546, commissioned by the Emperor Ferdinand I to look for pots growing in the ground. The reputation of the locality gained most, however, from the local pastor L. D. Hermann, who, much later on, dug up over 10,000 vessels and described his finds in his book, *Maslographia* (1711). Rudolph II initiated excavation of the urnfield at Gryżyce in 1577, to add to his Prague collections; he took a personal part in the operations and is said to have lifted vessels from the earth with his own hands. The emperor had a wooden column raised on the site to commemorate the event – the first monument to the fruits of archaeology.

The excavation of barrows was a much rarer occurrence, but in a few cases was of considerable significance for the future of archaeology. When P. Weisse-Albinus, professor at Wittenberg University, explored the site at Marzahna in Saxony in 1587, it was perhaps the first expedition of its kind that did not set out to find treasure or curiosities, to enrich a collection or to satisfy idle curiosity, but explicitly to investigate in the field a specific archaeological question (to assemble evidence that the excavated vessels were man-made). The record of this excavation given by Albinus in his *Chronicle of the Land and Mines of Meissen* (1589) can be called the first proper excavation report in prehistoric archaeology. Later, the motive for undertaking excavations was often a historical one, as when efforts were made repeatedly, after the middle of the seventeenth century, to find the grave of the mythical father of the Czechs, Čech, below the mountain of Říp in Bohemia.

We know relatively little about the techniques employed in field surveys during the age of antiquarianism. It is rare to find such observations as those in the chronicle of J. Długosz or the letter of Georg Uber, who noted that after digging up pottery it must be left to dry in the open air, to become hard enough to transport. This item of practical experience from the urnfields is actually the first instruction based on practice in the field that is known in the history of Central European archaeology. It dates from a time when the discipline was still a private affair of amateurs, carried on by enthusiastic individuals for their own satisfaction rather than for scientific ends. They were drawn by the romance of discovery, as has been well expressed in such rare documents as the poem by C. Stieff dedicated to the memory of the Silesian archaeologist L. D. Hermann (1746).

These votaries of the antique were few in number, and their equipment simple; they worked surprisingly fast. Careful investigators were few, and interest concentrated on what was dug up; practically no-one bothered to record the archaeological context. As time went on, however, a few experienced antiquarians began to reflect on the

6. Archaeologists of the antiquarian period: digging in a barrow in northern Germany (J. H. Nunningh, 1713).

methods used and came to realize that the contemporary approach meant in fact the inevitable destruction of historical relics. At the beginning of the eighteenth century A. A. Rhode in northern Germany expostulated at those who destroy 'the whole of a lovely barrow, from its foundations, grubbing like swine', and was ready to show anyone who was interested the right way to dig. Personal instruction was not enough, though, and so the first printed recommendations appeared, such as those inserted by G. Treuer into his book published in 1688; he had excavated over a hundred graves in Brandenburg. About the same time archaeologists began to use graphic illustration of the sites they investigated. Following the first diagrams of megalithic monuments drawn up in western Europe, the first picture of a grave to be preserved was made in Central Europe. This was the view into a stone cist grave with face-urns, and was drawn by M. Lilienthal of Gdańsk (see fig. 7). Archaeological information also figured in maps at this type, like the Lubin map of the early seventeenth century which marked a number of Pomeranian forts, and the map of Moravia drawn up by Comenius in 1627 (see fig. 8) and showing the Celtic oppidum at Staré Hradisko near Prostějov, as a place where prehistoric amber had been found.

Prehistory as seen by the Age of Antiquarianism
The Renaissance brought with it profound changes in man's attitude towards the ancient past, as in other things, but that did not mean that

7. Documentation in the antiquarian period: this view into the stone cist-grave with face-urns from Gdańsk, North Poland (discovered in 1656, published 1724) is the first known presentation of an archaeological find *in situ*.

the old attitudes had disappeared. For the Church, in particular, the biblical account of the earliest history of mankind was binding, although more advanced views were gradually accepted.

The principal contribution of the Renaissance in this field was the 'classical' model of prehistoric times, characteristic of Renaissance thinking. The study of classical literature and of archaeological finds in Italy and nearby countries enabled the humanists to form a general idea of the life of classical antiquity – or rather, of Roman life – which they then applied to the life of the 'barbarians'. While it is true that classical authors also referred to the barbarians, as a rule they were not very exact in their observations and their interpretation followed the Roman model ('interpretatio Romana'). Archaeological finds from territories beyond the Roman frontier were also recognized, in time, as historical sources, but in practice they remained passive illustrations of the presumed reality of the classical model.

8. Archaeology on the maps: 'Hradisko ubi myrrha effoditur' – the Celtic oppidum of Staré Hradisko, north of Brno, on J. A. Comenius' map of Moravia (1627).

Some scholars presented a neat picture of prehistoric society in Central Europe, a society of 'classical' beauty and nobility; others were so biassed against the pagan world that they painted a dark picture of human sacrifice and other real and imagined barbaric aspects of prehistoric man and his way of life. While both these schools of thought drew a sharp line between the pagan and the Christian world, there were already scholars (and even theologians, like the German T. Arnkiel, 1703) who realized that the pagans of prehistory were the ancestors of the nations of their own day, and who therefore tried to stress the positive aspects.

The classical model of prehistory was a decided advance on the old biblical model, and in some quarters survived into the nineteenth century. Nevertheless the growing amount of archaeological evidence and the recognition of the real nature of some types of source material (such as stone axes and adzes) gradually brought about a realization that in spite of resemblances there must have been many differences between the society of prehistory and that of classical antiquity. Philosophical ideas of the gradual advance of humanity (Francis Bacon), and experience gained during voyages of exploration all contributed towards this change – although the latter was rather slow in reaching Central Europe.

The new ethnographical model which thus came into being assumed that in Europe prehistoric man lived at about the level of the primitive peoples of other continents at this time, and especially that of the North American Indians. The sixteenth century laid the foundations for this approach, which was applied more extensively during the two centuries which followed. The classicist admiration for antiquity, characteristic of the time, was, however, an obstacle to a more profound understanding.

The ancient Germani, like the Gauls and the ancient Britons, were compared to the Indians of North America (J. G. Hauptmann, 1760). By the eighteenth century the importance of overseas exploration for the evolution of the ethnographical model of prehistory was clear; it was stressed, among others, by the German poet Schiller in his inaugural address as professor of history at the University of Jena in 1789. By this time two distinct versions of the model had evolved: one of a poor society living in hard conditions, in a fearful struggle for bare existence – the version Schiller himself accepted; and the contrary one of a 'golden age', an idyllic society of unspoilt children of nature. This was the idea on which was based the moralistic ideal of the 'noble savage', – found in literature, for example, in the works of Montaigne and Rousseau, and in Germany in that of J. G. Herder – which became so popular in the eighteenth century.

This general outline of prehistoric society naturally could not suggest details to fill in the picture of man in his surroundings. An important step towards weakening the hold of biblical dogma was the realization that man does not stand in opposition to nature, but is a part of it. The majority of antiquarians, of course, had little interest to spare for the ecology and economy of prehistoric society; the only aspect of social life that attracted their attention was pagan religion, which tended to colour their interpretation of archaeological finds, especially those rarer objects whose function was not clear. Yet it should be remembered that 'native' parallels with the pagan world of East Prussia and Lithuania, still alive in Renaissance times, were ignored.

The few exceptions were noteworthy indeed, like N. Marschalk in the early sixteenth century, who judged the Mecklenburg megaliths to be the tombs of nobles while the poorly furnished cremation graves were those of servants; or A. A. Rhode, who thought it was a sign of the social standing of the deceased whether his urn was covered with a dish or simply with a flat stone. Such observations, however, were isolated comments in particular cases, and were not developed or generalized; they could not contribute to socio-historical theory.

However static, simplified and idealizing the ethnographical model may have been, and however uncritical the parallels it tended to suggest, it was of immense significance not only for the classification and interpretation of new kinds of archaeological material, but as a standpoint from which the general character of prehistoric society could be comprehended. Much time was still needed, of course, and much more factual information had to be collected, before the principle of ethnographical parallels could be scientifically applied. The Age of Antiquarianism was only at the preparatory stage.

The Clear Light of Reason: the Age of Enlightenment

The historical background: Central Europe in the second half of the eighteenth century

Eighteenth-century thought and scientific inquiry in Europe developed in the atmosphere created by western European ideas of enlightenment, particularly those coming from France. The trend came later to Central Europe, and did not become the dominant feature until the second half of the 'enlightened' century. The political scene was determined by the long-drawn-out antagonism between the old and the new power – that of the Hapsburg Empire and of Prussia; exhausted in the military sphere, and having signed a peace treaty in 1763, the two continued their hostilities in the diplomatic field. The other German states, formally linked in the 'Holy Roman Empire', were of little significance, while Turkey to the south no longer presented a real threat to Central Europe.

The states of Central Europe shared the common features of a feudal system based on agriculture, with poorly developed industries and those only in a few limited regions (Prussian Silesia, Bohemia, Lower Austria). The bourgeoisie was still too weak to exert any influence on the traditional ways of life and thought, although Central Europe was not closed to influences emanating from France and some other countries in the west. Here enlightenment had already taken root and flourished towards the middle of the century, with scholarship working to loosen the bonds of dogmatism in science and the arts, to establish reason and empirical knowledge as the principal forces and criteria of progress.

The ideas of enlightenment, particularly as far as government was concerned, aroused interest in the ruling courts of Central Europe, while the newly forming social strata for whom enlightenment, as an ideology, was intended were only slowly becoming aware of it. 'Enlightenment' was thus something imposed from above. Reforms instituted by benevolent rulers, mild though they were, were welcomed by the as yet weak bourgeoisie and by the common people, who saw the reforms as the only help against the traditional forces of society, the nobles and the Church.

Change came about first in Prussia, in 1740. The militarist despot Friedrich Wilhelm I, who said of the greatest German scholar of the day, G. W. Leibniz, that 'the fellow's not even good enough to stand on guard', was succeeded by Frederick II, the disciple and admirer of Voltaire. His stance of enlightenment, however, was little more than a fasionable affectation, for his policies both at home and abroad had little in common with the ideals of the philosophers. This was particu-

Map 4. Central Europe in the Age of Enlightenment (1789).

Academies and	2 Berlin	*Localities:*	10 Hradec
learned societies	3 Erfurt	7 Lochovice	Králové
mentioned in this	4 Görlitz	8 Langeleben	11 Gagers
chapter:	5 Olomouc	9 Gaillenreuth	12 Podmokly
1 Halle	6 Prague		13 Prillwitz

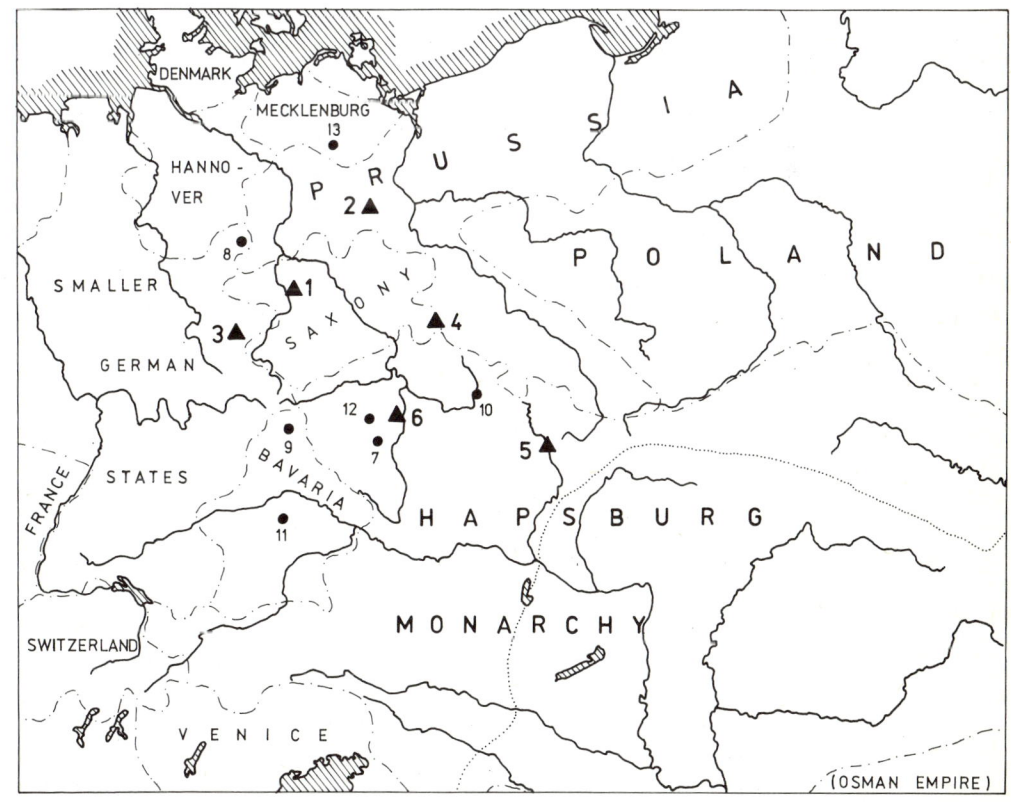

larly clear when he took the initiative in breaking up the kingdom of Poland, which was so torn by internal conflicts that there could be no question of an independent policy. The neighbouring powers struggled to strengthen their own influences, and finally decided to divide Poland between them. This happened first in 1772, on the Prussian initiative, and again in 1793. The unsuccessful rising with which the Poles replied to this abolition of their independent existence was crushed, and followed by the third division in 1795. This meant the end of a country whose last ruler, Stanislaw Augustus, was also an enlightened monarch, and where the ideals of the Age of Enlightenment had gained considerable influence among the nobles and the intelligentsia.

A much better example of the 'benevolent despot' than the King of Prussia was Joseph II, the Hapsburg who become Holy Roman Emperor in 1765 and ruled the Hapsburg Empire alongside his mother, Maria Theresa, until 1780, and then alone until 1790. Maria Theresa was a typical feudal monarch of the old type, while her son transformed his empire into an absolute monarchy of the enlightened kind, rationalized and bureaucratized, a state in which the ideas of enlightenment, modified to suit the specific needs of the situation, became the official ideology (Josephinism). Reforms were much more vigorously pursued than in Prussia, and not only encouraged the growth of industry and economic life, but even allowed a measure of free thought. The reforms inevitably made inroads into the old privileges and the property rights of the nobles and the Church in the different lands of the Empire, while systematic centralization of the imperial administration destroyed the traditional local features and privileges, and the introduction of German as the only official language meant that the languages of the non-German nations suffered.

The reforms instituted by Joseph thus met with opposition from many different quarters: from the Church, from the nobility (on traditionally patriotic grounds) and from the middle class (on grounds ranging from simple love of their own language to a reaction of national defence). Hungary in particular took advantage of Vienna's difficult military position to become somewhat less dependent, and thus avoided applying the reforms too consistently. There was strong opposition, too, in the lands of the Bohemian crown (Bohemia, Moravia and the remnant of Silesia). All these factors led to inconsistency in the measure of reform achieved, and in fact developments themselves limited the period of reform to the 1780s. It was not only the deaths of the two 'enlightened' despots, Frederick II (1786) and Joseph II (1790), that sounded a warning note; the explosion of the French Revolution at the same time showed clearly the dangers of relaxing absolute rule, and caused enlightenment to be viewed with suspicion. Many of the recently permitted benefits were withdrawn, and the nobles and the Church strengthened their positions once more. The common danger united the traditional rivals, Vienna and Berlin, and they became once again the pillars of the old feudal world.

The events around 1790 also broke the influence of enlightenment in Central Europe, never very strong and reflecting the weakness of the bourgeoisie, which was much more inclined to compromise than was that of France. In the struggle to come the middle class, fearful of revolution, supported the renewal of feudal despotism in the countries of Central Europe, replacing the cosmopolitan ideals of enlightenment with nationalism, the phenomenon which accompanied the birth of Romanticism during this period.

Science and scientific institutions in the Age of Reason

The age which set the 'light of reason' against the darkness of medieval and baroque superstition and prejudice based its philosophy primarily on the results achieved in the natural sciences. The sciences offered the most suitable forum for the scholars' aims of free research, the rational and empirical pursuit of bare facts, but their ascendancy also reflected the need to contribute to the development of the national economy, of industry, and of the new middle class.

Fundamentally, of course, this tendency did not favour the traditional antiquarian interest in the past, but a new trend in the historical sciences had emerged, committed to the intellectual struggle for enlightenment. In its methods the new school of historiography concentrated on critical analysis of existing knowledge, on the search for the truth, hidden beneath centuries of legends and error and dogma, and on the need to establish the original version of historical sources. In its theoretical stand it was at one with the philosophers of enlightenment, seeking in the past arguments for the present and the future, and bringing into history a new concept, that of evolution and progress. It was in this light that Montesquieu sought the 'spirit of laws' (1748) and Voltaire the 'spirit of nations' (1754); the history of civilization, so long neglected, was raised to the dignity of the foundation of history, and Condorcet finally worked out a general picture, however oversimplified it may have been, of the historical advance of the human mind (1794). The fact that Voltaire and his disciples stressed the importance of cultural history was not without its significance for archaeology, which presented one of the principal sources for that history. J.-J. Rousseau, on the other hand, took a quite different view of history; in some parts of Central Europe he was more popular among enlightened thinkers than Voltaire. Rousseau regarded the advance of civilization as a gradual degeneration in the human state, the loss of the original state of harmonious innocence. This modification of the Utopian ideas of a 'golden age', essentially romantic as it was, became as significant for archaeology as was the rationalist critical approach, because it aroused interest in the primitive stage of humanity and man's prehistoric ancestors.

Conditions were not as favourable for enlightened ideas and the enlightened view of history to the east of the Rhine as they were to the west. In Central Europe traditional historians still continued alongside the disciples of the new approach, and often won the day, collecting facts in the antiquarian tradition, with no critical assessment of their sources.

And yet we should not forget that for archaeology this was the time when J. J. Winckelmann was opening the eyes of Europe to the real significance of classical archaeology and the history of ancient art (1763), while the excavation of Pompeii begun in the 1730s was revealing the true picture of classical civilization and contributing to the birth of a wave of classicism. A typical example of the classically-minded enlightened thinker of Central Europe was the young Goethe, whose passionate interest in classical antiquities (inspired by a journey to Italy which included a visit to Pompeii) was a prelude to his active interest, later, in archaeology at home in Germany.

Often, of course, to visit Pompeii and other ancient sites in Italy was no more than a fashionable social event. The Emperor Joseph II himself went to look at them in 1769, and yet neither he nor any other Viennese exponent of Josephinism had any feeling for the past and its values. Not that they were against history, in principle; works on ancient history were written in those same circles, e.g. M. I. Schmidt, *History of the Germans*, 1778–85. They believed, however, that history should not attract good citizens' attention away from the present, and that it was only useful in so far as it encouraged even greater devotion to the interests of the state.

More fertile ground for interest in the past was to be found among the opponents of enlightened centralism, who came into conflict with the proponents of enlightenment because they preferred the traditional view of history to the rationalist and critical approach; an example of this conflict was the lengthy polemic among Czech scholars over the historical authenticity of the mythical 'father of the nation', Czech (Čech), carried on between 1761 and 1769. The traditionalists were also concerned with the spirit of the nation, but they sought its origins not in geographical or racial circumstances, but deep in the past, where the nation had its roots and whence it drew its strength. After the middle of the eighteenth century patriotism and traditionalism of a legalistic character evolved in Germany and in the German regions of Austria, but at the same time conscious nationalism, territorial and national patriotism, came into being. Against the utilitarian model of the protagonists of enlightenment a wave of interest in and sympathy for the old order arose, an interest in the traditional and specific character of each land and its people; writers began deliberately to idealize the distant past. J. G. Herder, the friend of Goethe and Schiller, did much for this trend not only in Germany, but throughout Central Europe, particularly by his *Observations on a Philosophy of Human History* (1784–91). Already in the mid-eighteenth century we find the outward feature of this trend in the first romantically conceived expressions of Neo-Gothic, which emerged alongside the classicism of the writers of the Enlightenment, who in their turn considered the very word 'Gothic' to be synonymous with barbarian obscurantism.

Tracing the evolution of archaeology in those countries of Central Europe where it was most advanced, we find north-eastern and central Germany to be in the vanguard, although at this period they were resting on earlier tradition, with no great personalities in the contemporary field. They were followed by Bohemia, where archaeology evolved in contact with German scholarship, and where achievements were again ahead of those in the German regions of the Austrian Empire; here it was mainly in Lower Austria and the Tyrol where archaeology developed, although principally concerned with Roman remains. In the Danube basin, both Austrian and Hungarian, interest was concentrated on finds dating from the Roman provinces for a time, and often only thanks to the interest shown by foreigners and by native travellers. F. Nicolai published an account of his travels in 1784, referring to the excavations led by General von Kettler near Vienna, and to his private collection.

The countries north of the Danube turned their attention to the archaeology of their own prehistory and early historical period. There were two notable personalities in Czech archaeology at this time, K. J. Biener of Bienenberg and J. Dobrovský. The former belonged to the traditional school of historiography, and in 1773 published the first survey of archaeological finds in Bohemia. Dobrovský, on the other

9. Archaeological publications in the eighteenth century: J. Dobrovský, 'On the burial customs of the ancient Slavs', the first scientific paper in Bohemian archaeology (1786).

I.

Ueber die Begräbnißart der alten Slawen überhaupt, und der Böhmen insbesondere. Eine Abhandlung, veranlaßt durch die bey Horin im Jahr 1784. auf einer ehemaligen heydnischen Grabstätte ausgegrabenen irdenen Geschirre.

Von Joseph Dobrowsky.

(Mit einer Kupfertafel.)

§. 1.

Auf die Frage: Haben die Slawen ihre Todten verbrannt, oder ohne Einäscherung begraben? sind die Antworten der Gelehrten noch getheilt. Unsere einheimischen Geschichtschreiber, wollen durchaus vom Verbrennen der todten Körper unter den Böhmen nichts wissen; auswärtige, als Ditmar, Bischof zu Merseburg, reden zwar von Slawen, allein nicht von allen, obschon der Mönch Alberich Ditmars Zeugniß, welches die Polen angeht, auf die Slawen überhaupt gedeutet hat. Wäre es nun nicht möglich, die sich widersprechenden Meynungen zu vereinigen? Wenn man annimmt, daß unter den Slawen der doppelte Gebrauch, todte Körper sowohl zu verbrennen, als sie ganz einzuscharren, beobachtet worden; daß also von einigen das in Wahrheit gesagt werden kann, was von andern mit Grund geläugnet wird, so verlieret die Glaubwürdigkeit der sich widersprechenden Zeugen nichts, und beyde Partheyen haben unter dieser Einschränkung Recht. Dieser Weg scheint mir nicht nur der sicherste zu seyn, die streitenden Theile mit einander auszusöhnen, ohne

T t 3   dem

hand, a scholar of European reputation and the father of scientific Slavistics, was a convinced believer in Josephinism, critically stripping bare the early history of his people not from lack of patriotic feeling, but on the contrary, out of the conviction that it was his duty to put before his countrymen 'the bare unvarnished truth, without being ashamed of it'. In 1786 Dobrovský published the first purely scientific paper in Czech archaeology, 'On the burial customs of the ancient Slavs' (see fig. 9).

In Poland conditions were somewhat more favourable than in the Hapsburg Empire, since King Stanislaw Augustus (1764–95) was a great connoisseur of classical and native archaeology; he himself instigated excavations and his example was followed by the nobles at his court. (The aristocratic character of Polish 'enlightenment' and archaeology was as typical as the bourgeois character of those trends in Bohemia.) It is not surprising that a plan for systematic archaeological research and for the establishment of a public museum devoted to it was drawn up as early as 1786 in Poland, although never realized. The cosmopolitan form of enlightenment was no more successful in Poland than elsewhere, against the nationalist standpoint put forward before the partition of the country (e.g. by A. S. Naruszewicz, *History of the Polish People*, 1780–6) and even more so afterwards. The ensuing time of deep national humiliation meant a break in the previous attitudes, bringing into being a new approach to the nation's past, one of idealization and heroization. In Poland, earlier than elsewhere, the emotional approach to national history overlaid the enlightened critical attitude with a new conception which was already that of Romanticism.

Slovakia, part of the Hungarian kingdom within the Hapsburg Empire, can serve as the example of a small country without its freedom and slow in awakening to nationhood; having no marked historical traditions, the Slovaks were only just beginning to consider their own past and their attitude towards it. Finding no suitable landmarks in their medieval or modern history, Slovak historians (serving the nation in the fight for its very existence, menaced by Magyarization) went further back in their defensive search for a historical identity, to the Great Moravian Empire of the ninth century. It formed the centre of attention much sooner in Slovakia than in Moravia itself. The historical works written in Slovakia during this period cannot of course stand up to the criteria of enlightened criticism, nor did archaeology have any role to play. When Dobrovský tried to collect reports of archaeological finds in Slovakia, in 1786, he found no-one capable of informing him. Indeed, archaeology struck no roots as yet in Hungary itself, although Hungarian thought was one of those more influenced by the ideas of enlightenment.

Not only the content, but the manner in which scientific research was carried on, had its specific characteristics in the Age of Enlightenment. The principal feature, and the bearers of new ways of thought and new paths in science, were the 'learned societies', which were the counterpoise to the atmosphere of the universities, still medieval in their spirit. In view of the general tenor of enlightenment in science, most of these societies centred their interest in the natural sciences. Learned societies and academies were established in the seventeenth century in the advanced countries of western Europe, in Paris from 1635 onwards and in England in 1645; in the eighteenth century they became the fashion at greater and lesser courts. In Germany the first was the Academia Leopoldina in Halle, Saxony (1670), followed in 1700 by the Brandenburg Electoral Scientific Society in Berlin, the foundation of the future Royal Prussian Academy of the Sciences (1744), and the Bavarian in 1759. The Society was set up on the initiative of Leibniz 'for the glory of the German people and the German language', but under the influence of Frederick II it became very French; while in the neighbouring Hapsburg Empire German officially replaced all the other languages, in Prussia it became the fashion at court to despise the German language and German culture as inferior to French. This francophile attitude persisted up to the end of the century, but was soon dissipated after Prussia was defeated by Napoleon. In the course of the eighteenth century regional learned societies and unofficial scholarly clubs arose and disappeared again. One of the earliest was the Academy of Useful Sciences established in Erfurt (Saxony) and functioning from 1754 to 1764. Archaeology was encouraged particularly by the Upper Lusatian Learned Society in Görlitz, founded in 1779.

Although the famous philosopher Leibniz was successful in Berlin, the fragmented condition of Germany did not provide the political backing necessary for his plan for an all-German learned society. It is of interest that Leibniz also considered making the Imperial Scientific Society of Vienna the centre for the sciences throughout the 'Holy Roman Empire', but this project, too, remained on paper. Vienna had little understanding for ideas of that sort, and probably the knowledge that suitable scholars would be hard to find also played its part. New plans drawn up around 1750 in Vienna also remained abortive. It was thus left to Bohemia and Moravia to take the lead in forming enlightened learned societies.

The first of a long line of such societies was the Societas Incognitorum, active from 1746 to 1751 in the Moravian centre of Olomouc, but enlightenment was not yet strong, and the society soon succumbed to the Jesuits and other traditionalists. Nor did the society take any interest in archaeology, although its founder and leading spirit, Baron Joseph Petrasch, had travelled in Greece and Italy and was a member of the academies of Florence and Cortona. It was not until the 1760s that the ideas of the Enlightenment gained strength in Hapsburg territory, and the centre of Czech scholarship was gradually formed in Prague with the Royal Czech Scientific Society which was taking shape from 1771. Although the Society was born out of Josephinist ideas, it gradually became the focus of anti-centralist Bohemian territorial patriotism. This influenced the members' interest in history, and archaeology also came into its own.

Learned societies were not founded in Poland until after the Partition. In 1800 the Royal Society of the Friends of Science was established in Warsaw, under the Prussians, and played an important role in developing Polish archaeology in the following Romantic period.

Like the university curriculum, collectors' activities were little affected by the ideas of the Enlightenment. The traditional attitudes of the baroque period persisted in the universities, although history had become an acknowledged branch of study at many of them during the eighteenth century. Collections, too, remained traditional in character, either prestigious or scholarly, but far from the idea of a public institution for educational purposes. Nevertheless the desire to collect archaeological material, even during this period, was often the impulse leading to exploration and the acquisition of important finds.

Independent of changes in ideology, theory and historical method, the number of publications dealing with archaeological material and its interpretation continued to grow. By the end of the eighteenth century Germany, traditionally the most productive area (taking into account the southern Baltic seaboard, Great Poland and Silesia), had seen the publication of about 2,000 papers, including those appearing in periodicals, increasingly popular in Central Europe from the middle of the century. Towards the end of the Age of Enlightenment the first independent regional archaeological bibliographies appeared (J. C. C. Oelrich, for Pomerania, 1771), as well as the first general bibliography (B. F. Hummel, *Library of German Antiquities*, 1787).

'Speaking documents' acknowledged at last

By the eighteenth century European archaeology had already passed through a relatively long evolution. Similarly, interest in ancient history had developed from the tales of chroniclers to a scientific conception of historiography – but there was no contact, as yet, between research into material sources and study of the written sources of history; archaeology and history followed their own separate paths. It is one of the positive contributions of the Age of Enlightenment that scholars began to stress the need to return to the primary sources, and that the importance of archaeological material as a material source for our knowledge of history prior to the broad emergence of written sources was finally acknowledged, at least in theory.

There were of course widely differing views, and the acceptance of archaeological source material was a long and slow business. Most historians regarded this material sceptically, and their attitude persisted right up to the early twentieth century. Others expected archaeology to throw light on the shadowy patches of history and to fill in the gaps. Those few scholars who were already prepared to give priority to the archaeological material in the modern manner now appear as real pioneers. In Central Europe this was the stand of the outstanding scholar of the Enlightenment, J. Dobrovský, the 'father of Czech prehistory', who pronounced archaeological finds to be the 'speaking documents' of our most distant past, documents capable of illuminating this as yet unknown period of national history even without the help of written sources. This was as early as 1786, and it is clear from the way he formulated his conviction that he was thinking primarily of the history of civilization.

The generally accepted attitude, however, is well expressed in this quotation from Germany in 1752: 'Here and there something unusual turns up in grave pots, and provides scholars with an excuse for discussion, but there are so many ordinary urns that no attention should be paid to them any longer.' The real problem was no longer insufficient material, but how to elaborate and apply the results drawn from that material, a problem which it was still too early to solve, and which therefore seemed discouraging. Even Dobrovský himself was not very successful in practice; it was not enough to recognize the importance of the archaeological material, and scholars had to learn to decipher it.

At this time, however, scholars were still enclosed in their studies and rarely if ever acquired their material in the field, by excavation. Such excavations as were carried out generally aimed at collectors' items alone. The first systematically organized and documented field investigation in Bohemia, for example, can be said to have been made in 1802–3 by J. H. Arnold, who excavated Hallstatt-La Tène barrows near Lochovice in central Bohemia. Dobrovský gave an interesting assessment of this campaign in the report printed in 1803, which in fact consists of an imaginary dialogue between a practical and a theoretical archaeologist, and gives as it were a compendium of contemporary Czech archaeology.

During the Age of Enlightenment scholars tried to popularize archaeology among a broader public (e.g. K. Kluk in his book *The Fossils*, published in Poland in 1781), but little new knowledge was deduced, and on the whole the level of the discipline remained where it was during the previous period. There were of course occasional finds significant not only materially but also for the stimulus they provided. Their exceptional character and the conflicting views they provoked led to scientific discussion, stressing the as yet unsolved problems surrounding prehistory, and the opportunities for solving them hidden in the archaeological sources. One such group of stimulating finds was the Celtic hoards of gold coins, particularly that of 1751, near Gagers, Bavaria, and the largest hoard of Celtic coins ever found, near Podmokly in Bohemia, in 1771 – the latter containing several thousand gold coins weighing altogether about 40 kilograms (see fig. 10). In the polemics provoked by these finds, especially the Czech hoard, the unknown coins were variously called Roman, Greek, Etruscan, Celtic, German, Slav, Avar, Arabian . . . The Podmokly find can be said to have started the first wave of wider interest in archaeology in Bohemia, but on the other hand the fate of the coins shows how little even 'enlightened' minds understood the significance of such a find. The Fürstenberg prince on whose estate the hoard was discovered was the first chairman of the Czech Scientific Society; he had almost all the coins melted down to mint others of his own, bearing his portrait.

Simpler finds from prehistoric settlements naturally aroused much less interest, and the observations made of pits on a site near Langeleben in north Germany, by J. C. Dünnhaupt (1778), are the exception which proves the rule. The lack of interest in searching for settlements was primarily caused by the apparently obvious assumption that our 'ancestors' had always lived on the sites occupied by present-day towns and villages, and that their homes differed little from the simple rural cottages of the day. It is interesting to note, however, that forts, the most noticeable type of settlement, did not arouse much interest either. Here the reason is more likely to be the habit of the archaeologists of the time of not venturing into the field. There was one notable exception, the foremost Polish archaeologist Count Jan Potocki, the first scholar in Poland to point out the existence and importance of forts, as early as the end of the eighteenth century.

Prehistoric man also made his home in caves, and here we must mention one of the greatest discoveries in the archaeology of the Age of

Enlightenment. In 1774 J. F. Esper, a Bavarian pastor, published the first scientific report on cave deposits, in which he proved that the human race dated from before the Flood, i.e. the Paleolithic Age. In 1771 human bones had been found in the Gaillenreuth Cave, together with the bones of extinct animals, in an undisturbed deposit. This was the time when mammoth remains in Germany were described as Roman war elephants, and ideas on the emergence and age of man were still bound by the fundamentalist biblical account. Yet Esper not only freed himself from narrow-minded theological views, accepting the objective facts deducible from the finds, but ably defended his opinions before the public. He was not successful in convincing them, however, because the time was not yet ripe, and his contribution to historical science fell into oblivion for many decades.

Graves, and particularly cremation graves, were usually paid more attention than dwellings. The urnfields of Silesia and Lusatia, in northern Bohemia and Moravia, remained in the forefront of archaeological interest and absorbed the attention of the scholarly world (in 1798, for example, A. Hirt gave a lecture on the subject at the Berlin Academy). Technical advance began to play an increasing part in helping to discover the graves; for instance, when the town of Hradec Králové in north-east Bohemia was to be fortified in readiness for a threatened Prussian attack, during the years 1768 to 1778, the clearing of large areas of ground revealed several urnfields; a large part of the finds were salvaged and published by a military engineer who later became regional governor, K. J. Biener of Bienenberg. Biener's three-volume work on Czech antiquities appeared between 1778 and 1785.

The archaeologists of Central Europe had a considerable quantity of pottery which could be studied, from the urnfields. Their interest centred mainly on shapes and ornament, but no writer succeeded in drawing valid conclusions for archaeology from the material observed. It was exceptional, for instance, that Dobrovský noted the technique used for the pottery, and concluded that not all vessels found in the graves were made specifically for funerary purposes. Under the influence of urnfield finds, scholars came to believe that cremation burial necessarily involved urns – but all vessels found in graves, and even shards found in pit dwellings, were considered to be cinerary urns; the pits themselves were interpreted as cremation graves or cremation pyres (*ustrinae*). Assuming that there was a single 'pagan religion', the evidence of two different funeral rites (cremation and inhumation, burial in the ground) caused some perplexity, and led certain authors to the view that the bodies were buried and the garments and funerary votive offerings burned. Others thought the different rites belonged to different tribes or nations, and tried to assign the finds accordingly. However, they were far from agreement when it came to attributing one or other rite (or a double rite) to specific ethnic groups. In general, of course, the question of religious ritual and burial customs was the most popular subject for research, and interpretations of the material were coloured by the writings of classical antiquity.

There was one special type of 'find' that appeared in the eighteenth century as the harbinger of Romanticism: supposed or forged evidence concerning pagan religion. The less this material had to do with actual

10. Archaeological finds in the Age of Enlightenment: 'barbarian' substitutes for the real classical antiquity: the largest hoard of Celtic gold coins ever found, from Podmokly, Bohemia, published in 1771.

fact, the greater the interest it aroused and the fiercer the debates that raged round it, for there was still so little known on the subject that it was indeed difficult to keep an open and critical mind when faced with such fabrications. The most important instance, which bedevilled Central European archaeology even as late as the mid-nineteenth century, was that of the Prillwitz idols from Mecklenburg. The fantastic picture of the pagan mythology of the ancient Slavs in the Elbe basin and on the Baltic coast, and of the ancient Prussians and Lithuanians, as it was created by chroniclers from the Middle Ages onwards, inspired the fabrication of a series of bizarre artifacts said to be pagan idols and even

to have 'Slav runes' carved on them (see fig. 12). As discovered much later, they were actually made by a goldsmith called Sponholz from the town of Neubrandenburg. His idols appeared on the scene in the 1760s and figured in dozens of polemic articles, as well as in an extensive monograph by A. G. Masch (1771); opponents appeared as rapidly as supporters. In the 1770s the whole affair quietened down without any conclusions having been reached, and it was not until the Romantic movement got under way that it was revived, principally by Count Potocki, in his book published in 1795. Thereafter the idols had quite a long life.

11. Archaeological maps: Prince Jablonowski's Polish map of ancient Central Europe, decorated with a small picture of the then famous urn from Maslow bearing a false inscription in Latin (1748).

12. Archaeological forgeries: 'Perun', one of the famous so-called 'Idols of Rethra' (Prillwitz), made in northern Germany in the eighteenth century.

These were the different types of archaeological material which were newly examined in the Age of Enlightenment. There was practically nothing new, however, in the way this material was interpreted, in the working methods used. Relative and absolute chronology had not progressed beyond the stage of the Age of Antiquarianism. There were only a few individuals who realized the vastness of the periods of time involved, such as C. G. Heinrich, who suggested in his history of Germany (1787) that the Germani might have been living in Germany a thousand years before the time of Tacitus, the chief informant about ancient Germany. Dobrovský, too, assumed in 1788 and later that the Slavs had already had a long evolution before they moved into Central Europe. At first he thought their homeland had been in the eastern Baltic region, but later he concluded it was between the Dnieper and the Volga. By the end of the eighteenth century it had become clear to him that all the archaeological finds in Bohemia could not possibly be attributed to the Slavs. The Tyrolean historian A. Roschmann assumed (1744, 1756) that Austria had been settled by the Celts before the Romans came, and that there were Celtic remains to be found there. In Bohemia Biener of Bieneberg tried in 1780 to distinguish Germanic from Slav pottery; his conclusions were incorrect, because the pottery he was studying came from the Lusatian urnfields, of the Bronze Age and Hallstatt period.

Towards the end of the century the possibility of distinguishing the archaeological remains attributable to specific ethnic groups or tribes became a matter for increasing speculation, but nothing at all reliable was devised. K. G. Rössig, for instance, in his *German Antiquities* (1797), declared that the characteristics of the Germanic tribes could be determined from their urns and barrows, but the only conclusion he reached was that 'the urns of the Westphalians and Thuringians had handles and lids'.

In practice, of course, the antiquarians did not bother to prove their contentions, and simply attributed their finds to peoples and tribes attested in that particular territory in classical antiquity or the early historical period. According to this system even stone implements were attributed to the ancient Germani or to the Slavs, and it was assumed that knowledge of metalworking was brought to Central Europe from Roman civilization at the beginning of the first millennium A.D. When K. von Dalberg assigned a relatively correct date to finds of Roman *terra sigillata* in central Germany, as early as 1777, it was indeed by mere chance, and was the exception.

Prehistory as seen by the Age of Enlightenment
The scholars of the Age of Enlightenment who set themselves the task of clearing away legends and fabrications from the early history of their peoples and countries soon found themselves in a difficult position. A critical assessment of the knowledge gained hitherto revealed that there was practically no reliable factual basis for that history. This discouraged most historians, and they dropped prehistory, but some turned to archaeology, previously neglected, to help in amassing what knowledge could be found. Thanks to them, by the end of the eighteenth century archaeology was being acknowledged as a scientific discipline.

The very modest sources at their disposal did not allow even those historians who were ready to use archaeological material to evolve a systematic account of prehistoric society, particularly since many of them were not concerned with cultural and theoretical evaluation of that material; critical editions and the 'purging' of sources became their principal objective. Other historians, even if they acknowledged the value of archaeological finds, in theory, nevertheless continued to approach their subject from the traditional historical standpoint. The thought of the eighteenth century was static, assuming that the world, created and unchangeable, was governed by a firm order and universal principles. Often the forces of nature and the physical laws governing them which had been elaborated by the thinkers of the Age of Enlightenment, were taken as the model for an understanding of history; history, freed from the domination of theological dogma, then fell victim to the dogma of rationalism. The only significant change in thought during this period was the acceptance of the new idea of constant advance in human civilization.

The very fact that archaeologists in Central Europe preferred analytical description of the facts to the formation of a synthetic picture of the past shows how small was the contribution of the Age of Enlightenment to all-round knowledge of prehistory. The conclusions drawn in the previous chapter, on the classical and the ethnographical model of prehistory, remained valid for this age too. The manner in which one or other model was applied depended on the author's general approach and his environment. Classicism, which formed public taste towards the end of the century, stressed the classical parallels, while ethnography was the main inspiration for those who, like Rousseau, were full of admiration for the supposedly simple and harmonious life of primitive natural societies, untouched by the harmful influence of civilization; or who, like Herder, sought the roots of their culture and of the 'spirit of the nations' far back in ancient history and in unsullied folk tradition.

The social sciences, with the development of enlightened thought, now began to form more systematic and fundamental ideas on the economic and social evolution of mankind. These ideas did not come from the antiquarians, but from historians and economists, accustomed to trace back to ancient times the roots of the contemporary state of affairs. Of the ideas which took root the most important was the theory of three stages of human society, based on the forms of subsistence: hunting, herding, and farming; we find this theory in Rousseau (1755) and later formulated by Adam Smith (1776). The serious thinkers of the time, however, were well aware of the complexity of the question and the dangers of treating it mechanically. The German philosopher Kant in his *Presumed Beginnings of the History of Man* (1786) stressed the significance of the 'great leap' from hunting to farming and animal husbandry, and thus first suggested the idea of the 'Neolithic revolution'. At the same time he realized that in fact the process may have been very long and slow.

This trend was typical of scientific thinking in the Age of Enlightenment, with its links to the national economy. The age contributed far less, though, to man's knowledge of prehistoric society. We have already seen, too, how ethnic problems began to affect archaeology in Central Europe, with the question of to which nation finds should be attributed, and hence who were the original inhabitants of each territory.

The latent danger of nationalism, so often to divide archaeology into hostile camps in the future, began to rear its head in the second half of the eighteenth century, with the rise of the middle classes in Central Europe. Indeed, as a form of reaction against the reforms of enlightened despotism, it also affected the traditional structure of society. Thus the Age of Reason prepared the ground for something which was far enough from its original ideals – a phenomenon which was to mark the whole succeeding Romantic period in Central European archaeology.

Our Glorious Pagan Forefathers: the Age of Romanticism

The historical background: Central Europe in the first half of the nineteenth century

The Napoleonic Wars brought the Age of Enlightenment to a close and also profoundly changed the state of affairs in Central Europe.

The new danger had drawn together two age-old rivals, Austria and Prussia, but to no avail. Napoleon's victories of 1805 and 1806 turned the two most important states in Central Europe into his unwilling allies, and the whole area came under the hegemony of France. The new order established in Germany by Napoleon meant the end of the Holy Roman Empire ruled for so long by the Hapsburgs; from 1806 onwards the monarch in Vienna was Emperor only of Austria.

When Napoleon attacked Russia, however, he drew disaster upon himself, and Prussia and Austria eagerly seized the chance to strike back at him. The Battle of the Nations at Leipzig a year later was the last act in the drama of French domination over Central Europe. In 1815 the Congress of Vienna succeeded in restoring the former balance of power and the Holy Alliance was formed to preserve for years to come the intimate collaboration of the most reactionary régimes of Central Europe, Russia, Austria (under the notorious Chancellor Metternich) and Prussia, which was only very slightly more liberal. These governments were underpinned by the system of feudal ties and maintained in power by a professional police force as well as a regular army. The lesser German states were allied in the German League, where it was again Austria that exercised the decisive influence.

Nor did the revolutionary year 1848 make much difference. In Central Europe, unlike the western part of the continent, the struggle was not only one for political freedom and social justice, but often for the nation's right to exist at all, for the right to self-determination, for national unity. The situation was all the more complex because the German and Magyar revolutionaries were unwilling to relinquish their belief that it was the right of their particular nation to rule over all the others in the Hapsburg Empire, an attitude which proved fateful for the outcome of the revolution. The feudal régimes of Central Europe were strong, the middle classes politically and economically weak, and the popular masses unenlightened. Deep nationalist conflicts made enemies of those who should have been allies fighting side by side for a common goal.

It was thus not too difficult for the forces of reaction to get the situation under control: in April 1848 the revolution was already over in Cracow, the heart of the Austrian part of Poland; in June the revolt in Prague was crushed, not long after the first great Congress of delegates from the Slav peoples had been there; in November the two capitals, Vienna and Berlin, were finally cleared of the threat. The Magyar revolution held out the longest, and was not crushed until the summer of 1849, with the help of the armies of Russia and of the smaller non-Magyar nations of Hungary whose right to independent existence was denied by the Magyar revolutionaries. The only permanent consequence of the wave of revolution in Central Europe was the breakdown of the feudal order, opening the doors to free capitalist enterprise.

The 1850s were marked by absolutism, particularly in Austria, and by the suppression of all civil rights. While Austria was becoming economically stronger, Prussia was advancing at an even faster rate. Although it was the most powerful of the German states, it remained under Austrian influence even after 1848, until Bismarck guided the country to political supremacy in the 1860s. Three wars helped Prussia to this goal. The Prussian victory over Denmark in 1864 was no surprise, but that could not be said of her victory over Austria in 1866, when the latter was aided by some of the smaller German states with Saxony at their head. The Peace of Prague meant the end of the German League and the end of Austrian influence in Germany altogether. Prussia finally became a great power in 1871, when she defeated France under Napoleon III, and Wilhelm of Prussia became the first Emperor of the newly proclaimed Second German Empire. United at last in a single national state (which, of course, had considerable non-German minorities in the eastern parts of the Empire) Germany took over the leading role in Central Europe.

The young nations

In between the defeat of Napoleon 'the great' and that of Napoleon 'the little', the political history of Central Europe was the history of states, but individual nations were already making their appearance within these states, and were making themselves heard as well. Some nations were tacked on to others, or some part of them, to form artificial super-states like the Austrian Empire; others, like the Germans, were split up into no less artificial states and statelets, or like the Poles, torn apart by force and annexed by powerful neighbours. These arbitrary divisions lay at the root of the growing troubles of the old monarchies.

The period following the French Revolution was marked by the growing economic and social importance of the bourgeoisie, and the ever more rapid decay of the feudal system. Country labourers, freed from their feudal bondage (a reform which was enacted by the Emperor Joseph II in Austria in 1781), were crowding into the towns, and the Industrial Revolution was under way. In this respect, however, Central Europe lagged behind the West; here feudalism was still strong and the bourgeoisie weak. Only a few regions were industrialized to any extent – the environs of Berlin, Saxony and Silesia in Germany, and in Austria the environs of Vienna and parts of Bohemia and Moravia. Elsewhere there were few or no changes, and it was not until after 1848 that industrialization gained momentum.

Besides these geographical factors there was the nationality question, which played a particularly material role in Austria The businessman who belonged to the ruling nation was closer to the authorities, was given preferential treatment, and found it easier to forge ahead; this made the gulf between him and his rivals among the underprivileged nationals even greater, and the latter felt they were being unfairly kept back. The struggle for equal rights, for a share in economic prosperity and in political power was the strongest moving force behind the nationalist movements of Central Europe after the fall of Napoleon – although an integral part of that struggle was always the fight for the right to use the mother tongue, the outward sign of national identity, and the right to foster the original national culture. The weaker the bourgeoisie of these smaller nations, the more significant was the role of the intelligentsia, moulding and nourishing the national spirit.

It was particularly important for those peoples whose political situation was oppressive to be aware of the ancient glory of their forebears – whether that glory was real or imaginary. And imagination ran riot, naturally, when there was little factual knowledge to build on. Here lay the roots of that typical phenomenon of historical romanticism, delight in the 'twilight of bygone pagan times'.

This is of course a very rough outline of the social background of romantic archaeology. It would be more accurate to say that there were as many forms of national movement and as many historical attitudes involved as there were nations in Central Europe. This applied equally to the great ruling nations. The Germans ruled in Austria, Prussia and dozens of smaller states and statelets, but scattered under so many feudal masters they were insignificant as a national entity. Their subjugation by Napoleon intensified the feeling of helplessness among German intellectuals and brought into being a passionate movement for the liberation and unification of the nation, drawing on the glories of the Germanic past. The prehistory of the ancient Teutons played a great role; the barbarian Germani of Roman authors were metamorphosed into the ideal embodiment of all the national virtues and took their place in literature, on the stage, and in the arts. Educated Germans longed 'like reindeer in the Spring' (to quote E. M. Arndt in 1816) to go back to the very sources of their nation's history, and to cast off the heritage of the eighteenth century. Before the war of liberation (1813–14) they had been full of admiration for the Romans, but now they glorified the victories of their Teuton forefathers over the legions of Rome. German archaeologists spoke of the times they lived in as the time of awakening and blossoming of archaeology. And it can indeed be said of the first ten years after the Battle of Leipzig that the foundations were being laid for a modern scientific approach to the prehistory and early history of Germany.

Before long, however, this nationalist movement led by students and intellectuals was suppressed, the initiative coming from the Holy Alliance. The great powers had no desire at all to see any change in the political situation in Central Europe, and it must be remembered that the idea of Pan-German unification also affected those parts of the Austrian Empire inhabited or ruled by Germans.

Archaeology as such was not substantially touched by these political events, but nevertheless the wave of interest in German prehistory subsided round about the year 1830, and activity was fragmented among innumerable local societies, isolated antiquarians and collectors. The second wave of interest, reviving after 1848, was weaker. It is true that for the first time in the history of German archaeology several nation-wide institutions were set up, but they lacked real viability. Little then changed until the end of the Romantic epoch.

The Magyars were not content with the German hegemony in Austria, for although the greater part of the population of the tradition-al Hungary, 'the lands of St Stephen's crown', were not Magyars, they considered themselves the ruling nation. There was little industry established in the country as yet, and it was the landed aristocracy that headed the nationalist movement. In the prevailing feudal context they were a powerful force, capable of standing up successfully to Viennese centralism.

Magyar nationalism, too, based itself on the nation's past. It was much less tolerant towards the smaller peoples than German national-ism was, and this stand did not weaken even during the revolution of 1848; indeed it contributed to the defeat of the revolution by uniting the Croats, Serbs, Slovaks and Transylvanian Rumanians behind the central government in Vienna, for the threat to their national culture and identity in the enforced unity of a single 'Hungarian' nation repelled them.

In the German part of the Hapsburg Empire it was the Czechs in Bohemia and Moravia who were the main opponents of the Germans, for the considerably smaller Slovene minority was only just beginning to awaken to nationhood. At first the Czech national revival, hastened towards the end of the eighteenth century by the increasing pressures of Germanization, took the form of defence of the national language and culture. As the Czech bourgeoisie grew in importance from the 1830s onwards, the focus of struggle shifted to the economic and political sphere, though with less success than was achieved by the Magyars. This became evident in 1867, when the Empire was divided into two parts, ruled by the Germans and the Magyars respectively, and called 'Austro-Hungary', while the Czech plan for a federal Austrian Empire was rejected.

History had a significant place in Czech nationalist thinking during the nineteenth century. The glorious era of the medieval kingdom of Bohemia, the great years of the Hussite Wars, had their message, and so did the 'prehistoric' Slavs of the legends kept alive by chroniclers from early medieval times. Long poetic forgeries came into being, in part to make up for the lack of Old Slavonic heroic epics, and in part to refute the German historians' biassed presentation of the ancient Slavs as savages. The *Dvůr Králové* and *Zelená Hora Manuscripts*, as they were called, were 'discovered' in 1817 and 1819, and recalled the *Works of Ossian* published in England. For almost the whole of the nineteenth century Czech scholars regarded the manuscripts as a reliable source for the early history of the Czech Slavs. After a long tug-of-war which often went beyond the bounds of scholarly argument, it can now be said that there is sufficient proof that the poems were a recent creation, although we still do not know who the author of the masterly and admirable literary forgeries was.

Of the non-Magyar peoples in Hungary it was the Slovaks who were closest to the Czechs. Linguistic affinities and the desire for strength through unity persuaded leading figures in Czech political and cultural circles to regard the Czechs and Slovaks as a single people; they found it hard to accept the fact that the Slovak nationalist movement went its own way after the middle of the century. It was a very weak movement, however, and fundamentally a literary one, formed by a handful of intellectuals to resist the constant threat of forcible Magyarization.

The strongest non-Magyar element in Hungary were the Croats, who were rapidly maturing both politically and culturally. Their centre was Zagreb, and it was the Croatian cultural institutions that were the principal propagators of the idea of Illyrianism, aiming at uniting all the southern Slavs (the Croats, Serbs and Slovenes), a movement which dated from the sixteenth century. Most of the Serbs lived under Turkish rule, however, and enjoyed a measure of autonomy which culminated in 1830 in the formation of a semi-independent princedom with its capital in Belgrade. In these lands with little or no industry and a great deal of political and cultural oppression, the southern Slav peoples had little chance to develop as nations; nor were the Rumanians in Hungarian Transylvania much better off. Their brothers on the other side of the Carpathians, in the lower Danube basin, had better luck. Thanks to conflicting attitudes among the great powers they managed to form an independent Rumanian state in 1862.

Once again the Poles were a special case. It was not until 1795 that this well-advanced western Slav nation lost its independence. The hopes the Poles had of Napoleon were not realized, and the Duchy of Warsaw he established very soon became a kingdom dependent on Russia, to be finally abolished after the rebellion of 1830. The national oppression suffered by the Poles under their Slav neighbour was no less severe than that borne by the people of Great Poland, annexed by Prussia. Relatively better conditions were enjoyed by the Poles in the Cracow region and Galicia, under the rule of Austria.

Poland was essentially an agricultural country, and the industrialists who emerged after the country lost its independence were for the most part bound to the new political situation. The ideas of Polish nationalism and statehood were therefore cherished mainly by the landed aristocracy, while the general masses of the people remained indifferent, and were ignored by the high-born patriots. This had disastrous consequences in the repeated failure of Polish rebellions. The aristocratic character of the Polish national movement was markedly different, for instance, from the Czech; the Bohemian aristocracy had been destroyed by the Hapsburgs after the 1618–21 revolt, and the Czech national movement of the nineteenth century was led by intellectuals from the professional class and petty bourgeois families who were much closer to the ordinary people.

This is only a very rough outline of the infinitely complex conditions in which the nations of modern Central Europe were coming into being. It is essential, however, to an understanding of why Romantic archaeology developed as it did, influenced to such an extent by national attitudes. On the other hand it must be granted that not all the extremist attitudes and political trends affected the attitudes and actions of the archaeologists themselves. Archaeology was a true child of the age, pulled in different directions by the urge to serve national aspirations, romantic passion for the mysteries of prehistory, and a critical search for historical truth.

Romantic archaeology
It is now necessary to look at what is meant by 'Romantic archaeology', especially in Central Europe. This is no easy task; the concept itself is a matter of dispute, accepted by some and rejected by others. It is certainly a trend in ideas rather than a clearly defined period, although we can roughly date the beginnings – growing from pre-Romantic roots – in the years following the Napoleonic Wars, trace its heyday in the 1840s and watch its decline in the 1860s. This means that the Romantic archaeologists were men born somewhere between 1780 and 1810, and nurtured on Romantic literature in their youth. At this time archaeology had much in common with literary Romanticism, for it sprang from the same social roots. Archaeology was the province of the middle-class intellectuals who were forming the programme and the principles of the nationalist movements; it played a part in their struggles, was influenced by them and influenced them in turn.

This inevitably affected the conception of archaeology itself. From being the pastime of rich noblemen and solitary scholars it gradually became a systematic science whose practitioners were aware of the social impact of their work and consciously put it at the service of their fellow countrymen. As yet there was little factual knowledge, and finds could be interpreted in various ways – and at this time, with the techniques of archaeological study in their infancy, interpretation was what mattered. These devoted archaeologists boldly idealized their prehistoric forefathers, to clear them of the odium of barbarity and place them on the same pedestal as the heroes of classical antiquity.

As always, there were chance discoveries to arouse wider interest in archaeology. In 1837 a gold hoard was found at Pietroaşa in Transylvania; in 1846 the vast burial ground of Hallstatt was uncovered, and in 1848 the 'Svantovit column' was discovered in Galicia . . . Of even greater significance, however, was the growing flow of 'ordinary' finds, the finds that provide the archaeologist with his primary source material, without which he could not vie with the heroic episodes of written history. It was the Industrial Revolution that set this tide in motion.

Digging the foundations for factories and railway stations revealed much, but the ideal hunting-ground for the archaeologist was the stretches of countryside through which the new means of transport were being laid – roads, railways and canals. Never had such vast archaeological trenches been cut through almost virgin terrain. The road network in the western provinces of the Austrian Empire was fairly dense, and the first railway to be built on the continent of Europe, originally horse-drawn, ran from Bohemia to Upper Austria (České Budějovice–Linz, 1825–32). By about 1850 there were several steam railways in existence, in particular those linking Berlin–Leipzig–Nuremberg–Munich, Vienna–Brno–Olomouc–Prague–Dresden, and Pest–Bratislava–Vienna.

Unfortunately the railway builders rarely bothered to preserve the immense wealth of archaeological finds turned up. A praiseworthy exception was the Czech engineer J. Perner, in charge of building the the Olomouc–Prague line, who turned a large number of finds from his site over to the National Museum in Prague. He lost his life in a tragic accident when the line was opened. There is yet another Czech whose name should be remembered here, the archaeologist V. Krolmus, who was perhaps the first to keep a systematic record of the routes followed by the new roads and railways, and did his best to see that the labourers on the sites understood something of the archaeological implications of their work.

The vast amount of material archaeologists were now collecting had of course to be classified. This could be done from the archaeological or from the historical standpoint. In northern Europe the former approach was used, for finds were fairly homogeneous and it was neither so difficult nor so urgent to present a historical interpretation. The result of this approach was Thomsen's system of the Three Ages: the Stone Age, the Bronze Age and the Iron Age.

In Central Europe the situation was reversed. The purely archaeological approach was made difficult for the scholars of the time by the great variety of the finds round this crossroads of prehistory, while on the other hand society had pressing claims on them. If archaeology was to be recognized as a 'national science' it had to contribute to the national endeavour – otherwise the public would lose interest. And the archaeologists of the Romantic era were more than ready to take their place in the social and even in the political movement for statehood. As early as 1843 J. E. Vocel had formulated the concept of 'Czech national archaeology'.

One of the basic assumptions for the existence of a nation is that its members are conscious of the historical continuity of a common past, and this is doubly true of a nation emerging anew or coming into being, and fighting for its identity. This is why historicism was so important in the nationalist programmes of Central Europe during the Romantic era. It was psychologically effective to draw comparisons between a glorious past and contemporary decline, and it helped to rouse the nation to work for modern goals. Those nations whose identity was not at this time threatened (the English, the French, the Russians, and even the Austrian Germans) did not experience such a fierce wave of romantic historicism, by far, as those nations who felt themselves endangered, whether large (like the Germans under the hegemony of France) or small (like the Czechs). Archaeology filled a greater or lesser role in this historicism in Central Europe, greater in the traditional German regions, where the first generation of scholars was coming on the scene, or in Poland where there was still a tradition from the not-so-long-lost days of independence; and lesser in Bohemia, where medieval history was a powerful rival to archaeology, still in its infancy. In the other countries of Central Europe archaeology did not play a significant role.

Essential to the make-up of the Romantic archaeologist was a love of the unusual and a longing for sensation, encouraged by the taste and the literature of the time. Literature sought its inspiration mainly in the Middle Ages, but themes from an earlier period, too, found their way into novels, stories and plays. The discovery of a prehistoric grave afforded excellent opportunity for the ever-popular meditations on the theme of death and the transience of all wordly things. It is no accident that interest in settlement sites did not grow until the end of the Romantic era. Reading the treaties of these Romantic archaeologists we are left with the impression that our far-off ancestors spent all their time in religious ceremonies and funeral rites, for this was the favourite interpretation of almost all the sites investigated.

It is not surprising that the Romantic archaeologist was not very critical in his approach. Even if he had not been influenced by the spirit and the demands of his time, he remained an isolated dilettante, in the best and the worst senses of the word; his interests extended over the whole of prehistory without distinction, and often took in the Middle Ages as well. There was little scholarly literature available and not much contact with other archaeologists. Even the larger antiquarian societies could usually only boast one or two really active members. There was, however, yet another characteristic which distinguished the archaeologist of the Romantic era from his predecessor of the eighteenth century: he was actively interested in field work.

Romantics in the open air

There was a great deal of the spirit of the age in the enthusiastic interest in Nature and in the landscape which transformed the scholar meditating in his study over chance finds, at second hand, into the Romantic archaeologist going out into woods and fields to look for his material. The great Polish poet A. Mickiewicz admired the founder of 'native' Polish archaeology, Count Jan Potocki, for 'having taken science out of the scholar's study into the open air'.

Surface monuments such as megaliths and barrows were typically Romantic and unusual features of the landscape, which is why they were so often imitated by landscape gardeners laying out manor parks in the fashionable 'English' style. In theoretical treatises on Romantic archaeology, however, these monuments and other finds in the field represented only one of the three more or less equally valuable sources; the second was the written evidence of classical authors and medieval chroniclers, so highly regarded by the previous age, while the third was a new source: folk lore. Romantic archaeology studied fairy tales and legends, folk songs and rural customs, seeking out their 'pagan' kernel, historical references, and evidence of the pagan view of life. In practice, however, most archaeologists concentrated on actual finds.

What interested them in the field? Primarily graves, those favourite subjects for the Romantic pen. Unfortunately there were not so many to be seen in Central Europe; megaliths occur only on the northern perimeter, near the Baltic coast, and their place was taken by a special type of grave described by F. M. Sobiesczanski in 1845, in the north-eastern part of Central Europe, a region known as Kujawy, in the Russian part of Poland. This of course did not mean that Romantic archaeologists did not spend a great deal of their time trying to find megaliths elsewhere as well. They were particularly assiduous in Bohemia, where as late as the 1860s the literature abounds in references to natural heaps of granite boulders, bearing a chance resemblance to dolmens. Menhirs were no less popular. It is true, though, that in the north-west quarter of Bohemia there are many isolated perched boulders whose age has still not been determined; this phenomenon, too, found its way into Romantic archaeological literature.

Barrows were much more frequent, but much less striking. In farming country many barrows had long since disappeared under the plough, and those which survived were usually well hidden in the depths of woods. At first they were discovered by accident, when woodland was taken over for cultivation. This was how the barrows near Lochovice in Bohemia, mentioned in the previous Chapter, were found. But it was the Romantics who first went out into the gloom of what they believed to be sacred groves, to seek the barrows which were to them what megalithic structures were to their colleagues in the north or the west.

13. Archaeological localities in the Romantic Age: a dramatic north German landscape crowned with a megalithic tomb (from a water-colour by W. Tischbein, 1820).

The most productive terrain was the wooded region covering both sides of the mountains forming the frontier between Bohemia and Bavaria. The larger barrow investigations on the Czech side were led by Count E. Černín of Chudenice, a disciple of J. Dobrovský and an oustanding collector of archaeological finds, mostly during the 1850s.

Flat skeleton graves were no novelty by this time, but the Romantics proceeded to excavate whole cemeteries. These were mainly cemeteries of the early historic period, with the graves laid in rows. In the 1830s the first large-scale investigations of Slav cemeteries of the ninth to the eleventh centuries A.D. took place (1834 Kopidlno, 1835 Prague–Panenská), while Germanic cemeteries dating from the middle of the first millennium A.D. were excavated in southern Germany (Fridolfing 1837, Nordendorf 1843, Oberflacht 1845), and in 1846 Ř. Volný conducted the first excavation of a Great Moravian Empire cemetery, dating from the ninth century, in Rebešovice.

The most famous find of all in the Romantic era, though, was the cemetery of Hallstatt in the Austrian Salzkammergut. The earliest record of 'heathen' graves here dates from 1710, but the bodies of prehistoric miners had been found in the salt mines as early as 1573. Digging for gravel in November 1846, a mining surveyor, J. G.

14. Documentation in the Romantic period: Isidor Engel, the skilled Austrian painter, recorded graves of the famous Hallstatt cemetery.

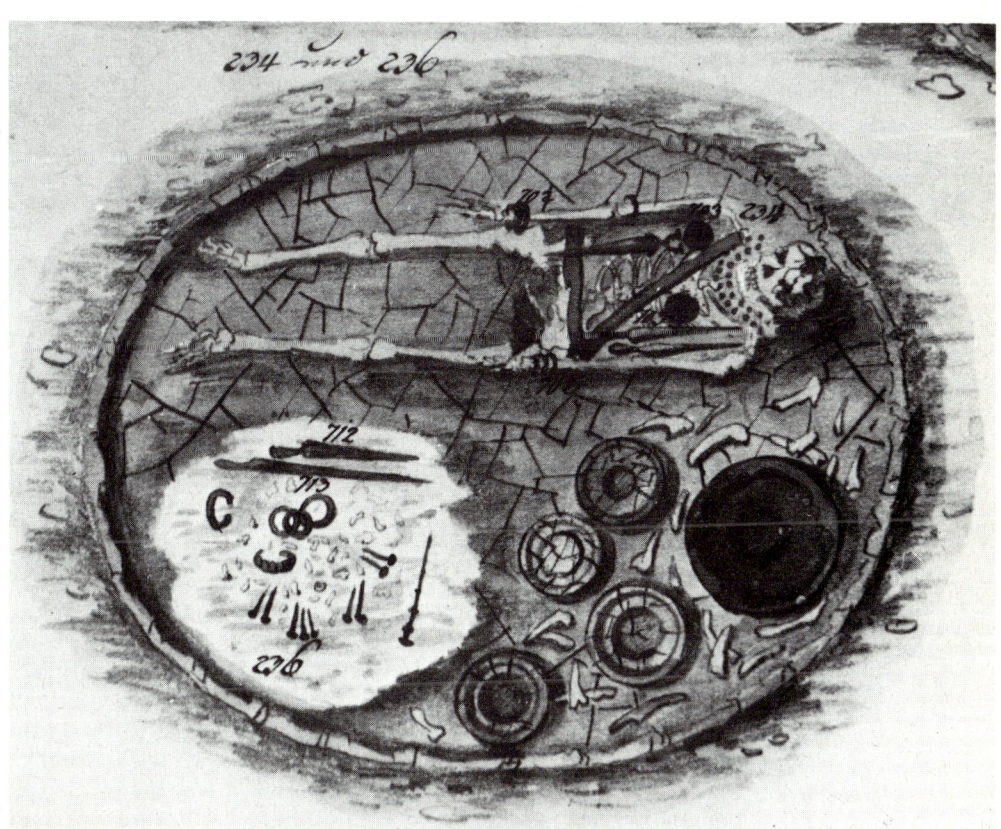

Ramsauer, turned up several graves which he took care not to damage. The following year he began an excavation, the results of which were analysed and published by J. Gaisberger in his book *The Graves near Hallstatt* (1848). This was the beginning of a research project which has had few equals. Ramsauer went on excavating until 1864 under the guidance of Baron E. von Sacken, director of the Imperial Cabinet of Antiques in Vienna. The Emperor Franz Joseph himself was keenly interested in the excavations and paid several visits to the site in person. Nearly 1,000 graves were excavated; the contents were deposited in Vienna and published by von Sacken in his *Hallstatt Cemetery* in 1868. The Hallstatt excavations revealed a prehistoric civilization previously unknown, but it was not until the following period that the significance of the finds became clear.

It was not often that a large cemetery of cremation graves was excavated. There were times when Nature herself did the work of the archaeologist, as when the Elbe flooded and uncovered several hundred cremation graves of the Late Bronze Age, at Neštěmice in north-west Bohemia (1845). Most of the finds from this urnfield were grabbed by collectors and dealers before a proper study of the site could be made.

Nevertheless, we find cremation graves mentioned frequently enough in the works of Romantic archaeologists, who often included dwelling and refuse pits under this head. In the Romantic era prehistoric dwelling-sites were practically unknown; pits and the foundations of dwellings hold little but potsherds and bones, and few people were interested in that sort of find. Nor was it clear, as yet, how these pits should be interpreted; the usual explanation was that they were cremation graves in which the darker filling was due to ash from the cremation bier. Alternatively, they were regarded as 'ustrinae', where the dead were burned. Other writers thought the pits were places of sacrifice, and the sherds and bones the remnants of sacrifices offered there. This approach was even applied to the cultural strata of dwelling-sites; when M. Kalina of Jäthenstein found a sequence of Eneolithic and Bronze Age layers, about 1m thick, near Slaný in Bohemia, he tried to calculate how long the sacrifical fire must have burned to form such quantities of ash.

There were of course theoretical treatises on what prehistoric man's home may have looked like, and occasional attempts to find it, usually unsuccessful. In the 1820s Büsching thought he had found dwellings when he discovered pits left by prehistoric quarrying on Ślęża (Siling) Hill in Silesia. The Romantic archaeologists were even less likely to recognize the purpose of the various 'workshops', which were much less frequent finds. It was only where a large quantity of any particular material was found that interest was aroused – as when F. von Hagenow discovered a chipped stone industry workshop at Lietzow on the north German island of Rügen, in 1828. H. Schreiber, in southern Germany, was writing of bronze foundries in 1842, but in most cases the finds were really bronze hoards, another category not yet distinguished. On the other hand, the Prague archaeologist V. Krolmus had excavated and correctly interpreted several iron-smelting furnaces of the Roman Iron Age, near Prague, as early as 1846. So little was known of the level of technology, however, that throughout this period it was the custom to deny that 'barbarians' had acquired the technique of bronze-working, and to declare as Italian imports all the more skilfully wrought bronze articles found north of the Alps.

It was special types of settlement that attracted the attention of archaeologists rather than ordinary farm dwellings: hill-forts, caves and pile-dwellings. Nor were hill-forts with their ramparts and moats always understood as dwelling or defensive structures. For a long time a Romantic explanation flourished, probably originating in Lusatia, that they were sacrificial and burial hills. In Lusatia and Saxony there had been a lively interest in the excavation of forts ever since the 1820s. M. Kalina, who was preparing a monograph on Czech hill-forts about the year 1840, was frequently in touch with Lusatian and Saxon colleagues. Kalina, who did not publish his work in the end, was inclined to see a primarily ritual purpose in the hill-forts, as did F. A. Wagner in Lusatia. The Saxon officer O. Schuster, on the other hand was more interested in their potentialities for defence. In the 1850s and 1860s Kalina's pioneer work was carried on by Czech archaeologists headed by two leading representatives of the Archaeological Committee of the National Museum in Prague, Professor J. E. Vocel and F. J. Beneš, who prepared an extensive survey of hill-forts in Bohemia.

While on the subject of hill-forts we must not overlook a specific problem of Romantic archaeology: 'vitrified forts', or hill-forts whose ramparts of stone and clay have been fired and even fused at some points. Since the end of the eighteenth century this curious form of rampart had been known primarily from Scotland, whence reports reached Central Europe especially after the publication in Vienna of a German translation of T. Garnett's book on his travels in Scotland, in 1825. The Romantic archaeologists began looking for vitrified forts in Saxony and Lusatia, where C. B. Cotta wrote about them in 1837, followed by K. B. Preusker in 1841. Then they appeared in Bohemia, where they were first reported on at the 1837 Natural Science Congress in Prague. The treatise on Bohemian vitrified forts published by J. E. Födisch in 1868 quoted a number of sites.

The most widely held view was that these forts were examples of a special prehistoric technique serving to strengthen the ramparts. Czech scholars from Kalina onwards, however, were more inclined to see them as the accidental consequences of the burning down of wooden stockades. In time this view was shown to be closer to the facts, and the once popular category of 'vitrified' forts disappeared from the archaeological literature during the second half of the nineteenth century.

Caves presented a much more hopeful subject for investigation, but they are confined to karst localities. In the eighteenth century caves were popular sources of fossil bones and in one case provided archaeological finds as well (Gailenreuth, 1771). Yet the Romantics showed surprisingly little interest in caves, even after the successful excavation of caves both in France and in England.

It was probably the influence of English excavations (and W. Buckland's contacts with the National Museum in Prague) that led to the first investigations of caves in the Bohemian karst near Prague, in 1824, during which archaeological finds were made. Later, however, interest shifted to the more extensive Moravian karst north of Brno. Here a physician, Dr J. Wankel, started excavations and in 1854 turned his home in Blansko into a museum of cave finds, and opened it to visitors. The first archaeological finds in caves in the Austrian Alps were at Badlhöhle near Peggau, in 1837, while in Bavaria there was a century of inactivity after Esper's discoveries at Gailenreuth, broken only by Engelhardt in 1866–8 – the beginning of a new era.

A new impulse, though rather an unusual one, encouraging interest in dwelling sites, was given by the now famous discovery of villages of pile-dwellings on the shores of the Swiss lakes (1854). The story of these truly sensational finds has been told over and over again, and when it reached Central Europe it was popular reading in newspapers and magazines for a long time. Archaeologists in Central Europe had hitherto known only urban settlements and military camps on the Danube frontier of the Roman Empire. Some of these, like Carnuntum near Vienna, had produced ancient objects ever since Renaissance times, while others were discovered and excavated by archaeologists of the Romantic era, like Schlögen near Linz, in 1838–40. Now it seemed as if the prehistoric equivalents could perhaps be found.

Scholars visited the Swiss sites and studied the finds, the first collections of which were finding their way into the museums of Central Europe. In the field, work went on almost everywhere along the shores of rivers, lakes and peat-bogs. In Germany work started as early as 1856 at Wangen on Lake Constance, and later on the Bavarian lakes, where the Swiss archaeologist E. Desor contributed his skills. In 1864 the Viennese Academy of Science sent Professor Hochstetter to search for pile-dwellings on the shores of Carinthian and Slovene lakes, but it was not a successful quest. The decisive year in this part of the world was 1870, when Count Wurmbrand made his first discoveries on the shores of Lake Attersee. (It was here that in 1910 a pile-dwelling 'skansen' was set up, a life-size reconstruction of a prehistoric lake village; during the First World War it suffered from neglect and soon afterwards was burned down during the shooting of a historical film.)

The fashion for lake villages spread to Bohemia and Poland, too, but all the discoveries turned out to be something else in the end. There was the extensive 'pile village' in Olomouc in Moravia, discovered by schoolchildren in 1864 when gas pipes were being laid. This was a highly popular discovery on the pages of scholarly publications as well as in the popular press, and the Swiss naturalists Heer and Rütimeyer studied material from the site. In the end the archaeological material turned out to date from different periods, and the piles to be the foundations of an early medieval town built on marshy ground. The Czeszewo site in Greater Poland, discovered the same year, came closer to being a pile village. It was a prehistoric fortified village of the people of the Lusatian urnfields, which had been preserved by water like the famous Biskupin site.

While the Central European pile-dwelling villages were real finds wrongly interpreted by the Romantic mind, the 'pagan shrines' were usually nothing but the product of the Romantic imagination, and as such, of course, a typical sign of the times. Antiquarians of the previous century had only talked about them, but the Romantics set out to find them in the field.

These shrines took various forms. Sometimes it was a hill-fort that was so designated, sometimes a storage pit. There were even 'discoveries' of complete shrines. In 1857 V. Krolmus published a book about his discovery of what he believed was the shrine of the supposed ancient Slav god of the underworld, Černoboh, at Skalsko in northern Bohemia. It was in fact a stone cellar dating at the most from the late Gothic period. The most frequent 'evidence' of pagan religious rites, however, was the sacrificial stones.

The interest in Central Europe in sacrificial stones, and particularly in cup-stones, was but a part of the vast wave of Romanticism that swept through Europe around the middle of the nineteenth century. Most archaeologists were convinced that hollows on the tops of certain boulders in some regions were the work of man's hands, and that they had served to catch the blood of sacrificial animals (and humans?) in ancient pagan rites. It did not worry them that these sacrificial stones were all to be found at fairly high altitudes, in thickly wooded country where there was no trace of prehistoric settlement, nor that the stone in question was almost always granite. Sacrificial stones had been written about in the West and in Central Europe ever since the late eighteenth century (J. A. von Riegger had previously described one such find, in 1792, in Bohemia), but had aroused little interest. It was after 1850 that the subject became popular, reaching its peak some 20 years later – one of the last outbursts of the Romantic imagination. Sacrificial stones were found in their greatest profusion in the mountains along the Bohemian–German and Bohemian–Moravian borders. It was not until the 1880s that the wave of fantasy entwining Ancient Slav and Ancient Germanic sacrificial altars began to recede, especially after H. Gruner of Berlin published his *Sacrificial Stones in Germany* (1881), and the fact that the 'cup' hollows were the result of natural weathering of the stone became generally known.

The same fate lay in store for the 'rocking stones' – another bizarre weathering effect on granite, where only a small surface of the stone is left resting on the rock beneath, so that it can be rocked. In the eyes of the Romantics these were sacrificial altars whose rocking motion was used by pagan priests to prophesy the future. This truly fantastic idea was not so widespread, however, and died an earlier death than the more stubborn superstition of the sacrificial stones.

Among the errors due to ignorance, which were later explained away, must be mentioned the 'idols'. Romantics gave the name to sorts of objects of strange shape and unknown function, objects which they could not date, but which aroused their imagination. The idols attributed to the pagans of Central Europe were most frequently metal figures which had originally formed part of medieval candlesticks or Renaissance lanterns, Romanesque aquamanilia shaped like lions or horses, and so forth. The most famous 'idol' in Germany was the Püsterich, a human figure in metal which was actually a gentleman's toy of the late Middle Ages made to illustrate the laws of physics, and was found near Sondershausen. The most famous find in Bohemia was a sacrificial bowl bearing the likeness of the Old Czech goddess Živa, as it was thought, found on Vyšehrad Hill in Prague, the traditional seat of the pagan Czech rulers. In fact this object was not much older than the Püsterich.

Among the Romantics the passionate urge to discover pagan idols knew no bounds. E. Raczyński carried on excavations at Gniezno in Poland with the sole intention of finding statues of the Ancient Slav gods, said to have been thrown into the lake when the land was converted to Christianity. He was not interested in anything else he found – and of course there were no gods. Others fared no better. That was why such excitement was aroused by the chance discovery of a stone column on the Austro–Russian border, on the river Zbrucz, in 1848. The column was taken to the Cracow museum where it can still be seen today; it bears a head with four faces, which is why it was thought to be a statue of Svantevit, a god of the pagan Slavs in north Germany, described in old chronicles. Although this identification is pure Romanticism, the column is nevertheless thought today to be one of the very few surviving monuments of religious significance from pre-Christian times, in spite of the doubts and suspicions of scholarly minds, both then and not so long ago.

The many reports of excavations by Romantic archaeologists naturally arouse our curiosity as to the methods used in the field in those days. One of the important advances made during this period was the introduction of methods of field survey, to discover and determine the site and to organize its protection, and to carry out an inventory of the finds and draw maps of the site. It was the Industrial Revolution that was responsible for this development, with its interference with the earth's surface on such an unprecedented scale. The main focus of archaeological interest, however, were the excavations which offered all the excitement of discovery, and provided antiquities of all kinds for private and public collections.

The more experienced archaeologists had already realized that not everybody who feels called to it knows how to work in the field. Few felt the sense of responsibility of the west Polish archaeologist W. Morawski, who wrote aptly in 1843 that 'to dig up an urn and not note down the circumstances of the find is sacrilege'. To prevent unnecessary losses the first guides to excavation were printed, and many writers incorporated good advice in their books, like J. G. C. Büsching of Wrocław (1824, following an independent article five years previously), K. B. Preusker of Lusatia (1829), J. E. Vocel of Prague (1845) and E. von Sacken of Vienna (1865). The Mecklenburg Antiquarian Society put out special instructions in 1837, in the form of a questionnaire reminding antiquarians of all that should be watched for and noted while excavating. This was also the purpose of a pamphlet issued in Berlin in 1835 for use of employees of engineering firms building communications, of the popular handbook of archaeology published by J. E. Vocel in Prague in 1845, and of the appeal issued by the Cracow Scientific Society in 1850 for aid to the local museum.

The rules laid down in these publications were of course pious hopes rather than an indication of what actually went on. Archaeological picnics were still a popular social event in the 1860s; the digging was all for fun and finds were distributed among those present. There is little record of how the actual work of excavation was carried on in the Romantic era, but it is sufficient for us to be able to form some impression.

The first surprising fact is the speed at which work progressed; it was not at all unusual for several graves or barrows to be excavated in a single day. This of course was due to the lack of interest in small finds, particularly in sherds, and to the perfunctory documentation. One of the most extensive archaeological campaigns of the Romantic era was Ramsauer's excavation of the Hallstatt cemetery. The Polish archaeologist Count K. Tyszkiewicz, who worked there in 1858, was amazed to see that every grave was carefully cleaned, sketched and written up for the record. The graphic documentation, which was entrusted to the painter I. Engel, was magnificent indeed. On the other hand we know that at least in earlier stages of the excavation potsherds and broken scraps of iron and bones were disregarded, and that some of the graves can no longer be reconstructed today. Nevertheless it cannot be denied that at Hallstatt the standard of documentation was remarkably high. Incidentally, this documentation has an interesting story. Ramsauer was the father of 24 children, and helped to keep the home going by copying shorter records and offering them to important visitors at the site in hope of reward. Many of them still survive, but the principal record disppeared in the last century, only to be found by chance in 1932, in a Vienna second-hand bookshop.

Apart from Hallstatt, really good excavation reports were rare. They probably meant too much plain hard work for most of the Romantics. The fact that the circumstances of the find may sometimes be more important than the object itself (as C. J. Thomsen had already remarked in 1831) was not generally accepted until the next period in the history of archaeology.

Archaeology becomes a scientific discipline

It is just possible for isolated scholars in their studies to indulge in scientific pursuits, but a branch of science implies a degree of organization, permanent institutions and premises, the possibility of publishing results and of training others to carry on with the work . . . all this was created for archaeology by the Romantic era, and from this point of view it is only just to call it the founding era.

Fieldwork improved not only in its professional aspects but organizationally as well. This was a slow process, of course, and at the end of the period most archaeologists in the field were still working on their own, mostly with a view to collecting. The rare working teams formed in Western Europe represented a more sophisticated form of private activity: Hoare and Cunnington in England, and later Lartet and Christy in France. A similar team, Stempkovski and Dubrux, worked on the Russian Black Sea coast around the year 1830. Another venture in Bohemia about the same time brought together a practical field archaeologist and a theoretical scholar who also provided the financial backing. The latter was M. Kalina of Jäthenstein, who worked with V. Krolmus; the results of their collaboration appeared as the first complete survey of Czech archaeological material, in Kalina's *Pagan Sacrificial Places, Graves and Antiquities in Bohemia*, published in Prague in 1836.

For a scientific discipline to develop properly, however, the acquisition of source material itself must be organized on institutional lines. In the conditions obtaining during the Romantic era this could only be done by scientific societies or by museums. There were several scientific societies of an academic nature in Central Europe, some of them founded as early as the eighteenth century, like the Czech society in Prague and the Upper Lusatian in Görlitz. Later, societies of 'Friends of the Sciences' were formed in centres of intellectual life in partitioned Poland: in Warsaw in 1800 (disbanded after the 1830 rebellion against Russia); in Cracow in 1816 and Poznań in 1857. It was characteristic of the situation in Austria that the Imperial Academy of the Sciences in Vienna was not established until 1847.

Archaeology had a place in all these societies, a bigger place in Poland and Lusatia, a lesser place elsewhere. Not much could be expected of them, however, for they were mostly loose assemblies of scholars from various branches of the natural and the social sciences, which could hardly provide a platform for intensive study of a narrower field. This remained the task of the institutions for which the collection of relics of material culture was of fundamental importance – the museums.

From the seventeenth century onwards museums had been growing around private collections, although the latter continued to exist as well. In Germany it was the basic collections made by field archaeologists that provided the nucleus of the new museums, while in Poland it was primarily members of the aristocracy who threw their own collections open to the public, like S. K. Potocki in Wilanów near Warsaw (1804), J. Ossoliński in Warsaw (1814), and Lubomirski in Lwow (1823). These men were inspired by the French Revolution, which threw open the gates of the Louvre in 1793, but they were also moved by the urge to strengthen the sense of national identity. The loss of the nation's independence was also the impulse for the establishment of the first private Polish museums of the Romantic era, the Shrine of Sybil and the Gothic House on the estate of the Czartoryski family in Puławy (1800 and 1809), concerned mainly with Polish antiquities. The largest collections of local archaeological material in Bohemia were those of Baron J. Neuberk and an engineer, J. Pachl, of Prague, followed later by Count. E. Černín of Chudenice with his collection in his Petrohrad manor house.

Collections of this type, particularly when they were made accessible to the public, were closest in character to the museums in royal residences created in the tradition of Enlightenment from royal collections. The Berlin Museum is a good example; in 1815 Frederick William III of Prussia, in the spirit of the late eighteenth century, decided to establish a museum, and from 1824 to 1829 the architect K. F. Schinkel was commissioned to build one of the first great museum edifices in the world specially designed for the purpose. It stood on an island in the River Spree, and was later called the Altes Museum. Inaugurated in 1830, the architecture bears witness to the classicist heritage; the columns of the façade imitate a Greek temple – as does the façade of the British Museum, begun in 1823, and that of the Hungarian National Museum in Budapest (1837–47).

Most of the Central European museums of the Romantic era, however, were linked with regional or local archaeological and historical societies, a characteristic feature of the German movement for national revival and its historicism. The first such society was founded in Bonn in 1814 in response to the idea sponsored by Goethe and many others: 'to nurture love for our common fatherland and for the memory of our great forebears'. Soon there were others in central Germany: Naumburg in 1817 (Unstrutverein), in 1819 the Thuringia-Saxony

Society for History and Antiquities (moved to Halle in 1823), and in the 1820s Wrocław, Leipzig and Dresden. There were many such societies by the middle of the century, of which several were of importance for archaeology, for example the Voigtland Society of Hohenleuben, founded in 1825, and the Society for the History and Archaeology of Mecklenburg, founded in Schwerin in 1835, in which G. C. F. Lisch was active. Most of these societies possessed their own collections, but these could rarely be dignified as museums.

As a result of the political situation in Germany it was not until 1852, when practically every German state already had its own museum or at

Map 5. Central Europe in the Romantic period of archaeology (1848).

National museums:	*Archaeological localities:*	11 Kopidlno	22 Hradec
1 Budapest	*University*	12 Fridolfing	Králové
2 Prague	*chairs of*	13 Nordendorf	23 Badlhöhle
3 Ljubljana	*non-classical*	14 Oberflacht	24 Attersee
4 Zagreb	*archaeology:*	15 Rebešovice	25 Olomouc
5 Belgrade	7 Vienna	16 Neštěmice	26 Czeszewo
6 Nuremberg	8 Prague	17 Pietroaşa	27 Vlence
	9 Cracow	18 Zbrucz	28 Strzegowa
	10 Hallstatt	19 Slaný	29 Skalsko
		20 Ślęźa/Siling	30 Mikorzyń
		21 Lietzow	31 Prillwitz

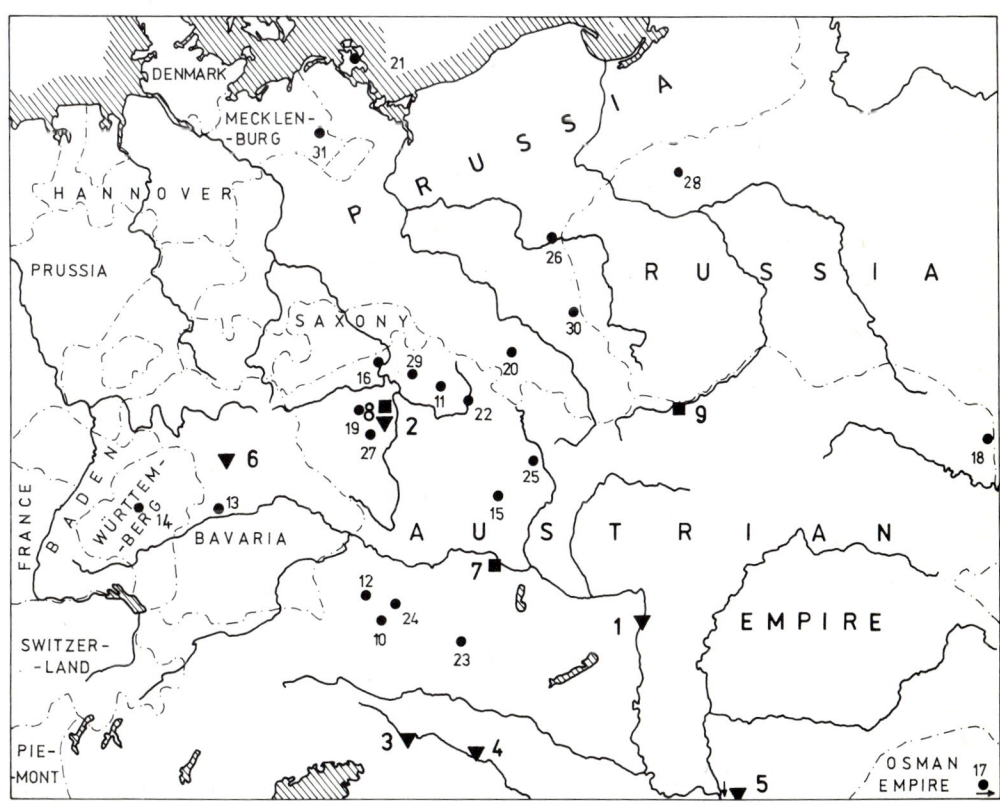

least its society collection, that a national institution was set up (the Union of German Historical and Archaeological Societies), and also a Germanic Museum in Nuremburg. At first this museum was no more than a private collection made by the first director, Hanns von Aufsess, and open to the public; von Aufsess was one of the Romantic proponents of a unified Germany, and was moved to transform his private collection into a public museum by the example of the Czech National Museum as reported by Goethe and King Ludwig I of Bavaria (Bavaria had its own 'national' museum in Munich from 1855).

The first Polish archaeological society was formed in Szamotuly in the Prussian part of Poland in 1840; it was a very active one, which led to its abolition as early as 1846, for the Prussian government had no intention of encouraging historicism in the non-German peoples. In 1857 the Society of the Friends of the Sciences was formed in Poznań, with archaeology very much to the fore, and a Museum of Polish and Slav Antiquities was established there at the same time.

This upsurge of German patriotic amateur societies did not occur with the same intensity in the Austrian Empire, where the government did not encourage German nationalist aspirations towards unity because of the threat they held for the integrity of the Austrian Empire itself. The museums that were established under the Austrians were of two different types, regional and national.

The national museum is the typical institution for the small nation fighting for recognition in the world; it is a psychological and ideological weapon, a centre for committed historicism and often the centre of the intellectual and cultural life of the nation. The regional museums were more in the nature of scientific *cabinets* attached to the administration of a given area. In Austria the role of the central museum was played by the imperial collections in Vienna, where archaeology came under the Imperial Cabinet of Coins and Antiques, headed by such scholars as J. von Arneth and E. von Sacken. In addition there were regional museums in the capitals of the German provinces of the Empire which also sometimes housed amateur societies for local history, geography and customs (Graz 1811, for Styria; Innsbruck 1823, for the Tyrol; Linz 1833, for Upper Austria; Salzburg 1834, Carinthia 1843, Vorarlberg 1858). The museum in Brno was similarly intended to serve Moravia (1817); the people of the province were Czechs, but Brno itself was the centre of a wealthy German bourgeoisie, and in this period the museum never transcended the bounds of German nationalism and purely local significance.

The non-German lands in the Austrian Empire, by contrast, were at this time setting up national museums which became lively centres of cultural and intellectual advance. In 1807 the Hungarian assembly decided to found the National Museum in Pest (later Budapest), based on collections donated to the nation in 1802 by Count F. Szechényi. The museum was opened in 1811, and from the outset archaeology held a prominent place in its activities, thanks primarily to finds of Roman remains in the Danube valley. The Czech nobility set up the National Museum in Prague (1818, opened in 1823), based on donations from the counts of Sternberg and other families; these were mainly natural science collections at first. Foundations were slowly laid for national museums of the Croat and Slovene peoples in Zagreb and Ljubljana respectively from 1821, while the Serbs had a national museum across the frontier in Belgrade, from 1844.

In Poland a national museum (in the pre-Romantic sense) had been discussed as early as the eighteenth century, but the partition of the country put an end to the plan. The Polish National Museum developed much later out of the Museum of the Fine Arts founded in Warsaw in 1862. The museum opened in Martin in 1863 was to have served the same purpose for the Slovaks, yet even these humble beginnings conflicted with the Hungarian government's plans for the Magyarization of Slovakia; the museum was closed down in 1875 and the collections moved to Budapest. Similarly the Rumanians in Transylvania only managed to establish local school museums, in Blaj (1850) and Braşov (1851).

The largest national museums were those of Pest and Prague, and they were also the most active in the pursuit of archaeology. The Hungarian National Museum formed an archaeological department early on (1814, although permanent exhibitions were not held until 1870), and from 1847 the department organized excavations. It was not until about 1840 that the original natural science character of the National Museum in Prague was broadened, mainly thanks to the efforts of the historian F. Palacký. On his proposal the archaeological collections were made independent in 1841 and two years later the Archaeological Committee began its existence as a separate section of the Society of the National Museum, headed by the poet J. E. Vocel, who was to become the leading figure in Czech Romantic archaeology. All the better-known archaeologists in the country were members of the Committee, which cared for the archaeological collections of the Museum and for monuments throughout the country, as well as for new finds. In 1846 the Committee began to finance excavation work and field surveys, and in 1852 started publishing an archaeological journal.

Elsewhere, too, archaeology was the subject of specialized attention. The Scientific Association in Cracow established an archaeological section in 1850, whose efforts resulted in the opening of an archaeological museum in 1859. There was another very active archaeological commission in Poland, that of Vilnius, the Lithuanian capital, where it also ran a museum; after the Polish rebellion of 1861, however, the Russian authorities closed the museum down. There was also an archaeological museum in Bavaria, at Munich (1867).

The care devoted to collections in the museums of the day was not excessive, and rarely went further than cataloguing of varying efficiency. There was no conservation of finds and the more perishable, such as iron objects, soon deteriorated. Bronze pieces were the most popular items, both for their appearance and because they were not perishable. As a rule only whole pottery vessels were kept, sherds being discarded.

It was the ideal of the museum custodian of the period to be able to put on display for the public absolutely everything the museum could boast of, and so there were no museum store-rooms. Besides the permanent collections on view, it was the custom from the middle of the nineteenth century to arrange special exhibitions of archaeological and historical monuments. These were very popular in Poland: Warsaw in 1856, Cracow in 1858 with a photographic album, first of its kind, Lwow in 1861, and others. The museums of Central Europe, however, were not at their best in the arrangement of their material. Unfortunately we have little pictorial evidence, the illustrations to the Cracow exhibition of 1858 or the Prague National Museum permanent exhibition of 1859 being an exception (see fig. 15), but the impressions of the most advanced curator of his day, the Danish archaeologist J. J. A. Worsaae, are explicit enough. He visited the museums of Germany and Austria in 1845, but only that of Schwerin, organized by Lisch, came up to his standards of museum management: the material was classified on the basis of the Scandinavian Three Age system, find associations were not disrupted, and different types of archaeological and historical material were not mixed up together.

The museums were centres where movable remains were preserved, but the Romantic era extended care to cover immovable monuments and material still hidden in the ground; the idea that this was national property and the heritage of all began to gain ground. As early as 1804 measures were taken in Mecklenburg to protect megaliths and barrows from wanton destruction, and in 1808 it became obligatory in Bavaria to report archaeological finds, and a reward for handing them over was offered from 1811 onwards. Another measure taken in Germany was the Prussian road law of 1835 which required a sketch to be made of all archaeological material turned up during road building. A similar law referring to material discovered when railways were being constructed was passed in Hannover in 1845. It was 1846 before Austria made reporting finds obligatory by law.

It must of course be borne in mind that law enforcement was not very effective in those days, and indeed there was only a superficial interest in regulations which were not directly concerned with state finances (it was a different matter when the earlier regulations about finds of precious metals were to be enforced). The laws protecting archaeological finds were thus of little practical value, and more was to be hoped for from the institutions established for the protection of historic monuments. In this respect Austria was to the fore, establishing a Central Commission for the Study and Protection of Historic and Art Monuments under the Ministry of Trade and Public Building; set up in 1850, it began work three years later with a network of surveyors in all provinces of the Empire, whose work was co-ordinated in Vienna. Although primarily concerned with buildings, this institution did much for archaeology as well.

The present survey of archaeological institutions has not yet referred to the universities, yet the omission is justifiable. The medieval atmosphere which still reigned in the universities was not conducive to scientific thinking, and archaeology was slow in finding a place there. Where it did exist, the subject was usually taken to mean the study of Greek and Roman 'antiquities' based on classical literature. Rarely did classical archaeology reach a higher level and an independent existence, as in Berlin (1832) and Tübingen (1829). Here and there, of course, there were professors who introduced the prehistoric archaeology of their homeland to the university curriculum, in the spirit of patriotic Romanticism; but they did so of their own accord, and only sporadically, like J. G. G. Büsching in Prussian Wrocław (Breslau) from 1815 to 1829.

In 1818 the first professorship of a new type was established; C. J.

Reuvens was the first to combine the two subjects of classical and prehistoric archaeology in his department at Leiden University in Holland. It was long before this official example was followed elsewhere; it was not until the middle of the century that two new university chairs of archaeology were set up in Central Europe, one in Vienna in 1849 and another in Prague a year later. Curiously enough, the first of these was devoted to Slav antiquities, a political gesture by the Austrian government in recognition of the work of the Slovak poet writing in Czech, J. Kollár. He was an uncritical Romantic in archaeology, however, and his period as professor in Vienna (1849–52) did nothing to further the field. On the other hand, J. E. Vocel, who held the Chair of Archaeology at Prague University from 1850 to 1871, was an oustanding archaeologist in his own right, seeking factual knowledge of Czech prehistory. At first Professor of Czech Archaeology, his field was widened in 1854 to cover archaeology as a whole (including also the history of art), and this chair can thus be considered the second of its kind in the world, after that of Reuvens.

Vienna and Prague had brought non-classical archaeology into the

15. Public museums: one of the two archaeological halls of the Bohemian National Museum in Prague as it would have appeared in 1859.

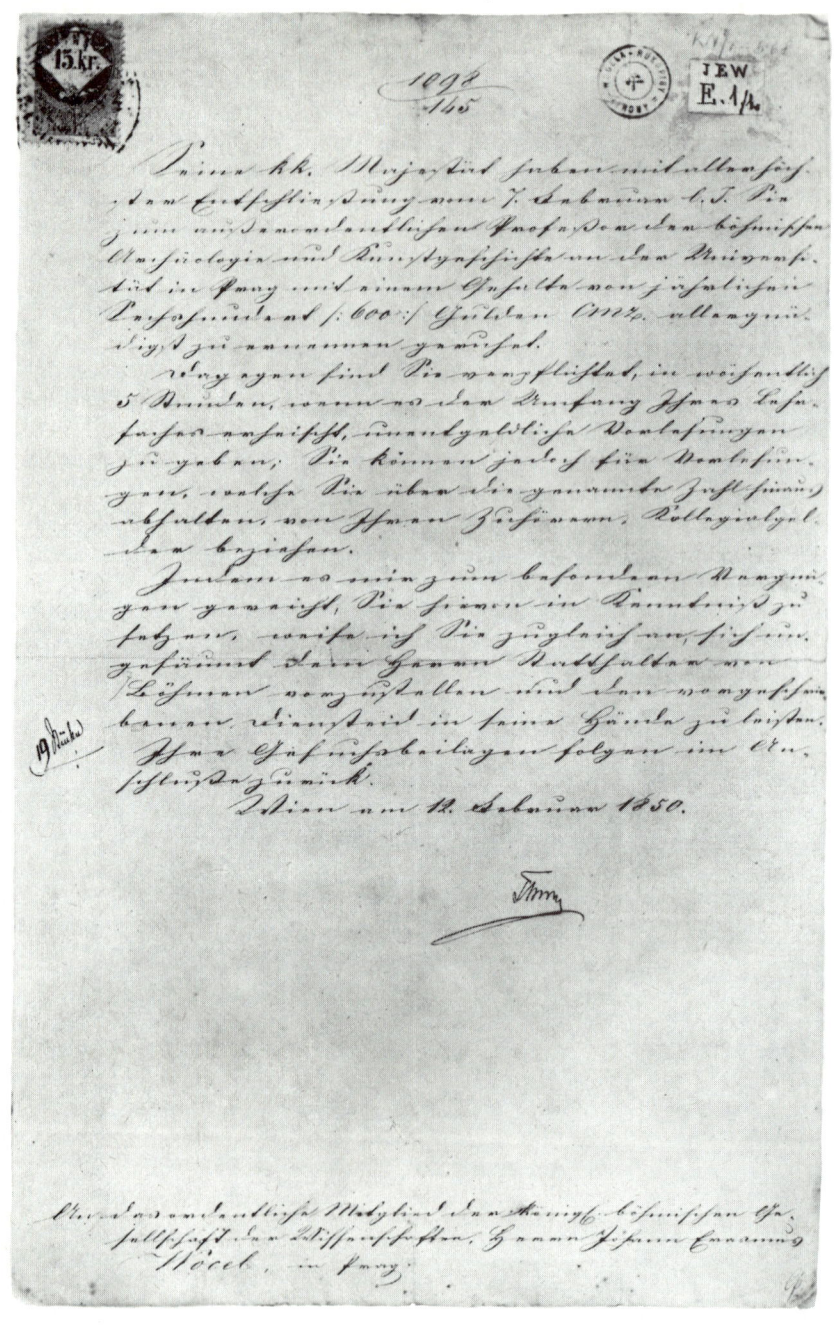

16. Archaeology in universities: by this *decret* J. E. Vocel was appointed the first Central European professor of non-classical, 'home' archaeology at Prague's Charles University.

universities, and Western and Northern Europe soon followed suit. J. Marsden was appointed Professor of Archaeology at Cambridge in 1851, Worsaae at Copenhagen in 1854 and N. G. Bruzelius at Lund in 1855. Cracow was the next town in the Austrian Empire to acquire a chair of archaeology, with J. Łepkowski lecturing at the Jagiello University there from 1863 and founding an important archaeological collection in 1866. It is interesting to note that Germany lagged behind, and that the University of Vienna, after Kollár's short tenure of the Chair of Slav Archaeology, did not establish a proper department of archaeological studies. This reflects the general state of affairs in archaeology during the Romantic era, with Bohemia well in advance of the other Austrian provinces both in the amount of work done and the level attained.

What contacts, then, were maintained between the Romantic archaeologists of Central Europe? This was primarily a question of

17. Archaeology in universities: the former Philosophical Faculty of Prague University. Here, in 1850, the first regular university lectures on prehistoric archaeology in Central Europe were given.

publication: as the ranks of the archaeologists swelled, so did the volume of their publications, although the standard did not keep pace. The first translations also appeared; at first scholars of the smaller nations – Danes, Poles and Czechs – published their works in one of the major languages, in order to reach a wider public, while in the second half of the century translations from major languages began to appear. The problem of language remained a serious one; while archaeologists of the smaller nations could draw on publications in the major languages, their own work remained confined to a small circle of their compatriots, and even when they appeared in translation, they did not reach a wide public. The 'great world' of archaeology was peopled by the British, the Danes, the French, the Swedes and to some extent the Germans, the Swiss and later the Italians. Around the middle of the nineteenth century the archaeology of the rest of Europe began to be excluded, although Central European authors followed their more famous colleagues' work and often had results to impart which should have been of interest to them.

The literature of the Romantic era of archaeology was already fairly varied. Works of a general nature were published in Germany (Klemm's *General Cultural History* began to appear in 1843) and in Austria (von Sacken's book *On the Prehistoric Cultural Epochs of Central Europe*, 1862). Important reference works were produced in Germany by J. G. G. Büsching (*Outline of German Archaeology*, 1824), Klemm (*Handbook of Germanic Archaeology*, 1836) and S. C. Wagener (*Guide to the Most Important Antiquities of Pagan Times*, 1842), as well as in Austria (von Sacken, *Handbook of the Knowledge of Pagan Antiquity*, 1865). A summary of Bohemian sites was published by M. Kalina (*Pagan Places of Sacrifice, Graves and Antiquities in Bohemia*, 1836), while J. E. Vocel produced a handbook (*Foundations of Bohemian Archaeology*, 1845) and a book conceived from the historical standpoint, *The Prehistory of the Land of Bohemia* (1866–8). Partitioned Poland also had its surveys of the archaeology of the various regions, in the *Galician Antiquities* of Ż. Pauli (1840) or E. Tyszkiewicz's *Review of the Sources of Local Archaeology* (1842). K. B. Preusker's work on Lusatia bore a similar title, *A View of the Prehistory of our Land* (1841–44), while surveys were published for the other German provinces as time went on. Monographs on single localities (e.g. Hallstatt) were rare.

The editions of source material were also directed towards individual regions, and often took a form popular at the time, in large format with full-page plates, frequently published in serial form. From 1820 to 1824 J. G. G. Büsching published his *Pagan Antiquities of Silesia*; from 1824 to 1828 F. K. H. Kruse's *German Antiquities* was appearing in Halle. Catalogues of museum collections were also occasionally printed, such as that of the Museum Friderico-Francisceum, the collections of the Grand Duke of Mecklenburg-Schwerin, in Ludwigslust, which was begun by Schröter in 1824 and completed by Lisch in 1837. Most of the printed catalogues of museum collections were much less elaborate, however (Berlin 1838, Prague 1859, Vienna 1866, etc.).

An important new feature in the Romantic era was the archaeological map. These were not yet cartographically accurate, but more in the nature of illustrations and aids to orientation in the field, but the mapping of finds in the region and annotation of the type or the age of the items provided essential information for the next generation of archaeologists to work on. These maps appeared first in German publications (F. K. Kruse, *Budorgis*, 1819; F. A. Wagner, *Temples and Pyramids of the Aboriginal Inhabitants of the Right Bank of the Elbe*, 1828). In the 1820s Z. D. Chodakowski mapped the hill-forts of eastern Poland; in 1836 Kalina of Jäthenstein published the first archaeological map of Bohemia. A map of the monuments on the island of Rügen was made by F. von Hagenow in 1829, and an *Archaeological Map of Bohemia* by A. P. Schmitt appeared in 1856. The Union of German Archaeological Socities had been discussing the mapping of German archaeological monuments according to the provenance, type and age of the finds, ever since its foundation, but the time was not yet ripe for such an enterprise.

Another typical feature of the time was the journal of archaelogical or historical and archaeological interest, mainly published in connection with the learned societies and museums. About the middle of the century the need for scholarly journals began to grow urgent. The publications of the learned societies and museums, as a rule, covered all the sciences with which the institution was concerned, and dealt with an entire region; there was little room left in their pages for archaeology. On the other hand, there were too few readers to support separate specialized journals. In the existing state of affairs it was most advantageous to publish journals dealing with both history and archaeology, or with historical topography and ancillary historical disciplines. In Germany the journals of the archaeological societies were mostly of this nature (especially the *Annals of the Mecklenburg Society*, the *Baltic Studies* published in Stettin, the *Variscia* of the Voigtland Society, and the *Bulletin for the Study of Ancient German History*, published in Nuremberg by von Aufsess 1832–39 and later, 1853–81, by the Germanic Museum).

For Austria the *Chronicle of Archaeological Finds* was the most important, published regularly by the Imperial Cabinet of Coins and Antiques, at first in the *Vienna Literary Journal* and then in the *Austrian Historical Archives*. The *Chronicle* covers the years 1840–66. *The Report of the Central Commission for the Protection of Monuments*, appearing in Vienna from 1856 onwards, also published archaeological information from all over the Empire. It was Prague that led in the Empire, however; the Archaeological Committee of the National Museum endeavoured to get a journal going from the 1840s onwards, and was at last successful with its *Archaeological Papers* in 1852. When this failed because it aimed at too narrow a public, a broader conception resulted in the *Archaeological Monuments* (*Památky archaeologické*) which began to appear in 1854 and is still going strong. In 1868 the journal *Archaeological Information* (*Archeologiai Értesitö*) began to appear, published by the Hungarian National Museum, and this journal, too, is still appearing regularly today.

The Three Ages in Central European prehistory
It was no mere coincidence that the system of relative chronology known as the Three Age System, which was the greatest contribution made by the Romantic era to the evolution of archaeology, should have taken its final form in Northern Europe. In this region (which can be

taken to include northern Germany as well as Scandinavia) archaeological finds were relatively homogeneous compared with those in Central Europe, where the mixture of remains left by many different cultures was complicated still further by the presence of the Romans on the Rhine and the Danube. Conditions were far from favourable for classification of the archaeological material, which explains the long persistence of the traditional approach in Central Europe. This approach was a simple division of history into 'pagan' and 'Christian', although the word 'pagan' had already acquired a more attractive sound for the nationally-minded Romantics seeking relics of their 'glorious forefathers'. The idea of the pagan age, however, was still very imprecise, and the 'age' was regarded as a single entity, with no subdivisions.

The first criterion for differentiation within the age was the realization that the different materials used to make tools and weapons had appeared in succession. The idea had already occurred to thinkers in classical antiquity, and was known in eighteenth-century Central Europe, but nobody had tried to apply it to the practical questions of archaeology. This was left to the Danes. It is well known that it was the historian S. Vedel-Simonsen who first clearly formulated the idea of the three successive ages, the Stone Age, the Bronze Age and the Iron Age, and that it was C. J. Thomsen who showed its practical application in his new arrangement of the collections of the Copenhagen National Museum opened just before 1820. He did not publish the system until much later, in Danish in 1836 and in German in 1837. This has often been cited as the date of the formulation of Thomsen's Three Age System, but it was widely known much earlier through correspondence and reports by visitors to Thomsen in Copenhagen. This must be borne in mind when considering the claims sometimes put forward for the German archaeologists who published the same idea (though much less explicit) at about the same time; they were J. F. Danneil (1835) and G. C. F. Lisch (1837). It is difficult to imagine that they had come to their conclusions entirely independently. M. Kalina of Jäthenstein, the Czech archaeologist, also attempted to distinguish stone, bronze and iron artifacts chronologically in his book published in 1836.

By this time, however, the Three Age System was no longer the property of Copenhagen alone; it spread rapidly throughout Scandinavia, where it was very suitable for classification of the local material. In Germany finds were more varied and the system less obvious in its application; there were also other factors retarding the German scholars' acceptance of what they scornfully called the 'Nordic' or 'Scandinavian' system – the long-drawn-out hostility of Prussia towards Denmark over Schleswig-Holstein, for example. Worsaae's critical book entitled *National Archaeology in Germany* made things even worse. Opposition was strongest in northern Germany, where the militant professor at Stettin, H. L. T. Giesebrecht, the Pomeranian archaeologist, attacked Lisch as early as 1838 for adopting the Three Age System. Leadership of the opposition to 'Scandinavianism' passed to C. Hostmann of Lower Saxony and the well-known L. Lindenschmit of Mainz; the latter had accepted the Three Age System in 1858, in the first volume of his famous *Antiquities of our Pagan Prehistory*, only to discard it later as out-dated. The Germans maintained their opposition to the system more or less to the end of the century, although the number and importance of the antagonists decreased.

Of the Slav archaeologists the Poles were closest to Denmark. W. Morawski brought the first report of the new system in an article (based on Lisch) printed in 1843. In 1844 T. Tripplin published his travels, including a description of the Copenhagen museum, and two years later the well-known archaeologist E. Tyszkiewicz brought out an account of his Scandinavian travels. It was at about the same time that the Three Age System was adopted in Bohemia; the custodian of the archaeological collections of the National Museum in Prague, J. V. Hellich, applied it explicitly in a manuscript handbook of Czech archaeology written in 1843. The German opposition to the system was long felt, however, in the Austrian Empire.

It was not easy to get the system accepted in Central Europe, and this meant that Lubbock's later suggestion that the Stone Age should be divided into Paleolithic and Neolithic periods was also slow in gaining ground. In this part of the world there were no striking Paleolithic finds for a long time, nothing to compare with the material from the caves of Dordogne and the gravels of the Somme. Nor was there much information available, and Cuvier's suspicions of the idea of Pleistocene man died hard. It is enough to recall the German scholars' reactions to the Neanderthal finds of 1856. There were of course attempts to find traces of Paleolithic settlement, but ignorance led to wrong deductions, like the presumed 'antediluvian' vessel found at Vlence in Central Bohemia in 1859 by the geologist J. Krejčí. In fact this was a vessel dating from the latest Roman Iron Age, found in secondary location, allegedly in deep fluviatile sediments. Real finds were slow to appear. They included the discovery of bone tools in the Badlhöhle cave near Peggau in Austria, by the geologist von Haidinger (1837); finds from Strzegowa in Poland in 1846; and then finds from southern Germany, Moravia and Bohemia, all around 1870.

There was much more Neolithic material in all the major collections, but opposition to the Three Age System prevented full understanding of its significance. For the most part the simplified view of 'pagan prehistory' persisted, not even divided according to Thomsen's system. But in general, although Romantic archaeology was not equipped to solve problems of absolute chronology, it achieved much in relative chronology.

While we may see the Three Age System as the application in practice of an ancient philosophical idea, the task of working out a more detailed classification within the system was one which could only be tackled by archaeologists. Some scholars tried to base their approach on the different types of graves found, but this led nowhere. Stratigraphy was a much more promising method; it was taken over from geology and based on the realization that the deeper you dig, the older the strata you reach, and hence the lower the stratum the greater the age of the finds. Worsaae used stratigraphy to prove the validity of the Three Age System, in the 1850s, and it is worthy of note that the Czech archaeologist M. Lüssner used the method, on his own initiative, when he was excavating culture layers under the city of Hradec Králové, in 1853.

At that time the methods used in the natural sciences raised great hopes among archaeologists, who had not yet worked out their own;

comparative methods were still in their infancy and so was style analysis. Problems began with the interpretation of the purpose of the finds turned up. Nobody any longer suggested that the stone axes and adzes of the Neolithic and Eneolithic periods were thunderbolts, but discussion was still going on as to whether they were weapons, tools, cult objects, symbols of rank, votive offerings, and so forth. The question of whether stone could be bored through without the use of iron caused a great deal of trouble, and most scholars, believing the answer to be 'No', thought this sufficient reason to deny a separate entity for the Neolithic period and to regard both stone and iron artifacts as the products of a single age.

Bronze finds posed similar problems. Büsching, for example, still thought in the 1820s that bronze pins were *styles* for use with wax tablets. Socketed axes were thought to be sacrificial knives until G. Klemm disproved the idea; others thought they were used for hurling wild-fire. The term 'celt' caused much confusion; it was derived from medieval Latin, from an assumed noun 'celtis', and first appeared in 1696. It was mainly used by the Romantics, frequently to cover all forms of bronze axes, while Scandinavian archaeologists introduced the term 'paalstab' for unsocketed axes.

Bronze finds of course made the best showing, and the Romantics concentrated on them, to the neglect of pottery and iron finds. It is not surprising that bronzes were involved in the first concentrated attempts to solve the problem of relative chronology in the Bronze and Iron Ages by the aid of chemistry.

In the northern third of Europe chemical analysis of bronze finds had started in the 1820s and 1830s, and it was soon found that the alloys used varying proportions of copper and tin, and that other metals, particularly lead and zinc, were also present in varying small quantities. Little work was based on the fact; but the Czech archaeologist J. E. Vocel endeavoured to apply these results to archaeological material, aiming at establishing a relative chronology of bronzes, on the basis of their chemical composition. From 1847 he collaborated with chemists at the Charles University in an analysis of the bronzes in the collections of the National Museum in Prague. Work went forward very slowly, and so Vocel developed an analytical method of his own, rougher but faster, using a goldsmith's touchstone. He collected a large amount of data and classified his material into three groups or evolutionary stages, 'classes'.

Later scholars laid greater stress on analysis of style and shape, while Vocel – although himself an excellent art historian – was concerned mainly with chemical results. Although the great German prehistorian R. Virchow praised his method, it fell into oblivion. A new study of Vocel's results nevertheless brought to light an interesting fact. In his articles published in the *Proceedings of the Vienna Academy of Sciences* in 1853 and 1855 under the title *Archaeological Parallels*, Vocel had already presented a more or less correct sketch of the sequence of bronze artifacts. His Class A covers finds dating from the Bronze Age; there are La Tène objects in his Class B; and his Class C includes early historic Slav bronzes.

The next generation of archaeologists drew more on the work of the Scandinavian founders of typology, but here, too, it is interesting that the scholars of Central Europe had been attempting this approach much earlier. G. Klemm was dealing with the evolution of the bronze axe as early as 1836, and H. Schreiber's book, published in 1842, included tables of typological series of axes. Vocel himself was not a collector, and finds interested him as a historical source, which was why he was not content to use only the Three Age System for classification, and tried to work out other more exact historical and ethno-historical approaches. While he contributed to archaeological practice the chemical method of analysis described above, his principal contribution to archaeological methods was the regressive method for tracing the presence of the Slavs back through prehistory by means of the archaeological material, a method he published in 1869. Based on an understanding of find associations and find horizons, it was the same method used later by Montelius to trace the history of the Germani back from the Middle Ages to the Stone Age; under the name of the 'retrospective method', G. Kossinna regarded it as his personal contribution to archaeological method, and the basis of his school of settlement archaeology (*Siedlungsarchäologie*).

For the Romantic archaeologists of Central Europe it was not the description of finds that mattered, nor their typological classification, nor determination of their exact age; all this was to become the focus of interest during the next period. The prime question now was: to whom did these finds belong? Who had made these artifacts? Who was buried in those graves? Celts, Germani or Slavs?

Celts, Germani or Slavs?
Even if all the other questions raised by archaeological discovery were to remain unanswered, this one had to be settled in the case of every find, and it was almost the patriotic duty of the Romantic archaeologist to settle it in favour of his own people. This archaeological nationalism, whose roots we have already traced, was the strongest bond with the political reality of the first two-thirds of the nineteenth century. The ethnic determination of a find not only transformed it into a weapon in the arsenal of the national consciousness, but taken to its logical conclusion meant that, in theory at least, it was possible to claim the territory where the object was discovered in the name of those who were, or felt themselves to be, the modern descendants of the presumed authors of the artifact.

This was not only a Central European phenomenon; the role of universal authors of all archaeological artifacts fell very often to the Ancient Britons in Britain and to the Gauls in France. But while in those countries it was a matter of national history, in Central Europe the question was part of the drama of contemporary politics.

Characteristically, conclusions about the ethnic provenance of finds could not be drawn solely from the archaeological material. There were ancient written records to be taken into account, however uncritical they may have been; and there was philology to call upon. This branch of learning had assumed respectable proportions towards the end of the eighteenth century, in both the German and the Slav world, and by the Romantic period it enjoyed almost unlimited confidence as practically the only reliable foundation for palaeoethnological conclusions. The Indo-European concept evolved in the German sphere, and in 1823 J. Klaproth introduced the nationalistically tinged term 'Indo-Germanic', which gave the Germani a privileged position in the prehistory and ancient civilization of Europe, deriving them first from Asia and later from Northern Europe.

In theory it was sometimes suggested that there might have been pre-Indo-European inhabitants of Europe, to whom the primitive era of the Stone Age could be attributed, and according to the Finnish scholar A. J. Europaeus they were of Finno–Ugrian origin. No-one in Central Europe took up their cause, however, and so we rarely meet with them in interpretations of the archaeological material. The autochthonic school of thought was much more influential; according to the writer's

18. Archaeological reconstructions: ancient German warriors according to the ideas of the mid-nineteenth century.

own nationality, he designated the earliest settlers in Europe as Celts, Germani or Slavs. These three groups played the decisive roles in the Romantic archaeology of Central Europe.

The Celtic school suffered the least from nationalistic considerations, not being tied by political assumptions. The Romantic quest for a Celtic past was not confined to England and France, but spread somewhat later to the German and Czech areas, and to some extent to Poland, encouraged by the evidence of classical writers as to which regions were inhabited by the Celts. Interest had already been aroused in Renaissance times, but during the nineteenth century it grew into Celtomania; the Celts were regarded as the most ancient people of the world, and traces of their civilization were soon being found everywhere. There were many devoted Celtomaniacs in southern Germany, but they lost ground after the middle of the century under growing pressure from German nationalism. (This conflict was due in part to the fact that they attributed all bronze artifacts to the Celts, which left nothing to the prehistoric Germani but primitive artifacts of stone, and that was inadmissible in the eyes of the nationalists.)

Outstanding among the philological-archaeological Celtomaniacs of the 1840s was H. Schreiber, who went so far in his efforts to ensure priority to the Celts that he changed the order of Thomsen's Three Ages so that the Bronze (Celtic) Age preceded the Stone (Germanic) Age. Another was C. Keferstein, who attributed the whole of European civilization to the Celts in his *Observations on Celtic Antiquities* (1846). In Austria, J. Gaisberger declared in 1848 that the Hallstatt cemetery was a Celtic burial ground, and his argument is so typical of the times that it is worth reproducing here: at Hallstatt bronze finds are more numerous than iron, and there are very few weapons in the graves, whereas Tacitus testified to the Germani's love of arms; bronze axes (celts) are present, and local place-names in the vicinity of Hallstatt show, says Gaisberger, innumerable Celtic roots!

F. Keller (1854) and others after him saw the people of the Swiss lake villages as Celts, while K. Rogawski in Poland (1856) credited them with Stone Age artifacts. In Bohemia (this Latin name is derived from the Celtic tribe of the Boii) interest in the Celts was understandable. It had existed since the sixteenth century, and now followers of the autochthonic school, philologists and historians alike, came forward with the idea that the Boii (and therefore all the other Celts as well) were really Slavs. They did not get their theory accepted, any more than their counterparts on the other side of the nationalist barricades succeeded in proving that the Celts were really Germanic. There were even Celtomaniacs in Bavaria (V. von Pallhausen and others) who tried to establish a philological link between the names of the Boii and the early historical tribe of the Baiuvari, later to become the Bavarians.

Celtomania gradually died away after the Three Age System came into general use. The realization that bronze was a feature of a culture, not of an ethnic entity, took root – and then, even the writers of antiquity had been quite explicit about the iron weapons of the Gauls. In the 1860s L. Lindenschmit, in Germany, thought the Celtic craze was over. Nevertheless it is worth noting that the first ethnic specialization in Central European archaeology was the study of Celtic antiquities.

The wave of interest in the early history of the Germani was more militant, and at a congress in Frankfurt am Main in 1846 specialists in the field decided to call themselves Germanists. Here, too, the roots of the movement are to be sought in the Renaissance, while Romanticism provided fertile soil for growth. Among the scholars who laid the foundations of the study of their Germanic ancestors during the German national revival were J. C. Adelung (*The Earliest History of the Germans*, 1806), Donop-Wackenbarth (*History of the Great Teutons*, 1821), J. Grimm (*German Mythology*, 1835), C. Zeuss (*The Germans and their Neighbours*, 1837), and J. G. G. Büsching (*Outline of German Archaeology*, 1824). They began to seek the original home of the Germani in the North, where Germanic culture had survived in its purest form, and in Central Europe there was a growing interest in Scandinavian antiquities. In Northern Europe bronze artifacts were automatically attributed to the Germani. In Germany itself non-Roman finds were more and more frequently designated as 'Germanic', and complicated interpretations of the words of classical authors, particularly of Tacitus, were evolved, in order to attribute each find to a specific tribe of the ancient Germani. After unsuccessful attempts to develop a compromise theory of Celto-Germanic culture and ancient Germanic Druids, the Celtic element had to fade into the background. Even the Romans suffered an eclipse, in spite of persistent but vain efforts in Germany and Bohemia to find evidence of Roman settlement far to the north of the Danube.

The problem was not so simple to the east, beyond the Elbe and the Saale, nor even in Bavaria, where early historians attest the presence of the Slavs for several centuries. Serious research into the Slav past was slower to develop among archaeologists. Those nations who would have liked to pursue it were not free to do so, except for Russia, during the Romantic period when these studies were being founded. In Russia Slav archaeology was not a focus of interest; in the North it was the Baltic Germans who led the field in archaeology, while in the Black Sea region it was mainly French *emigrés*, and the first storm of scientific enthusiasm was aroused by the wealth of Scythian finds from the royal burial mounds, *kurgans*.

It was thus mainly the western Slavs – the Poles, Czechs and not very numerous Lusatian Serbs – who devoted themselves to Slavonic studies and Slav archaeology. The founders of the discipline were J. Dobrovský, the leading scholar of the Czech Enlightenment, and P. J. Šafařík, a Slovak scholar working in Prague. An oustanding Slavonic scholar in Poland was W. Surowiecki, author of *Seeking the Origins of the Slav Peoples* (1824), who first identified the Slavs with the Veneti of Tacitus. In the practical field A. Czarnocki (under the pseudonym of Z. D. Chodakowski) was primarily interested in tracing the Old Slavonic pagan culture suppressed by Christianity (*The Pre-Christian Slav World*, 1818). At first Slav archaeology was studied mainly in Poland, but the conclusions reached by these and other authors were Romantic in the extreme. Interest died after the failure of the Polish revolt of 1830–1, partly because of persecution (the universities were closed and learned societies disbanded) and partly because the younger generation became more violently anti-Russian.

The Romantic fantasy was still hard at work, however. The Slavs were seen as arriving from India, or aboriginal in Central Europe and responsible for the Etruscan alphabet, or for Celtic coins . . . We need only name the greatest of the Slavophiles, the Slovak Jan Kollár, 'a scholar in poetry and a poet in scholarship', author of *Ancient Slavonic Italy* (1853); V. Krolmus, the Czech field archaeologist; or A. V. Šembera, the philologist (*The Western Slavs in Prehistory*, 1868), and T. Wolański the Polish mythologist. In 1830 Bohemia became the centre of Slav historical studies; here P. J. Safařík published his *Slavonic Antiquities* in 1836–7, the first history of the early Slavs to be based on serious scholarship, and established that Eastern Europe was their original homeland. In 1836 the first volume of F. Palacky's monumental *History of the Czech Nation* also appeared, as well as the outline of archaeology already referred to, by M. Kalina of Jäthenstein, which put forward an interesting theory that the autochthonous Slav population had been subjugated for a time by the Celts and then by the Germani. All these writers share Herder's Romantic view of the ancient Slavs as men 'of a dove-like nature', peaceful farmers endowed with all possible virtues, and suffering at the hands of the rude Germani.

It is not without interest that the first serious attempts to classify Slav archaeological finds were made in Germany (in fact as early as the sixteenth century, by Marschalk-Thurius). The problem was particularly difficult on the Germanic–Slav borderline to the East, because in the early Middle Ages Slav settlement had penetrated deep into Germany (covering practically the whole of the plains now forming the main part of the GDR) while in the Romantic era, on the contrary, German expansion spread over many areas of Slav settlement in Greater Poland, Silesia and Pomerania. To the west and south of these regions all finds were attributed to the Germani wherever possible, while in Bohemia and eastern Poland they were credited to the Slavs. From the 1860s onwards, however, the German minority in Bohemia began to propagate the contrary view. It was not easy to find objective criteria, but ultimately the archaeologists succeeded.

G. C. F. Lisch of Mecklenburg started trying to distinguish Germanic from Slav graves as early as 1832. In Bohemia M. Kalina was still attributing graves with weapons to the Germani and graves of 'farmers' or 'craftsmen' to the Slavs. In 1847 Lisch recognized an engraved wavy line as a typical feature of Slav pottery in north-east Germany. Six years later M. Lüssner, clearly independently, reached the same conclusion for Bohemian material, and this was confirmed in 1858 by L. Šnajdr. Yet their contribution fell into oblivion, mainly because of J. E. Vocel, whose authority carried great weight, but whose shortcomings unfortunately included a lack of interest in pottery.

These were of course the high points of archaeological research. More frequent were the attempts to attribute the richer finds in any one region to one ethnic group or the other, or to prove that border-line regions with a mixed population had always been either Germanic or Slav. The approach here was different: attributing territory to the Germani served primarily to justify modern domination or aspirations thereto, whereas on the Slav side the claim almost always sprang from the need to defend their right to exist, and indeed could not have meant more, at the time. Thus Schröter of Mecklenburg attributed graves with straight weapons to the Germani and those with bent weapons to the Slavs. Where the cremation graves were richer and more numerous than the skeleton graves, the former were attributed to the Germani (e.g. J. G. Worbs,

Are the Urnfields of Eastern Germany Slav or Germanic?, 1824). The same approach, on other occasions, had the Germani lying in skeleton graves (G. W. Adler, *Barrows and Places of Sacrifice in Orlagau*, 1836). Where the Slav element could be overlooked, it was passed over in silence; for this reason D. Popp remained alone in his attempt to determine the boundaries of early historic Slav settlement of the Upper Palatinate, in 1821. (Popp was in at the birth of the identification of the Suebi of Tacitus with the Slavs, later to become a popular theory.) On the other hand, reading J. E. Vocel on the subject of Bohemian prehistory, it cannot be surprising that the Germans were not satisfied with the scrap of space left to their forefathers, squeezed in between the Celts and the Slavs.

While it was a matter of day-to-day tactics to attribute each archaeological find to a certain ethnic group (one's own), the long-term strategy was to create the noblest possible image of the earliest history of one's land and people. The 'classical' model of interpretation presented by the writers of antiquity still persisted, strengthened by study of their descriptions of the ancient Celts and Germani, but at the same time new tendencies were emerging.

In the first place it was essential to suppress the idea, fostered by the Age of Enlightenment, that our forefathers were savages; the unfavourable passages had to be extirpated from the literature and the favourable passages stressed, regardless of what the writer had in mind at the time. The Germans naturally quoted Tacitus on the high moral qualities of the ancient Germani – passages which he had written, in fact, with an eye to the need for reform in decadent Rome. The Germans further intensified the effect of these quotations by describing the barbaric level of the ancient Slavs, of whom there is no mention in the classical texts. The Slav scholars, on the other hand, stressed those passages in Tacitus which describe the primitive way of life of the ancient Germani, comparing this picture with the descriptions of the advanced Slav civilization given by somewhat later Greek (Byzantine) authors. However, when Vocel compared the society of the ancient Germani to that of the North American Indians, he aroused a storm of protest.

All these ideas of what the life of the ethnic groups in Central Europe was like long ago were static, as though the period of 'pagan' prehistory was a changeless state which never developed further. The Romantic view of prehistoric society was affected neither by the evolutionary theories of the natural sciences nor by the concept of dialectical evolution worked out in classical German philosophy by Hegel.

Nevertheless new facts being discovered by explorers were beginning to influence the picture. In the Romantic era the study of contemporary man became a scientific discipline; the first ethnological societities were formed and the first scientific treatises written on the subject of ethnology, ethnography, the 'natural peoples' (Vollgraf 1853, Waitz 1859, Bastian 1860, in Germany). Observations of tribes in America, Australia and Oceania gave Europeans their first realistic socio-economic models of a pre-class society, more scientifically arguable than Rousseau's picture of the 'noble savage'. The fact that the material culture of these tribes showed affinities with the archaeological material found in Europe made it possible to postulate affinities on a more abstract level as well.

Central Europe had never possessed great navies or vast colonial empires, and knowledge of these matters was gained slowly and at second hand. From the outset of the nineteenth century translations and extracts from magazine articles on the life and customs of distant peoples began to appear, and much later the knowledge so acquired was systematized and used for comparison with prehistory, for example by the Czech evolutionist J. S. Tomíček in his work *The First Age of Mankind* (1846). An awareness that economic conditions had also passed through an evolutionary process became stronger; in Bohemia it was as early as 1817 that J. L. Ziegler proposed the sequence: food gathering, hunting and fishing, nomadic pastoral life, settled farming. This concept, developing slowly in Europe since the end of the eighteenth century, was made popular in the 1830s by the Swedish author S. Nilson. The socio-historical concepts of 'savagery', 'barbarism' and 'civilization' date from the end of the eighteenth century as well, but in Central Europe they were practically unknown, and no scholar there had ever attempted to apply them to archaeological material. It was much more satisfying to ponder over the nationality of those buried in prehistoric graves, or to imagine their religious rites.

Nevertheless a more advanced model of prehistoric society, one might say an ethnographical model, was slowly taking shape, however static and poor in detail it remained for the moment. It was the first realistic picture of prehistoric society, cleared of the false aura of nobility taken over from the classicists. The classical model differs from the ethnographical one in the same way as the historical approach based on written records differs from the archaeological approach, which already draws on the help provided by ethnography and the natural sciences. About the middle of the nineteenth century these two trends began to separate: history 'proper' remained sceptical of the value of material remains (and therefore of archaeology altogether), and the historians' view of prehistory was petrified in the Romantic-nationalist version of the old model, adding to it features of early medieval society, partly under the influence of various successful literary forgeries. It is this parting of the ways that marks the decline and fall of the Romantic era in archaeology.

The image of the distant past of the Slavs and the Germani that we have noted above did not remain the special preserve of historical scholarship; it was taken over by the arts, which stressed still further the nationalistic and Romantic elements. The 'Theatergermanen', as they were called, far removed from historical reality, appeared not only in historical plays but on the canvases of the official academic painters of historical scenes. The first marked success was that of K. Blechen's 'ancient Germani' at the Berlin Exhibition of Paintings of 1828. They were given three-dimensional existence by such popular sculptors as L. Schwanthaler of Munich, who provided the sculptures for the Regensburg 'Walhalla' set up in 1835 – and they even found their way into commercial advertising. They lived on well into the twentieth century, although with considerable loss of dignity as time went on.

Their Slav counterparts were equally dubious in their antecedents, depicted not from historical fact but from 'ancient legends' and from the supposedly Old Slavonic epics in the *Dvůr Králové and Zelená Hora*

Manuscripts. We have already seen how these manuscripts were forged with literary ambition and a profound sense of what the Romantic reader wanted to be given: heroic and lyrical scenes depicting the bravery, noble sentiments and moral superiority of the ancient Slavs, combined with deep feeling; their determined struggle and ultimate victory over the barbarian enemy – the Germani; an ideal democracy in the ancient Czech world . . .

In the atmosphere of the time it was not easy to doubt the authenticity of the *Manuscripts*, and not even his great age and authority protected the founder of Slavonic studies, Dobrovský, from accusations of lack of patriotism when he dared to express scepticism. Šafařík and Palacký, who belonged to the younger and more Romantic generation, came out in support of the *Manuscripts*, making them an article of faith for the nation, something which was not open to discussion. They were supported by J. E. Vocel, whose description of Old Slavonic civilization in his *Prehistory of the Land of Bohemia* (1868) was largely based on the *Manuscripts*, and is therefore one of the less reliable parts of his work. From the 1850s onwards attempts to disprove the authenticity of the epics were made, principally by German writers and more from nationalistic motives than in the interests of pure scholarship; this of course meant that the Czechs were obliged to reject their arguments in advance.

It was the positivist generation of Czech scholars at the end of the nineteenth century who succeeded in giving the *Manuscripts* their true place in Czech cultural history and clearing the way for historical research. In the meantime the figures and the episodes depicted in the *Manuscripts* had become part of the national consciousness, and to some extent live on even today. When the Czech Slavín – the counterpart of the Regensburg Walhalla – was set up near Mělník in 1846 it was the same Schwanthaler of Munich who carved the academically conceived figures of the Czech heroes. In the 1850s and 1860s a strongly individualized figure of the ancient Slav was moulded, based on the *Manuscripts*, and found immortality in drawings, paintings, statues, and on the stage. The tradition is still alive, in spite of the fact that these Slav heroes armed with stone battle-axes and bronze swords are evidence of the meagre archaeological equipment of scholarship around the middle of the nineteenth century.

Forgeries were not limited to literature, although the archaeological forgeries of the time, too, frequently set out to prove the high level of scholarship attained by our forebears, as shown by their writing. Runes were very popular indeed in the Romantic era. There were plenty of them to be found in Northern Europe, but in Germany, where runes were declared to be the script of all the ancient Germani, hardly any were to be found. And so the forgeries began. The first, dating from 1804, appeared in Bavaria in 1830 – and the fraud was exposed that same year, by police officials.

This dubious profession flourished even more in the Slav regions. Here there were no runes at all, but the devotees of Slav prehistory could not allow their forefathers to lag behind the ancient Germani in this respect. From a few allusions in the written records they built up a popular Romantic theory of pre-Christian Slav runes; it then became necessary to find them.

19. Archaeology and politics: the huge romantic monument of Hermann-Arminius, the 'Liberator of Germany', in the supposed area of his victorious battle against Roman legions (E. von Bandel, 1838–46; completed 1875).

Some of the evidence was provided by the misguided enthusiasm of the Romantics, proffering such proof as the cracked surface of the sandstone boulders of Krolmus's 'shrine of Černoboh' in Skalsko in 1852, or the cracks and channels on the surface of the 'rune vessel' of Neu-Käbelich in Mecklenburg (1853), which has unfortunately not survived, but was discussed by many scholars including Lisch and Schwerin and Vocel in the Danish *Memoirs of the Society of Antiquaries of the North.*

The rune theory was propped up at first by the Rethra idols from Prillwitz, notorious forgeries of the seventeenth and eighteenth centuries (see fig. 12). Their story did not end until the Romantic scholars of authority (Lewezow, Šafařík, Worsaae, Lisch and others) condemned the strange creations. Besides lack of proof, the most telling factor was probably the naïvety of the forgery, which no longer suited the spirit and requirements of the Romantics.

A more effective substitute was soon found: in 1855 and 1856 several stones were discovered in the village of Mikorzyń in Prussian Greater Poland; they bore Slav runes which aroused great interest in Polish scientific circles and among the broader public. Discussion centred on the reading of the inscriptions, and there were practically no doubts of their authenticity. The stones were published in the literature and Count A. Przezdziecki delivered a paper on the subject at the archaeological congress in Antwerp in 1867. It was not until 1872 that a commission set up by the Society of the Sciences in Cracow came to the conclusion that the stones were a forgery, perpetrated by means of prehistoric corn-grinding stones.

The Mikorzyń stones were only a typical example from among the host of lesser forgeries and errors in the history of Slav runes. In most cases they were meant to strengthen the national consciousness and provide arguments against the biassed assumption that the Slav culture was inferior to the Germanic, an argument constantly called into operation during the repeated attempts to Germanize or Magyarize the Slavs living in Prussia or Austria. It was not a convincing argument, however, and for that reason did not survive the Romantic era, at least not in scholarly circles.

The anecdotes we have retailed in our account of the Romantic period show how complex it was. On the one hand scholars were doing their utmost to maintain scientific standards and establish a scientific discipline, while on the other hand everything that served the sacred cause of the nation was worthy of credence (here, of course, the poor level of knowledge available was at fault). On the one hand the archaeologists stressed the importance of precise recording of the circumstances surrounding a find, and of exact description of the material; while on the other hand archaeological detail was of little weight in the interpretation of material in support of a given ethnic or cultural (ritual) significance. There was the best will in the world to achieve a sober academic approach, but the spirit of the times, in education and in cultural aims, was Romantic in the extreme. On the one hand there was delight in the beauty of the past, while on the other the evidence of the past was often deliberately misused for 'higher ends'.

In spite of all this, the Romantic era remains one of the most attractive periods in the history of archaeology. The modern scientific approach grew from these badly balanced beginnings. In this exciting atmosphere the teachings of the rationalists of the Age of Enlightenment and the ideas of the late eighteenth-century early Romantics combined to form a serious scientific discipline, bound up with contemporary reality and moving forward with the *élan* and faith of youth towards the unlimited opportunities that lay ahead. The whole movement reflected the rise to power of the 'middle classes' of Europe, their optimism and the scientific upsurge which settled down after the middle of the century to produce the calm objectivity of positivism. It only needed a few years around the date of 1870 for the entire world of archaeology to change substantially.

Tracing the Evolution of Things: the Age of Positivist Analysis

The historical background: Central Europe in the second half of the nineteenth century

After Germany had emerged victorious from the struggle for dominance, Central Europe enjoyed a relatively long period of peace and stability, and of comparative prosperity. It was only in the south that major political change occurred after Russia and the southern Slavs were victorious in the war against Turkey; Rumania and Serbia gained their independence in 1878, while the Austro-Hungarian Empire expanded by first occupying (1878) and later annexing (1908) the former Turkish territory of Bosnia and Herzegovina.

The major factor in Central European politics at this time was the German Empire formed in 1871 when a number of small German states united, on the initiative of Prussia, although some of them (like Prussia itself, Saxony, Bavaria, etc.) retained a degree of autonomy. The first emperor of the 'second German Empire' was William I of Prussia (1871–88), but policy was determined by the 'Iron Chancellor', Bismarck. The Hapsburg Empire was overshadowed; ruled from 1848 until 1916 by Franz Josef I, after being defeated by Prussia in 1866 it became a second-rate power. Like Germany, the Austrian empire gradually found itself isolated in European politics, a situation which led to co-operation and ultimately to the alliance of the two former rivals in 1879. In 1882 a secret agreement between the two and Italy created the Triple Alliance, directed mainly against France and after the retirement of Bismarck against Russia as well. Thus emerged a power group in Central Europe which was to be a significant factor in the history of the continent up to the year 1918.

There were significant differences between the two leading Central European powers, however. Germany was strong and on the whole a united national state, rising rapidly to a position that far outdistanced its hitherto insignificant standing in world politics. Industrially strong, Germany had a powerful army and relatively stable internal political conditions, liberal to a degree, yet firmly directed. Austria, on the other hand – since 1867 Austro-Hungary – was internally weak and traditionally unable to develop at a faster rate. Inside the Empire there were marked differences between the industrialized regions (Bohemia, Moravia, Silesia and Lower Austria) and the much vaster agricultural regions; more significant, however, were the national discords, the principal cause of political weakness. The Austro-Hungarian agreement of 1867 had left the Hungarian aristocracy and newly arisen bourgeoisie (which was represented by the lower gentry up to 1848) in political control, opening the way to a Hungarian national state. Expectations of conciliation within the Empire were not fulfilled, however; the ruling

Map 6. Central Europe in the period of positivist analysis (c.1870).

Localities:

1 Únětice, Řivnáč	4 Tószeg	7 Šipka	11 Cracow
	5 Stradonice	8 Předmostí	12 Vače
2 Ljubljana	6 Býčí skála, Kůlna	9 Weimar, Taubach	13 Kuffern
3 Attersee	Pekárna	10 Willendorf	14 Duchcov

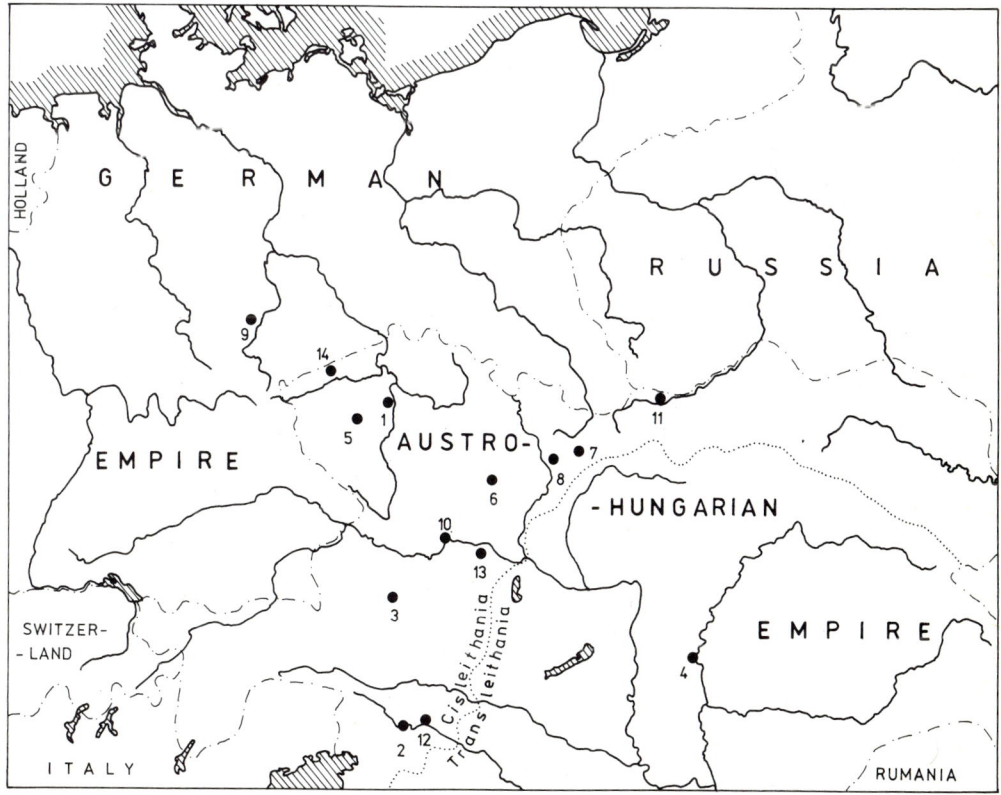

class in Hungary still vehemently opposed Vienna and fought for the upper hand in the Empire. The other peoples remained hostile, too, after their proposals for a federal Austrian state were disregarded in 1867; the Slavs were the most important element, since they formed the majority of the population of the Empire. In the relatively liberal conditions of 'Cisleithania', west of the river Leitha, the Czechs, Slovenes and Poles of Galicia were better off than the smaller peoples in Hungary (the Slovaks, Rumanians, Ruthenians and somewhat better-off Croats), who could do little to protect their identity. The latter were deprived of their fundamental political rights and subjected to uncompromising Magyarization, by which means the Hungarian rulers hoped to attain a homogeneous Magyar state.

It is clear from these few observations that the nationality problem in Central Europe was far from any solution – and that without mention of the considerable Polish minority subjected to the Germans in the eastern regions of the German Empire. After the constitutional gains of 1848, however, the struggle became political, and was not so clearly reflected in science as it had been in the Romantic epoch.

Archaeology as anthropology

Economic progress suffered no serious setbacks after the crisis of the 1870s increased its tempo, especially in Germany. The new horizons opened by technical progress, by advances in the natural sciences and their application to industry, all helped to create the illusion that progress in all fields of human endeavour was inevitable and irresistible. The idea of progress from the simplest to the more perfect was then applied to the past history of man and his evolution, as well as to science.

In 1867 Gabriel de Mortillet summarized the progress made by archaeology in three points: the law of human evolution; the law of parallel development; and realization of the immense age of Man. It is quite clear what the evolutionists, the most progressive of the archaeologists, considered most important and used as their base for the future. When the Three Age System was broadly accepted as the basic system for European archaeology (in the scientific sense) a new era began, one of more modest aims but more thorough study. This meant that archaeology was of less interest to the public than it had been in the previous period of Romantic, socially committed research.

After 1848, inevitably, Europe had changed, and Romanticism had outlived its *raison d'être*. From the 1850s onwards a new spirit is apparent, one which can be called 'archaeological' as against the 'antiquarian' spirit of earlier times. Scholars were now primarily concerned to confirm and work out in detail the system of prehistory which had won acceptance, born of the Romantic epoch, yet surprisingly enough archaeological and not ethnohistorical. It can be said, roughly, that this tendency could be observed earlier in countries less burdened by nationalism and Romantic ethnocentrism, and more clearly in those branches of research where such phenomena were of less account, such as the study of the Paleolithic. During the 1860s Romanticism faded out, still echoing only in various ethnic obsessions and on the amateur periphery of the discipline.

The 'archaeological' period had its own clear tendencies, three being marked: the first was a positivist approach to source material; the second was the application of principles of natural science in the study of that material; and the third was the endeavour to achieve a complex anthropological approach in the final assessment of the material. We shall be returning to the first and second tendencies; for the present let us consider the last.

About the middle of the nineteenth century the traditional antiquarian approach began to disintegrate. Prehistoric archaeology was breaking its bonds with its mother, 'pure' history (although she was more of a stepmother as far as material sources were concerned), yet it did not join the natural sciences, but became one with the new science of man, anthropology in the broadest sense of the word; here archaeology found new partners in physical anthropology and ethnology. The combination of these three disciplines is typical of the first (analytical) phase of the archaeological period, the 1860s to 1880s, when the general conclusions of the archaeologists were cultural and anthropological rather than historical. Where the Romantics were looking for nations, anthropological archaeologists sought the 'pure, nameless individual' beyond the nation; that was how the Berlin scholar Rudolf Virchow expressed it in 1884 – Virchow was the leading representative of anthropology in this sense of the word.

In practice, of course, it was not so easy to achieve complete integration of the anthropological sciences. Professor Virchow moved gradually away from physical anthropology towards archaeology, while another well-known German anthropologist, Professor H. Schaaffhausen complained in 1873 that archaeology was dominating the German Anthropological Society at the expense of the other branches. There was a great advantage for archaeology in this contact, however: the resultant co-ordination of research and the availability of results from neighbouring disciplines revealed new aspects and shed new light on archaeological problems. Perhaps one of the most important areas was ethnology, where contacts contributed to the gradual understanding of economic and social conditions in prehistory – an aspect the Romantics had sorely neglected. On the other hand, these links did not feed nationalism; where Romantic archaeology had been ethnocentric, anthropological archaeology was deliberately international, anthropocentric. It emphasized those things that primitive people had in common, and not what divided them.

It was not by chance that the term 'prehistory' became widely used at this time, signifying as it does a scientific discipline preceding that of history proper, and having little in common with it. The sense of a clear line of demarcation between international, scientifically informed prehistory and nationalist history, which was typical of the entire period, was reinforced by the amateur nature of prehistory, which took time to overcome and which aroused suspicion and lack of respect among professional historians. But the prehistorians were optimists. In 1873 Virchow doubted whether prehistory was or would ever be a scientific discipline; in 1880 he was already able to declare: 'We have made German prehistory an independent discipline'.

The archaeologists start organizing
The concept of 'local' prehistoric archaeology as one branch of

anthropology was thus of considerable significance throughout Central Europe in the 1870s and 1880s. Since it also influenced the external, organizational forms of scientific life it is perhaps appropriate to sidetrack for a moment and consider this aspect of the history of archaeology.

In the relative sense we can regard the 'archaeological' period as the phase of professionalization of the discipline, particularly in the museums and universities, in spite of the obvious fact that professional archaeologists were still few. This fact also left its mark on the organization of work; museums increased their importance and the universities progressed rapidly. The older scientific societies were stagnant, but the idea of scientific association was revived in the emergence of specialized bodies.

Some of these bodies were formed within the academies and societies; the Vienna Academy of Sciences set up a Prehistoric Committee in 1878, at the instigation of F. von Hochstetter, which was attached to the Natural Science section. The Bavarian Academy took similar steps in 1886. The Academy of the Arts which was set up in Cracow in 1872 established an Archaeological Committee the next year and an Anthropological Committee in 1874. In Bohemia the Royal Czech Scientific Society took no part in the development of archaeology, where its place was taken by the newly founded Czech Academy of the Sciences and the Arts (1890), which set up an Archaeological Committee in 1893. The discipline was also represented in the Southern Slav Academy of the Sciences and the Arts, in Zagreb, which had been active since 1867.

After the middle of the nineteenth century specialized scientific societies began to play a forward-looking role in the institutional sphere. It was the 'anthropological' societies that were typical of the first phase of the archaeological period, i.e. prehistoric-anthropological-ethnological societies. One was founded in Berlin in 1869, later to become the most important of the branches of the German Society for Anthropology, Ethnology and Prehistory, founded in 1870 with Professor Virchow at its head. Another important branch of the society was formed in Munich. At the same time the Vienna Anthropological Society came into being (1870), mainly archaeological in its interests; most of the archaeologists of Cisleithania were members. The success of the world congress of anthropologists and archaeologists held in Budapest in 1876 resulted in the formation of the Hungarian Anthropological Society two years later, with the outstanding archaeologists F. Pulszky, J. Hampel and F. Rómer among its members. Another important regional anthropological-archaeological society was that of Lower Lusatia, founded in 1884. In all these societies, in the course of time prehistory became much more influential than the other disciplines.

Another typical feature of the time, and one hardly seen before, was the organization of scientific congresses; these came into being in answer to the needs of increasing numbers of research workers with insufficient means of contact and opportunities to exchange views, and also because the ever stronger position of the discipline called for some form of representation. The most important were the world congresses of anthropology and prehistoric archaeology, the first of which was held in Neuchâtel in Switzerland in 1866. The first to be held in Central

Europe was the eighth congress, which took place in Budapest in 1876, and the venue was the result of the increasingly rich finds of the bronze industry in Hungary, especially in Transylvania and Slovakia.

Elsewhere in Central Europe a similar role was fulfilled by conferences of the German and the Vienna anthropological societies which were held every year, sometimes together. This was the clearest expression of a degree of unity in the scientific life of Central Europe which was more evident in this positivist anthropological phase than either before or after. These conferences presented very full programmes and were attended by most of the serious archaeologists of the German-speaking peoples as well as the Slav archaeologists of Austro-Hungary; the latter had fewer opportunities to arrange conferences of their own, the Czech anthropological-archaeological conferences held in Prague in 1880 and 1882 being the exception. Prehistoric-anthropological exhibitions became an important traditional feature of the German conferences, the first being held in Munich in 1875, while the most famous was that held in Berlin in 1880; a combined German-Austrian exhibition arranged in Vienna in 1889 was also significant.

During this period museums were developing slowly but surely, and in a progressive direction; they were becoming more specialized, and more archaeological museums were being opened. There were 165 publicly and 92 privately owned archaeological collections in Germany in 1876, while by 1880 the registered figures for collections were 213 and 311 respectively. The attempt to set up a central archaeological museum on the French model was unsuccessful in Germany, however, and the large regional museums became the centres for archaeological research: these were in Jena (founded by F. Klopfleisch in 1863), Kiel (1873), Dresden (the Saxon Museum, 1874), Berlin (Museum of the Mark of Brandenburg, 1874), Halle (Saxon-Anhalt Provincial Museum, 1882), Munich (State Prehistoric Collections, 1889), and Weimar (Museum of Prehistoric Thuringia, 1892). Prehistory found a place in other specialized museums, too, as when a Prehistoric Department was set up in the Berlin Ethnological Museum in 1874, under A. Voss.

In neighbouring Austro-Hungary independent departments were also set up in the large museums of Cisleithania, in Vienna in 1876 (the Anthropological-Ethnological Department of the Natural Science Museum, under F. Heger and J. Szombathy), and in Prague in 1893 (the Prehistoric Department of the National Museum, under J. L. Píč); while archaeology had been a separate department in the Hungarian National Museum of Budapest for some time, now under F. Hampel. Of the regional museums that of Olomouc became increasingly important as the centre of Moravian archaeology (1883). At this time the Provincial Museum in Lubljana formed the basis upon which prehistoric archaeology was established in Slovenia, when K. Dežman (Deschmann) began research there after 1875.

As the number of museums of various types grew, so did the arguments between centralists and regionalists, the former holding that finds should be concentrated in one place and copies exhibited regionally, while the latter stressed the importance of growing public interest, regional studies, and the larger amount of material thus made available.

Finally we must consider the situation in the universities, where archaeology was finding a place in the syllabus and in research. In the universities of Austria independent chairs of classical archaeology were set up (Vienna 1869 and Prague 1872) after the Romantic chairs of archaeology set up in mid-century, the first being in Vienna (J. Kollár, 1849) and the second in Prague (J. Vocel, 1850). Around 1870, however, a further development took place, and chairs of anthropological prehistory were set up or adapted from existing chairs of medical anthropology. The Munich physiologist Professor J. Ranke had been lecturing on prehistory since 1863 and in 1866 was given the formal title of Professor of Anthropology and Prehistory. Professor Schaaffhausen of Bonn lectured on anthropology and prehistory in alternate semesters, and the Berlin Professor of Pathological Anatomy, R. Virchow, also included prehistory in his courses. F. Klopfleisch, professor at Jena University from 1875 to 1896, came to prehistory from the history of art. There were no more chairs of this type founded in Austro-Hungary, however, and the Prague chair ceased to exist with the death of J. E. Vocel in 1871. Prehistory had no place in the curriculum in Vienna nor in Budapest, and only appeared as an occasional voluntary activity by interested university lecturers (in Budapest the classical archaeologist J. Hampel, and the anthropologist A. von Török).

The typologists and others

Let us now return to the three main tendencies to be traced in the 'archaeological' period: along with the 'anthropologization' of archaeology there was also positivism, and a way of thinking based on the natural sciences. Perhaps the best definition of positivism in archaeology would be sober concentration on the material, and a putting aside of the great questions raised by Romanticism in favour of closer and more realistic questions – archaeology, in the narrow sense of the word, rather than history. The failure of Romantic attempts to approach the discipline from any other than archaeological positions showed that it was too soon to attempt to solve the majority of historical and ethnohistorical problems, and that it was first necessary to collect sounder and more reliable facts and classify and systematize them. This shift mirrored the mood of the whole of this period, which, in contrast to the era of revolutionary Romanticism, was slowly losing the adventurous spirit, the flexibility and the capacity for action of those days. Now it was time for reducing down ideas, pigeon-holing them and setting them in definite order – as unchangeable an order as possible. The rational spirit of the 'technical age' prevailed in archaeology, too: instead of the 'history of nations' it was the 'history of labour' that was to be written. This was the theme of the successful archaeological exhibition arranged as part of the World Exhibition in Paris in 1867, and the archaeological section of the World Exhibition in Vienna in 1873 was of a similar nature. For the most part scholars no longer shared the Romantic fascination with the mysteries of a dark and distant past, but faced their subject with cool reason; for them 'pure observation of the facts' was the basis for all knowledge.

This systematic arrangement of facts then moved into the sphere of the natural sciences, whose determination of unambiguous facts and consistent systematization of them, since immense progress was being made, proved most attractive for other sciences; it was precisely these favourable features that archaeology sorely lacked. The archaeologists tried to apply and overtake the methods of natural science in their own discipline, to see archaeological finds and sites as natural phenomena and to apply to them the principles of geology, stratigraphy, Darwin's theory of biological evolution and Linnaeus' systematic method of classification: to understand the laws of social development in the manner of natural laws. This discipline was most readily applied in the study of the paleolithic period, which attracted scholars of the natural sciences rather than archaeologists throughout the period we are discussing.

From the point of view of the historian, of course, this concentration of interest on the descriptive approach to material sources was a step backwards. On the other hand, at this particular time it was of fundamental importance, since it made up for the previous neglect in the matter of treatment of source material, and thus brought about considerable progress in the classification of that material. (The well-known Austrian scholar M. Hoernes summed up the achievements of the period in his *Basic Systematics in Prehistoric Archaeology*, 1893).

Of the methods in earlier use, the comparative method made further

20. Archaeology in schools: the teacher with his pupils visiting an archaeological excavation (an illustration from a German book for children, 1877).

progress and was extended to types of material which had previously been neglected, and particularly to pottery, the importance of which had already been stressed by Virchow in 1872 in his famous saying that the sherd is the principal fossil in archaeology. (On the other hand, insufficiently critical comparison led even Virchow to draw false conclusions, as when he suggested a Phoenician origin for the Pomeranian face-urns, in 1876). Analogies were also drawn between prehistoric finds and similar forms in contemporary use both in Europe (e.g. A. Voss in his correct interpretation of the spindle in 1875) and in exotic lands (as when Virchow interpreted vessels with holes in their walls as fumigators, on analogy with Somali pottery). Growing importance was attached to comparative study of European finds throughout the continent; the most valuable contributions in this sphere were made by the Norwegian scholar I. Undset, who was impressed by the wealth of bronze industry in finds in the Danube basin, and the Swedish archaeologist O. Montelius, who travelled all over Europe in search of material and whose judgment was not impaired by narrowly nationalistic views.

Naturally, superficial and erroneous conclusions were often reached, but fundamentally, following the lead of palaeontology, it came to be accepted that certain types of objects which were susceptible to change in shape and decoration could serve as the 'principal fossil' in determining the chronological horizon or assemblage to which the find or the site should be attributed.

One important result of the use of comparative study was the determination and classification (at first only in outline) of archaeological associations of distinct character, usually representing settlement of a specific area at a specific time. These gradually became known under the name of the locality or region where they were first recognized or where they were found in greater measure, and thus in time produced the concept of a culture. For example, German archaeologists called the finds in the urnfields the Lusatian culture, a name which was later generally accepted. The gradual determination of a distinct culture on the basis of an association from an important locality can be traced, for instance, in the development of the term 'Únětice culture' (Bronze Age), from the burial ground at Únětice in central Bohemia. The literature offers the following terms of comparison: finds similar to those at Únětice – finds of the Únětice type – Únětice-type of finds (still a purely classificatory term in the comparative sense) – the Únětice culture. Other cultures were named after some marked feature of the material (e.g. 'face-urn culture'). The term 'Burgwall culture' for that of the proto-historic Slavs in Central Europe was not suggested because forts were a specifically Slav phenomenon, but because it was in forts excavated in the German-Polish marginal region that Slav pottery was first recognized and classified. (It was in the 1870s that R. Virchow used the term 'Burgwalltypus' pottery, preceding the concept of the Burgwall culture.)

This process went on independently of the development of relative chronology (systems of periods); culture as a cultural-historical category and period as an archaeological-chronological category were concepts of a different nature. The use of various analytical methods taken over from the natural or the technical sciences was an attempt to make comparison more objective and more exact. The chemical analysis of metal objects aimed more at investigating the technology of production or the source of the ore, rather than dating (E. von Bibra dealt with the subject in his *Chemical Analysis to the Aid of the Archaeologist*, 1872). Ethnographical parallels began to play an important role in discussions of the production techniques of stone tools.

Carried to higher levels, the comparative method became the more sophisticated typology. If we leave aside the first attempts at something of the sort in the Romantic period, it was not until the last third of the nineteenth century that typology took final form and came into broad use, particularly in Northern Europe, where prehistoric archaeology in its isolation was forced to find a way forward from the Three Age System in assessing its source material. While the Three Age System was struggling for recognition in Central Europe the importance of the closed association was gradually accepted, although Montelius was the first author to coin this precise term. He is regarded as the father of typology, although this is not really justified, just as Thomsen is considered the father of the Three Age System. The idea of gradual development from simpler to more complicated forms was already known to the auxiliary historical disciplines in the seventeenth century and to archaeology in mid-nineteenth century, as we have seen in the preceding chapter; the typological series was no longer a novelty. This was no simple application of Darwin's theory of evolution, however; like the Three Age System, the typological series was adopted for practical aesthetic and exhibition reasons when dealing with museum collections. It was Montelius, however, who turned what was a practical expedient into a method, elaborated the theoretical aspects and applied it as a way of determining the relative chronology of finds, and later, by transference, absolute chronology.

We shall be returning to the story of the development and significance of typology later, in discussing the synthesizing phase of archaeology, but we must mention at least the east German scholar O. Tischler alongside the Swedish archaeologists of this generation; as early as 1880 Tischler had classified Iron Age finds from the Baltic regions with the aid of typological series and closed (grave) associations. His detailed typological division of the Halstatt and La Tène periods became more relevant in Central Europe than in the Baltic regions, where there were relatively few bronze finds in the material.

There were serious problems, however, when it came to the application of the typological method, first among them being the lack of a well-thought-out terminology. Agreement was reached on many terms, but attempts to create a unified terminology (for instance, one applicable to the whole of Germany) always failed. Individual terms which proved their suitability gradually became generally accepted, deriving from various authors of whom Tischler and Virchow were the most prolific in Germany.

The need to arrange the comparative material clearly in order to use it for typological consideration was also felt from the point of view of geography; this led to greatly increased use of type maps (chorology), a new trend in archaeological mapping. Up to now the maps had merely registered sites, but type maps helped to determine the inter-relation of various types and cultures and their relation to their geographical setting, helped to trace trade routes and relationships, and to gain a better insight into economic and cultural conditions in prehistory. With type and distribution maps the archaeologist was able to work in space as he did in time with the help of typological series.

Co-ordination of mapping activities, unification of the signs used, and the systematic publication of maps were all discussed at conferences and congresses, beginning in Copenhagen in 1869; Central European research played an important part. The Polish archaeologist Count Przezdziecki was the initiator (at the Bologna congress in 1871) of an international committee for type maps; work went on for several years with no concrete results to show for it. Germany developed on its own, with a committee headed by O. Fraas established by the second congress of the German Anthropological Society in Schwerin in 1871; most of the work was done by E. von Tröltsch. By 1873 work was in progress on 142 distribution maps, covering the whole of Germany, on the scale of 1:200,000; it was proposed (the suggestion came from Voss in 1875) to draw in 115 types of signs in different colours. In the end only 15 such maps were completed, relating to Bavaria (Ohlenschlager, 1879–90). The idea of distributing the vast number of signs over different versions of the same map had meanwhile developed into that of maps of the different types of material: von Tröltsch began working in this way, and it soon became clear that this was the most important aspect of the problem. The idea of a comprehensive archaeological map of the whole of Germany was dropped and in 1889 the committee was disbanded.

It was not long, however, before these type maps too came up against insuperable technical problems. The voluntary institutions of the day were not yet capable of successfully carrying out such large-scale undertakings.

The archives of sources underground
The extent of the archaeological material, which rapidly grew from mid-century onwards, brought little change as far as quality is concerned, nor was there fundamental change in the composition of the finds. One addition to the types of movable material were the suspect eoliths, while greater attention was paid to microlithic flaked industry. Real progress can be seen, however, in the field of immovable monuments; in the case of graves this applies to cremation burials in particular. They were cleared of erroneous interpretations, partly because the function of pit dwellings was properly understood at last, and partly because hoards were recognized for what they are, and established as a new category. Hoards became a favourite subject for positivist and typological studies, but even more significant for the future was the recognition of settlements as a specific type of archaeological site, and the fact that their importance was acknowledged. We are not concerned here with special dwelling sites such as caves, which for long enough were not even regarded as settlement sites, in spite of the long tradition of their study; in the 1870s and 1880s excavation work and interpretation was directed to ordinary types of settlement sites, farming hamlets, pit dwellings, post-holes, and later to the ground-plan of dwelling structures.

That archaeologists began to study seriously the question of dwelling structures, and to realize some of the specific problems connected with them, was due in large part to the excavation of pile dwellings as the introductory phase of the archaeology of settlement sites. The dawn of this interest, as we have seen, lay back in the 1850s and 1860s, still influenced by Romantic conceptions. Methods of research became increasingly more scientific, however, particularly in Switzerland, and the growing popularization of their results was eagerly welcomed in Central Europe. Significant finds of a comparable nature were discovered by Lake Attersee in Austria, in 1870; on the moors round Ljubljana (Laibach) in 1875; and elsewhere. Another example for Central European archaeologists to follow came from Italy, where *terramare* were excavated. A similar interpretation was then given to some important sites like those in the Tisza valley in Hungary (Tószeg), and thus the term 'Terramara culture' persisted in Central Europe for assemblages of the Copper Age (Chalcolithic), or of the transition from the Eneolithic to the Bronze Age.

Gradually forts, too, were interpreted and studied as settlement sites. Celtic oppida were the most striking forts; a counterpart to the oppida which had been excavated in France since the 1860s was found in Central Europe in 1877, when a hill-fort near Stradonice in Bohemia (see fig. 22) was discovered (although not fully appreciated until the end of the century). During the 1870s and 1880s excavations of Slav forts in the plain between the Elbe and the Oder were more important; studied

21. Archaeological localities in the Positivist Age: a realistic landscape with ramparts of the well-known prehistoric fortified site of Lengyel, Hungary.

mainly by Virchow, these forts gave their name to the newly distinguished Slav pottery – the 'Burgwall type'.

During the 'archaeological' period work in the field was carried on at many more sites, of greater extent, and using more efficient methods than before (stratigraphy, for instance, was now being adopted). Nevertheless most archaeologists had to find out for themselves how to work better, a slow process and one involving error and damage. Helpful handbooks on practical archaeology were published at this time, such as O. Tischler's booklet on how to excavate cremation graves (1883), and particularly a handbook issued by the Prussian Ministry of Education and widely known in Germany, *Introduction to the Excavation and Protection of Antiquities* (A. Voss, 1888) – an archaeological questionnaire and a publicity leaflet from this book were published separately under the title *Short rules for the preservation of antiquities*.

However, the standard of work of individual archaeologists varied very much in practice, and although there are progressive features such as the use of photographic documentation in the field as early as the 1880s, the average level of work was low (as indeed it was everywhere). This is not surprising once we remember who these active archaeologists for the most part were. The well-known German historian T. Mommsen declared at the time that archaeology was a harmless but useless hobby 'for regional doctors and government officials, retired army officers, village teachers and superannuated village priests'. He gave voice to the typical scorn of the professional 'pure' historian, an attitude towards prehistory shared by classical archaeologists as well,

22. Archaeological localities in the Positivist Age: the discovery in 1877 of the Celtic oppidum at Stradonice, Bohemia (the terraced hill on the left side) was one of the greatest discoveries in Central European archaeology.

23. Archaeologists of the positivist period: a skeleton grave is prepared for transportation to the National Museum in Prague (1893).

yet it was true that in the absence of trained professionals and with growing public interest, excavation and work in the field was carried on mainly by members of the middle class who could afford it, cultivated men interested in their country's past, collectors, landowners whose estates yielded interesting finds, and so forth. In such conditions it is no wonder that irresponsible amateur 'friends of antiquities' could very often be more appropriately called their 'enemies'.

There were of course many other enemies, and more powerful ones: increasing industrialization of some regions, more efficient farming methods (including the use of the steam-plough for deep ploughing, which became common in the last quarter of the century), the rapid growth of communications – railways in particular – from the 1870s onwards. Demands that antiquities be protected grew more and more vociferous. The responsibility for conservation passed to an ever-increasing extent to the public authorities, whose work in this field was hampered by red tape and ineffective methods as well as by the consistent upholding of the rights of private property.

The conservation of antiquities took various forms. In Germany the government appointed the first curators of antiquities as early as 1872, on the request of the Anthropological Society, and district authorities as well as public works officials were informed of their duties in a government decree. In the same year Saxony passed regulations to protect archaeological finds turned up in the course of government building operations; a similar regulation applying to the whole of Germany came soon afterwards. Other regional authorities passed similar laws for their own territory (Bavaria as early as 1877), but the proposal put forward by the annual anthropological-archaeological congresses in Mainz (1887) and Bonn (1888), that there should be an Imperial law on the protection of monuments, did not meet with success. The German Anthropological Society established its own committee to preside over the conservation of archaeological material.

Conservation was organized earlier and more systematically in the Austro-Hungarian Empire. In 1873 the competence of the Central Commission for the Investigation and Protection of Monuments was extended to cover all objects of artistic and historical value, and the Commission was divided into three sections, of which the first dealt with prehistory and classical archaeology. A network of curators and correspondents set up at that time went on with the work until the fall of the monarchy. In 1887, on the initiative of the Commission, the Ministry of Education again called upon government departments to report all archaeological finds, but the measure had little effect.

Practically speaking, the Commission dealt only with 'Cisleithania', while Hungary had its own Commission set up in 1868 and replaced in 1881 by the Regional Office for Art and Monuments. It was in the Austro-Hungarian Empire that the first scholar to deal with the theoretical aspects of archaeological conservation emerged; the Polish archaeologist W. Demetrykiewicz, later to become well known, made it the subject of his doctorate thesis presented to the University of Cracow in 1886.

A deeper insight into prehistory
Thus the archives of sources underground began moving more and more

rapidly towards the surface, and although they were not as yet more than chance samples, in the positivist age they began to form a more complete picture. The material found its way to the public partly in museum collections and exhibitions, and to a greater extent in the archaeological literature.

This literature fell into several principal categories. Publications offering a synthesis were not yet popular, except for such isolated cases as the popular *Prehistoric Man* by W. Baer and F. von Hellwald (1874), which found a wide public in Germany; or K. Čermák's *Prehistory of European Man* (1887) in Bohemia. It is typical of the age that the first attempts at a synthetic view were devoted to cultural history (F. von Hellwald, *The History of Culture in its Natural Evolution up to the Present Day*, 1875).

It was more in the spirit of positivism that factual summaries and reports of finds in the various regions were published: Lindenschmit's *Antiquities of our Pagan Prehistory* continued to appear in Germany (vol. 3, 1871–81); a work by F. Hampel, *Antiquités préhistoriques de la Hongrie* (1876–77) appeared in Hungary, while the first review of archaeological finds in Rumania was presented by G. Tocilescu in *La Dacie avant les Romains* (1880). Finds in Poland were dealt with by J. N. Sadowski in his *List of Prehistoric Monuments on Polish Territory* (1887), several years later a similar work was written by L. Šnajdr in Bohemia, *The Beginnings of Prehistoric Topography of the Czech Land* (1891). The Cracow Academy was preparing serial publication of the *Monumenta Poloniae Praehistorica*, but only one volume was actually published, in 1879.

Bibliography became a serious problem after 1870, since the numbers of publications increased so rapidly that it was soon out of the question for the individual scholar to follow everything. Certain periodicals attempted to keep pace with the literature (e.g. the German *Archiv für Anthropologie*, 1866–75), but none of these efforts were either systematic or permanent. In Germany there were at least local bibliographies for some regions (Bavaria and Hessen 1884, Mecklenburg 1889, Prussian Silesia 1892–1900).

A typical feature of the time was the popular scientific literature intended for a wide public interested in archaeology because of information about finds in Europe (pile-dwellings) and even more distant excavations such as those of Schliemann at Troy. Among the authors were Hellwald and Čermák, mentioned above; one of the pioneers in the field was Virchow, who had started publication of the *Collection of Popularly Comprehensible Scientific Lectures*, in Berlin (1866), and had written the first volume himself, dealing with megalithic and pile structures. There were similar popular series elsewhere, too, naturally covering more than one discipline.

Regrettably, it is beyond the scope of our survey to give a more detailed account of archaeological publications in Central Europe in the 1870s and 1880s; this is unfortunate, for it is a period relatively neglected from the point of view of the history of science, although it is of crucial importance for an understanding of how modern archaeology came into being. Taken as a whole, the literature also shows how the age regarded prehistory.

The principal question in the formation of the positivist image of prehistory was of course the relative chronological structure, the 'system'. There were still sharp arguments being carried on over this question, deriving from the divergent attitudes towards the Three Age System round the middle of the century, and still very much alive at the end of it. The focus of opposition to archaeological 'Scandinavianism' was still in Germany, where the attitude combined misunderstanding, nationalism, and political and personal motives. There were few German scholars as objective in their views as Virchow was. The ideological attacks on Scandinavianism were led by L. Lindenschmit Sr, C. Hostmann, and others of the older generation (L. Giesebrecht, G. Klemm, the Englishman J. M. Kemble who had become a naturalized German). The opposition to the Three Age System was less strong in Austro-Hungary, and based on factual rather than ideological grounds; the principal opponents of Thomsen's system here were the Austrian Count Wurmbrand, the leading Czech positivist J. Smolík, and the greatest of Moravian archaeologists of the day, J. Wankel.

The principal objections raised by opponents of the Three Age System were these:

1. Stone artifacts have been found alongside bronze and iron objects in some graves, therefore there was no specifically Stone Age – Hostmann went so far as to say that iron artifacts had been found in the earliest known graves. These objections were overcome when the significance of the closed find was recognized, and critical assessment of finds reached a higher standard.

2. Nor was there any Bronze Age, because bronze artifacts came by trade routes from the South to Central Europe during the Iron Age. (This was disproved as typology and the relative chronology based on typology provided more information.)

3. Stone tools could only have holes bored in them by steel. (This widely held belief was only shaken after experiments by O. Tischler, who exhibited his results in Berlin in 1880 on the occasion of the Congress there.)

4. The decorative motifs on bronze artifacts must have been imprinted by means of steel dies. (This, too, was disproved in experiments by Tischler.)

The climax of the fight against the Three Age System in Central Europe came with the publication of a long polemic by Hostmann in 1875, reprinted in 1890 by L. Lindenschmit with his own introduction. By this time it was only a vain attempt to prolong a struggle already decided by the success of relative chronology in the 1880s; however, it should not be overlooked that the argument helped to make it clear that the three Ages could not be mechanically understood as clearly and sharply defined closed stages of development, each with its unified content and universal validity. Nevertheless the majority of archaeologists had still not achieved a more profound and critical attitude towards existing schemes, and were content to subdivide and classify each period in ever greater detail.

The ideas of a previous Bone Age or Timber Age did not find favour, in spite of isolated attempts to propagate them and suggestions based on doubtful finds (e.g. in caves in southern Poland, by G. Ossowski); the main difficulty was the lack of finds to substantiate these ideas. Investigation of the Stone Age made great strides, however, primarily thanks to archaeologists in Western Europe who had already divided the period into earlier (Paleolithic) and later (Neolithic) stages. It was now possible to speak of four periods. Increasing knowledge of the Paleolithic period was also due to the work of scholars in the West; as the Romantic age was dying out, it was Paleolithic research that headed the new trend of scientific positivism, and became the domain of natural scientists, geologists and anthropologists; paleolithic studies went their own way independently of the other branches of prehistoric archaeology.

The natural sciences played an important role, for instance in determining the climatic changes which had come about during the Pleistocene, on which was based the new science of glaciology which emerged after the middle of the century, particularly in the Alps (the foundations of the system of four alpine glaciations were laid by A. Penck in his book *Man in the Ice Age*, 1884). The natural sciences were responsible for research into the origin and development of man as an animal. The discussion centred round Darwin's theory of evolution, which had been applied to the evolution of man by German writers as well as by T. Huxley (and indeed earlier, by the zoologist K. Vogt in lectures delivered at Neuchâtel in 1862, and by E. Haeckel in 1863; these were later included in his *Natural History of Creation*, 1868). Opposition to Darwin's theories was strong, and was led by Virchow, out of principle; the conflict came to a head at the congress of the German Anthropological Society in Munich in 1877. The story of Fuhlrott's discovery of Neanderthal man is well known as an illustration of the difficulties encountered in trying to establish new paleoanthropological ideas against the forces of tradition. Neanderthal man was better received in the West than in the land where his remains were found – although it was the German anthropologists G. Schwalbe and H. Klaatsch who finally rehabilitated him, about the year 1900. In the meantime several important finds of remains of this extinct type of human being had been made in Central Europe (particularly in the Šipka cave in Moravia, 1880). Virchow's authoritarian attitude made discussion of possible pre-Neanderthal types of human beings impossible for many years.

Eoliths were not of particular interest to Central European archaeologists, except in northern Germany, nor was it possible to prove Early Stone Age settlement. The earliest finds were all from caves, which were being investigated in many parts; here and there the terms established by G. de Mortillet for French archaeology were already being applied to local finds.

The first site where important investigation of Paleolithic caves in Central Europe took place was the Moravian karst, where the 'father of Moravian prehistory', Jindřich Wankel, had been working since the early 1850s, and where Martin Kříž joined him later. The first Paleolithic finds on what is now Czechoslovak territory came from Wankel's excavations at Býčí skála (1867), and two other cave sites were also productive, Kůlna and Pekárna. After 1880 Karel J. Maška explored the Šipka cave in northern Moravia. Open sites were also discovered, including the now well-known Předmostí, where in 1894 Maška excavated a common grave of about 20 individuals of the Late Paleolithic. Excavation of caves developed in Germany during the 1860s and later in Franconia and Thuringia, but the most significant results came from open sites: Oskar Fraas explored Schussenried in 1866, and in the 1870s Munzingen, Weimar, Taubach and other sites were investigated. From 1884 onwards the famous Willendorf site in Austria was being studied as well as caves in the Alps, the latter without success. Another classical cave region was that around Cracow in southern (Austro-Hungarian) Poland, where Count J. Zawisza had been digging since 1871, followed later by Godfryd Ossowski.

The later period of agricultural prehistory did not provide such sensational finds, but the Neolithic period deserves detailed comment, because of its crucial importance for the prehistory of Central Europe. The archaeological aspect of the Neolithic, and indeed its very existence, were among the main problems of the 'archaeological' age.

For the broader public the Neolithic period (still considered as a single whole, and not yet distinguished from the Eneolithic) was represented by villages of pile-dwellings, an identification which persisted up to the end of the century, thanks to the detailed picture of prehistoric life filled in by the wealth of finds of organic substances there. In contrast to the Paleolithic, however, the West made little contribution to knowledge of the Neolithic. Neolithic remains in Central Europe presented a much richer but also a much more intricate picture, and the situation was further complicated by German refusal to accept the existence of a Stone Age at all. Nevertheless it was here that significant facts about the beginnings of an agricultural civilization in Europe were gathered.

The Neolithic was one of the touchstones in the struggle for and against the Three Age System. It is not easy to trace the involved history of the gradual distinguishing of different cultures of this epoch of prehistory. It is in Germany that such work began, when Friedrich Klopfleisch of Jena University, originally an art historian, first commented on the different types of ornament used by prehistoric potters. He had already tried to classify Neolithic pottery in 1874; later he distinguished Central European pottery with a ribbon-like ornament from that of the more northerly megalithic culture, and called it 'Bandkeramik'. In the early 1880s he distinguished Corded Ware from Bandkeramik; Corded Ware was then studied in Central Germany by his student Alfred Götze, author of the first doctorate thesis in prehistory to be presented at a German university. At first no distinction was made between Corded Ware and Stroke-ornamented Ware (Late Neolithic); the category was first established in Germany by Virchow (1878) and in Bohemia by Ludvík Šnajdr, although it was the Czech archaeologist Karel Buchtela who introduced the term 'Stichbandkeramik' (Stroke-ornamented Ware) in 1899. Klopfleisch himself did not study Stroke-ornamented Ware, although an important Late Neolithic site had already been found in the region (Rössen, 1879). Nevertheless the information so far collected was still insufficient for a systematic classification of the Neolithic.

The specifically Central European problems concerning the Neolithic were, however, already taking shape; a 'transition age' between the Stone Age and the Bronze Age was sought, after the idea of mechanical succession due to arrival of new populations had been dropped. Chemical analysis proved that among bronze artifacts there were some which were more or less of pure copper, and the evolutionist position led to the conclusion that copper must have been used in prehistory earlier than copper alloyed with tin – bronze. (J. E. Vocel had already suggested this in 1853.) The wealth of copper artifacts from some regions of Hungary led to the appearance of the question of a new period – the Copper Age – on the agenda of the world archaeological congress held in Budapest in 1876. First raised by the Swiss archaeologist F. Keller in 1863, it was then put forward by the Hungarian archaeologists F. Pulszky and J. Hampel, but opposed by Montelius who compared this material with finds from the Near East, proving that the suggested Copper Age was the first stage in the Bronze Age as he saw it.

Nevertheless the idea of a transitional Copper Age (Chalcolithic, Cyprolithic, Aeneolithic – the last from the Latin *aeneus*) was a very topical one for Central Europe, where neither Mortillet's system nor that of Montelius was quite satisfactory. Besides the works of F. Pulszky (*The Copper Age in Hungary*, published in Hungarian in 1883 and in German in 1884), and J. Hampel (*Antiquities of the Bronze Age in Hungary*, published in Hungarian in 1886 and in German in 1887), the outstanding Viennese archaeologist Matthäus Much dealt with the subject in his *Copper Age in Europe* (1886, rewritten and supplemented for the 1893 edition). The *terramare* of northern Italy produced a number of finds which could be compared with those of Central Europe, and in the 1870s the idea of an Eneolithic period was also voiced there by Pigorini. Towards the end of the century the term 'Terramara culture' appeared in the Central European literature, roughly equivalent to the last stage of the Neolithic and the earliest stage of the Bronze Age as accepted today. In 1875, after making acquaintance with the collections in the Prague National Museum, Virchow pointed out the striking similarities between terramara finds and Czech Eneolithic pottery of the Řivnáč culture, a branch of the broad category of channelled ware which had not yet been identified; he knew of no analogies in the German material.

Research into the Bronze Age proceeded more calmly and in a more balanced fashion than that into the preceding period, and views changed only gradually. The views of Montelius on the classification of the Bronze Age, published in the 1870s and 1880s, aroused considerable interest in Central Europe; the first of his six stages included the 'Copper Age', while the sixth covered what is now accepted as the Hallstatt period. In practice the system was not accepted, however, as it was elaborated from the North European standpoint.

A more vital question concerning the Bronze Age was the origin of bronze industry, and here the old Romantic arguments were echoed in a new form. There were rich finds in northern localities in Central Europe where neither copper nor tin are found. The old idea that bronze finds were imports from Italy, and particularly from Etruria, lingered on in the beliefs of the last opponents of the Three Age System. The new approach was heralded by Western scholarship's 'discovery' of Central European bronze industry at the time of the Budapest congress referred to above. I Undset had realized as early as 1880 (*A Study of the*

Hungarian Bronze Age) that the Carpathian basin had served to transmit this culture northwards, and also recognized the connection with the Near East on the other hand, a connection which was to be strongly stressed later. Some scholars (Virchow, 1889) linked the bronze artifacts to the arrival of the Indo-Europeans on the scene, but this theory was short-lived.

The concept of an Iron Age going up to the early historical period was the least clear of his three Ages to Thomsen himself. It was not until the 1870s and 1880s provided a number of new discoveries that the picture became clearer and a relative chronology could be worked out. Like bronze, iron technology too was now believed to have come to Central Europe by degrees, from the South-West (I. Undset, in particular, in his *First Appearance of Iron in Northern Europe*, published in Norwegian in 1881 and in German in 1882); previously it was thought to have originated in the South, in Italy. At first the Iron Age was divided into pre-Roman and Roman, the post-Roman period being thought contemporary with the earliest history of each people. After the middle of the nineteenth century new discoveries made it possible to distinguish two main pre-Roman phases in the cultural history of the Iron Age in Central Europe. The evidence for the earlier phase came from the years of investigation of Hallstatt in Austria, beginning in 1846 and published by E. von Sacken in 1868 (*The Burial-Ground of Hallstatt in Austria*), while the later phase was most clearly seen in the wealth of iron industry discovered at La Tène in Switzerland, where excavation – mainly after 1874 – gave the results published in 1885 by E. Vouga and in 1886 by V. Gross.

It was material from Central Europe that served the Swedish scholar Hans Hildebrand as the argument for a division of the Iron Age in Europe into two periods, first in 1872 and later at the Stockholm congress in 1874; the earlier period was to be named after the Hallstatt site while the later was to be called the La Tène period. It was also Central Europe that provided grounds for a further subdivision of these two periods. O. Tischler divided the Hallstatt period into an Early and Late phase (1881), and the La Tène period into three phases (1885); his ideas persisted even after archaeologists opted for the more detailed system proposed by P. Reinecke. Tischler also distinguished two different regions for the Hallstatt culture in Central Europe, an eastern and a western. Significant finds in several countries of Central Europe soon helped to fill in the details of the scheme: more finds in the Hallstatt style came from regions south-east of the Austrian Alps, in particular bronze situlae (bucket-shaped vessels), finely decorated (e.g. from Vače in Slovenia, 1882, and Kuffern in Lower Austria, 1891). In Moravia J. Wankel excavated an unusual 'grave' in 1872, that of a wealthy East Hallstatt community in the Býčí skála cave. Confirmation of a detailed subdivision of the La Tène period came from Bohemia, where a votive treasure of 2,000 pieces of bronze jewellery, known as the Dux hoard, was found in the medicinal hot springs at Duchcov in 1882.

There were scholars who attributed the Hallstatt culture to the Celts at this stage, but the most significant step forward was that of linking the La Tène culture, hitherto considered as German or Etruscan, to the Celts. G. de Mortillet proposed this at the Bologna world congress in

1871, but it was Undset who finally achieved its acceptance ten years later, pointing out at the same time that finds of La Tène artifacts did not necessarily mean the presence of ethnic Celts.

Roman remains in the Danube valley and to the south of the river continued to be excavated along the accepted lines, but the culture of the native peoples beyond the Roman sphere still waited to be discovered.

Not nations, but mankind

From the eighteenth century onwards the proto-historic period had formed one sphere of archaeological interest – the period of chaos after the fall of the Roman Empire in the West which saw the gradual rise of early mediaeval tribal and national entities known from the earliest written sources of local history. During the Romantic Age this interest had been coloured by the nationalism of the emerging nations seeking their roots, their ancestors and their traditions.

During the positivist, 'anthropological' phase, however, archaeology laid clear stress on the general economic, social, and especially on the cultural history of the inhabitants of Europe; this change of attitude came about at the expense the ethnohistorical approach which had suffered from the crisis of Romanticism in the transition from one epoch to the next. Archaeological work changed in character, and at the same

24. Archaeological finds in the nineteenth century: a picturesque group of bronze objects framing a Romantic view of its finding place – Hallstatt in Austria (from Hoernes' *Urgeschichte des Menschen*, Vienna, 1892).

time its aims changed. Positivist archaeology was concerned with the bare facts, and scholars tried to exclude from their conclusions fantasy and emotion, the passions which had so often encumbered arguments for specific ethnic sources of archaeological material. The anthropological approach deliberately transcended national boundaries, and was furthered in this direction by the trend which brought archaeology closer to the natural sciences. The conferences and congresses which became such a feature of scientific life during this period played an important part in making archaeology more international in spirit.

Such broad questions as the Indo-European problem were most typical of the spirit of this phase in the history of the discipline. (The term 'Aryan' came into general use during this period, alongside 'Indo-European', which took the specific form 'Indo-Germanic' in the work of German writers.) The philological aspect of the question was clarified particularly by German linguists (K. Müllenhof and others), but it was not clear whether and how philological arguments could be applied to archaeology, although the ideas of the Romantics that the Germani or Slavs had arrived directly from Asia (India) had already died a natural death. During the positivist period the tendency at first was to believe in the archaeologically verifiable home of the Indo-Europeans and the 'Caucasian' race in the Caucasus, which was why Virchow conducted excavation campaigns there. Later on it seemed that Northern Europe was the cradle of the 'Indo-Germani', according to 'linguistic palaeontology', which traced the words for some northern plants and animals common to the Indo-European group of languages. It was not yet clear how far a pre-Indo-European population should be assumed in Europe, whether the people should still be regarded as Finno-Ugrian, and what date and which archaeological culture should be attributed to the arrival of the Indo-Europeans in Europe. According to A. Götze the latter would be Bandkeramik pottery; according to M. Hoernes, Corded Ware. Linguistic palaeontology as developed in the Indo-Germanic spirit by V. Hehn (*Cultivated Plants and Domesticated Animals*, 1870) and O. Schrader (*Comparative Philology and Prehistory*, 1883) tried to prove that the diversification of the original single Indo-European language had come about before man acquired a knowledge of metalworking.

Many complications were also caused by attempts to identify culture, language and race, in which the Aryan race = the Nordic = the Indo-Germani. It was at this time that the fair-haired, blue-eyed, dolichocephalic northerner became the prototype of the Germani (P. Poesche, *The Aryans*, 1878; K. Penka, *The Origin of the Aryans*, 1883), in opposition to the French school of anthropological thought which was more inclined to see the original Indo-Europeans as typically brachycephalic.

Clearly, a degree of sublimation of nationalism in the archaeological period hampered objectivity in research. The ideological motivation of the ever more powerful and ambitious German Empire found a new outlet in the racial theory of Indo-Germanism, which was to reach its peak in the subsequent period at the height of German imperialism. Celtic archaeology lacked this political motive force, and in Central Europe tended to retreat into the background during this period, after being in the limelight in the Romantic Age. At the same time the growth of archaeological research among the Slav nations meant that the Slavs acquired special significance in the ethno-archaeology of the eastern regions of Central Europe. There are two main trends to be perceived in this sphere, one of scientific objectivity and one of moribund Romanticism. The former was based on earlier Slav philology (particularly the work of P. J. Šafařík) and produced important syntheses in the following period. The latter took the form of autochthonism, rejecting the view already propounded by Dobrovský and Šafařík that Central Europe was not the original home of the Slavs. Jan Kollár and some of the Polish Romantics were the spiritual fathers of this movement, which later found a focus in Moravia, where J. Wankel and his followers were active in Olomouc in the 1880s, along with the Slovene M. Žunkovič, the author of several uncritical autochthonist works.

The main problem for archaeology in practice was still that of distinguishing Germanic from Slav finds in the German–Polish–Czech border regions. Both sides were interested, and since power politics gave German (Prussian) archaeology a better start, it was here that the question was decided. In these plains forts were a noticeable feature of the archaeological material, and had been regarded as Slav monuments ever since the cremation burial grounds formerly known as Wendenkirchhöfe ceased to be attributed to the Slavs. In 1869 and 1872 Virchow had declared these burial grounds to be older Germanic remains and the forts to be later Slav monuments.

Here pottery was an important criterion. In the more involved archaeological situation in Bohemia and Moravia, M. Lüssner's correct observations in eastern Bohemia (c. 1853) and those of L.Šnajdr in central Bohemia, on the hill-forts historically proved to be Slav, fell into oblivion. To the north of these regions, in an area where the range of ceramic finds was rather simpler, the view of G. Lisch held good; he had asserted in 1847 that sherds with parallel horizontal lines and wavy ornament, common in finds from these forts, were of Slav origin. This was confirmed by an officially commissioned team led by J. Worsaae and G. Lisch after studying finds from the fort of Arcona on Rügen Island off the Baltic coast. It was known that this fort had never been rebuilt after its destruction by the Danes in 1168, and all the remains were therefore necessarily Slav. Virchow finalized the attribution of this type of pottery ornament to the Slavs at the world congress in Stockholm in 1874 and again in 1878; he called it the 'Burgwalltypus' because it was found in connection with forts.

The principal criterion for ethnic attribution of graves was still the shape of the skull; Virchow, A. Lissauer and others classified the dolichocephalic skulls as Germanic. It is interesting to note that as early as the 1850s the Czech archaeologist J. E. Vocel knew that the S-ended hair-rings associated with Slav skeleton graves of the early historic period were of Slav provenance, and yet did not draw the logical conclusions; nor did Lisch in 1863. That is why (the language barrier also playing a part) the credit for recognition of this ornament is generally given to the young Danish archaeologist S. Müller, who published his conclusions after a study trip to Silesia in 1877.

Virchow continued to explore the archaeological material from this border region, and found that the occurrence of these hair-rings was limited to the Slav regions in the eastern parts of the German Empire, as defined in the earliest written records, as was his Burgwall pottery with wave ornament. He presented his theory at the congress of the German Anthropological Society in Kiel in 1878, concluding in opposition to Montelius that the Slavs had inhabited these parts before the Germani. In later contributions to the discussion, and particularly at the congresses in Breslau (Wrocław) and Halle in 1884 and 1900 respectively, Virchow tried to break down prejudice and bring the views of German and Slav archaeologists more into line with each other, but without success; the changing mood in the German Empire did not favour such reconciliation.

On the Slav side of this national barrier the objective scientific trend was still struggling against moribund Romanticism with its picture of the Slav past. The idea that the Lusatian urnfields of the Bronze Age and the Hallstatt period were Slav in origin was of great importance for the future development of archaeology. The view originated in Germany, where Virchow at first wrongly believed that the stratification of urnfield pottery and 'Burgwall' pottery in the forts proved the genetic sequence of two phases of Slav settlement (1869). By 1872, however, in view of the difficult delimitation of the Germanic element in the Bronze Age, he decided rightly that there could be no genetic sequence where the two cultures were chronologically so far apart. (Less correctly, he was willing to see Germani in the people of the urnfield culture.) Autochthonist Slav archaeologists, on the contrary, believed the urnfields were Slav, and sought confirmation in decorative motifs common to urn-field pottery and contemporary Moravian folk embroidery and costume.

It should be noted in passing that it became the fashion during the positivist period to introduce into the discussion of ethno-archaeological questions linguistic-historical entities little known and therefore entirely vague, such as the Basques, the Thracians, the Illyrians, the Iberians, the Ligurians, and so on, while the earlier Romantic manias of this sort, postulating the Phoenicians or the Etruscans, gradually subsided to more realistic dimensions.

The ethnographical model of the beginning of history
Apart from such striking but uncharacteristic exaggerations as we have just discussed, it is obvious how much clearer and more credible the archaeological picture of prehistory and early history had become during the positivist period, and how much had been done to set a relative chronology. (Absolute chronology, as yet unaided by the natural sciences, was slower in developing.) The positivist approach and the anthropological basis of archaeological research had helped to free the discipline of the remnants of earlier mechanical classifications and had encouraged the acceptance and further elaboration of an ethnographical (ethnological) model of prehistoric society. It was no longer a matter of correlating certain finds with certain ethnographical backgrounds, but the generalization of conclusions leading to theories of a primitive classless community. There theories were based either on the recognition of general laws followed by human society in its historical development (the system of Marx and Engels and their predecessors) or on broad comparative material from the sphere of culture and anthro-

pology–ethnology, the typical approach of Anglo-Saxon scholars (E. B. Tylor and others).

Central European archaeology, too, existing in symbiosis with other 'anthropological' disciplines, was much closer to ethnographical parallels than before, and this was bound to be reflected in the interpretations put forward. The scientific journals of the time alternated between description and interpretation of prehistoric times and the description of the cultures and customs of primitive backward peoples. This could not remain simply a formal question, but led in time at least to individual cases of co-ordination of the archaeological and the ethnographical material. For the time being there was no synthetic approach to these two related social sciences.

In itself static in character, the ethnographical model was dynamized in two ways, often functioning together. The earlier impulse was that of evolutionism, still often mechanically understood in the spirit of the natural sciences: man everywhere passed through the same evolutionary stages, which have only to be recognized in the archaeological material and given names; everywhere the evolution led to the discovery of agriculture and metalworking; man developed mentally in the same way

25. Archaeological reconstructions: 'Funeral song on the battlefield of Tursko', drawn by M. Aleš in 1890, shows typical examples of the notion of 'classical' Ancient Slavs, created by Czech artists during the nineteenth century.

as he had developed physically during the Pleistocene. This attitude was typical of the analytical, positivist phase of archaeology, and was abandoned later when it was realized that the stages of relative chronology are not definable in strict sequence, sharply delimited and universally valid, and that regional differences existed both in the direction and the rate of development.

The second impulse, which became dominant, took into account these developmental irregularities and explained them by external events and influences. At first the idea of invasion was popular, explaining changes in the material culture by the appearance on the scene of new populations; the favourite argument of trade was also used: in the 1860s and 1870s trade appeared the all-powerful factor in the explanation of the occurrence of new products or new Technology in prehistory, even to the extremes of Etrusco-mania, Phoenicio-mania and so forth. Later, towards the end of the century, diffusionism became the archaeologists' preferred standby.

As yet there was little interest in the social context and the economy of prehistoric society. The positivist approach to archaeology here came up against the broader and more complex approach of the anthropologists and ethnographers, which led to the realization that co-operation with natural scientists was essential (H. Schaaffhausen, *The Methods of Prehistoric Research*, 1872). The former approach prevailed still, however, because it agreed better with the mood of amateurism among most of those interested in archaeology, still basically antiquarians and collectors. The find and its description were preferred to study of the site and the broader context of the finds.

Some scholars had already stressed the influence of climatic factors on prehistoric settlement and agriculture, but research in this field had not yet developed, perhaps partly because the soil of Central Europe had preserved far less evidence of natural conditions in prehistory than the pile-dwellings of Switzerland or the peat-bogs of Northern Europe. Evidence of animal husbandry in the form of animal bones was much more plentiful. Yet even this evidence was not systematically utilized, interest centring at most on the classification and quantifying of the species represented.

It was from outside the archaeological sphere that awareness of the significance of economic conditions came, the result of studies in national economy and ethnology. The system of the three stages of economy, that of hunting and gathering (Palaeolithic, Mesolithic), pastoralism (Neolithic, Eneolithic), and agriculture (Bronze and Iron Ages) found both supporters and opponents. Some scholars assumed that agriculture had already begun in the Neolithic period. Nevertheless the system persisted into the early twentieth century, when it was definitely replaced by the two-stage system in which the non-productive mode of life (hunting and fishing) was followed by the productive mode (agriculture and animal husbandry). The subject gave rise to a number of studies on the beginnings of farming, e.g. A. Nowacki, The *Development of Prehistoric Farming*, 1880.

The social and cultural evolution of prehistoric man also seems to have been studied more by writers in other disciplines than by the archaeologists themselves. Of the various aspects of tribal society, tribal and family relationships and the question of the matriarchal community received most attention. Unfortunately the discussion was purely theoretical, taking no account of the archaeological material. The historian of laws and civilization, J. J. Bachofen, assumed in his *Mother-right* (1861) that there had been a straightforward development from promiscuity through matriarchal to patriarchal law; others dated patriarchal law earlier than the matriarchate.

The classical evolutionists, whether German, English, or of other nations, ignored individual differences and regarded prehistoric ('primitive') society as a single whole, developing along one line of 'progress' from the simpler to the more elaborate; the facts were arranged to fit this universal model, moving towards the highest form, that of European civilization in their own day. This was not so much the influence of Darwin as the tradition of eighteenth-century French philosophy. The foundations for this theory were laid by the American scholar L. H. Morgan and developed further by Marx and Engels around the year 1880. Karl Marx presented the most progressive and best elaborated theory of prehistoric society as a whole, beginning with his essay *To the Critique of Political Economy* (1859). His theory of social-economic forms was not directly concerned, of course, with the subject of primitive community life, and was not reflected in the archaeology of the day.

Friedrich Engels was more closely concerned with the subject, and carried Morgan's views further, particularly in *The Origin of the Family, Private Property and the State* (1884). The three-stage history of man proposed by Morgan and Engels (savagery, barbarism and civilization, each with three sub-divisions) was the first consistently materialist conception of the economic, social and cultural history of the human race, and to some extent took into account the contemporary state of archaeological knowledge.

In opposition to the evolutionists were those who arranged the facts acquired by research not in time but in space, regarding as the principal agent of cultural change not evolution, but migration or diffusion. This school developed somewhat later and will be discussed in the next chapter, but it should be noted that neither trend exercised much influence on archaeological practice. 'Pure' positivist archaeology developed alongside but independently of either, showing little interest in broader economic and social issues. It was not until the next period, one of synthesis, that these different trends merged.

130

Tracing the Evolution of Cultures:
the Age of Typological Synthesis

*The historical background I: Central Europe on the eve
of the First World War*
The 1890s were a time of great significance for Europe; trade and
industry expanded rapidly, monopoly capitalism grew more powerful,
and together with the need for new sources of raw materials and for new
markets, brought to a climax the era of imperialism. The policies of the
great powers were almost entirely directed towards completing colonial
expansion, dividing up the remnants of as yet unexploited territories
between them, disappointing those who entered the game too late, and
creating international tension as a result. In home policy this situation
was reflected in official encouragement for nationalist attitudes often to
the extremes of chauvinism. Relations between the powers became
strained.

Europe was already split into two camps, following the lines of
existing secret agreements: the Triple Alliance made public in 1891, and
the Triple Entente which emerged as its counterweight, in spite of some
difficulties in holding it together. The Triple Alliance was focussed on
Central Europe, with Germany playing the principal role, Austro-
Hungary as its fairly reliable political satellite and Italy as a shaky third.

Kaiser Wilhelm II, who came to the throne in 1888, was a typical
representative of belligerent German imperialism and, after forcing the
ageing Chancellor Bismarck to retire, opened the way to an official
policy of expansion abroad and the build-up of the strongest army in the
world at home. The social life of Germany, where patriotism was
whipped up on various grounds, especially in the last years before the
war, was marked by pan-Germanism and the popularity of bellicose

associations in support of national armament, and by the suppression of any self-expression by non-German nationals in the Empire, particularly by the Poles. For all its internal problems and crises, to the world outside Germany appeared a stable country, exceptionally strong in the military sense, and determined to give its ruling class the share of power in Europe and the colonies which they were demanding. The German colonial empire was small, and could no longer be expanded by traditional means; the consequent tension between Germany and the more 'fortunate' England became the decisive factor in international relations in Europe.

Austro-Hungary was not a prime participant in this power game, neither possessing colonies nor anxious to acquire them; in this still backward state the role of colonies was played by the vast hinterland to the east and south-east, including Bosnia and Herzegovina annexed in 1908. In addition, the Empire had its own internal problems. The fact that the ageing Emperor Franz Joseph I had been on the throne since 1848 (he died in 1916) created an illusion of continuity and unity, although the Empire had been split in 1867 into two independent parts engaged in hostile rivalry: Cisleithania which formed a more or less constitutional monarchy, and Transleithania (Hungary) where there was an abysmal gap between the ruling Magyars and the other peoples. The Hungarian nobles and the nascent bourgeoisie exercised ever growing pressure in their policy of Magyarization, nipping in the bud any attempts by the non-Magyar peoples to maintain even their cultural identity; the Croats, who were the strongest of the subject peoples, were the only force strong enough to resist to any degree. In Cisleithania, too, political life centred almost entirely on the nationalist question; the Poles enjoyed a measure of autonomy (their situation under Austria was better than that of Poles in the region annexed by Russia and very much better than in Silesia and Greater Poland under German rule), the Czechs wavered between loyalty and opposition in their still unanswered demand for equality, and even the Germans were increasingly influenced by the pan-German propaganda for a Greater Germany issuing from their imperial neighbour.

It was only the strength of tradition that held the Austro–Hungarian Empire together, and any more serious shock could prove fatal, and yet it was Austria that became, almost by accident, the first link in the chain that dragged Europe into a vast military conflict in 1914.

Archaeology grows up and becomes a modern science
Like the Romantic wave before it, the positivist movement exhausted its strength and the ebb took with it the recent enthusiasm for an anthropological integration. Neither of these tendencies influenced archaeology for a longer period than the Romantic wave: in all, two decades. And once again, what happened in archaeology cannot be separated from what was happening in the history of Europe as a whole. The end of the ninteenth century gave free rein to those currents which corresponded to the spirit of the age in this field as in others.

The great powers were naturally looking for allies on the ideological front in their rise to power, and the historical sciences again became a ring where there was no room for unprejudiced anthropologists who were only interested in humanity as a whole. The spirit of the age had no interest in scholars at work in their studies, nor in connoisseurs of ancient monuments who were content to describe in infinitesimal detail the characteristics of their finds. The time had come to open the ancient arsenal of nationalism once more, and to compose the facts determined by the previous era of scholarship into vast images of the past, as far as possible assimilable in a composite picture of modern times.

This concern remained a distinctive feature of archaeology and the literature from the 1890s to the First World War, and it is this which allows us to define the period as one of archaeological (typological) synthesis. Objectively, the scholars of this period, like the Romantic synthesists before them, were trying to fill in the picture of prehistoric times, and thanks to the factographic approach fostered in the meantime, they were also better equipped for the task. And yet it was this routine positivism that made them unable to rise above their material, fascinated as they were by the quantity and variety of it, and all the opportunities it offered for classification in various ways. There were still no objective methods of dating to come to their aid, and they were not accustomed to draw on other social sciences nor on the natural sciences; most of them lost sight of their goal and failed to see man behind his vessels and his bronzes, man who had made these artifacts. They got no further than ingenious attempts to classify all the material from a given territory, in itself an important step at that stage of development; they constructed archaeological systems in which the sequence of cultures, groups and types took the place of a real history of prehistoric society. The synthesis they achieved was an archaeological and not yet a historical one.

When archaeology sobered up after intoxication with the natural sciences it returned to the motherly embrace of historical science – however much the stepmother it still seemed. The ethnohistorical approach again found an important place in the theory and strategy of archaeological work, although it was now based principally on positivist methods and on the results of typological studies. This change in the times was reflected in the German-speaking regions in a new name for the discipline; the newly revived historical approach rejected the term 'prehistory' (Vorgeschichte) as a survival of anthropological thinking: 'prehistory' meant that pre-history, i.e. non-historical man whether in prehistory or in the primitive cultures of the contemporary world, was regarded as distinct from history in the narrow sense of the word. The Germans found a convenient substitute in the term Urgeschichte (especially K. Jansen, 1886), which stressed the continuity of prehistory with history proper. Naturally the traditional concepts persisted in German as well as in other languages.

Thus the archaeological period between mid-nineteenth century and the outbreak of the First World War was marked by a distinct change from one theoretical outlook to another, although in method they were similar, both being based on the positivist approach to material and with the stress laid on the archaeological aspects. The second of these two phases, which we have called synthesizing (or historicizing, as contrasted with the previous analytical, or anthropologizing, phase), was moving in the direction of the outlook which would be adopted later, but in itself was too brief to formulate this outlook and give it currency. Archaeology was still the spiritual heir of the nineteenth century, and indeed represented the climax of its intellectual development, in that thanks to the strong positivist tradition it achieved an archaeological synthesis in the narrower sense of the word.

It is of course difficult to trace a clear boundary between these two phases of the archaeological period – partly because the image of the discipline at this time was a very varied one. New tendencies appeared alongside the older trends, 'minority' tendencies alongside established ones; even the Romantic-synthetic trend was not yet dead, and revived in the atmosphere of the turn of the century. The distinction between amateurs and professional archaeologists grew clearer, and so did that between those whose researches contributed to the advance of the discipline theoretically, and those who dug merely for pleasure and amusement. (By no means all 'diggers' and collectors took sides in the scientific and political struggles that will be described in this chapter.) It

Map 7. Central Europe in the period of typological synthesis (c. 1900).

Universities:	6 Vienna	12 Cluj/	16 Krapina
1 Munich	7 Budapest	Koloszvár	17 Willendorf
2 Berlin	8 Cracow		18 Szeleta
3 Leipzig	9 Lwow	*Localities:*	19 Vinča
4 Wrocław/	10 Szeged	13 Jevišovice	20 Ariuşd/Erösd
Breslau	11 Warsaw	14 Buch	21 Lengyel
5 Prague		15 Předmostí	

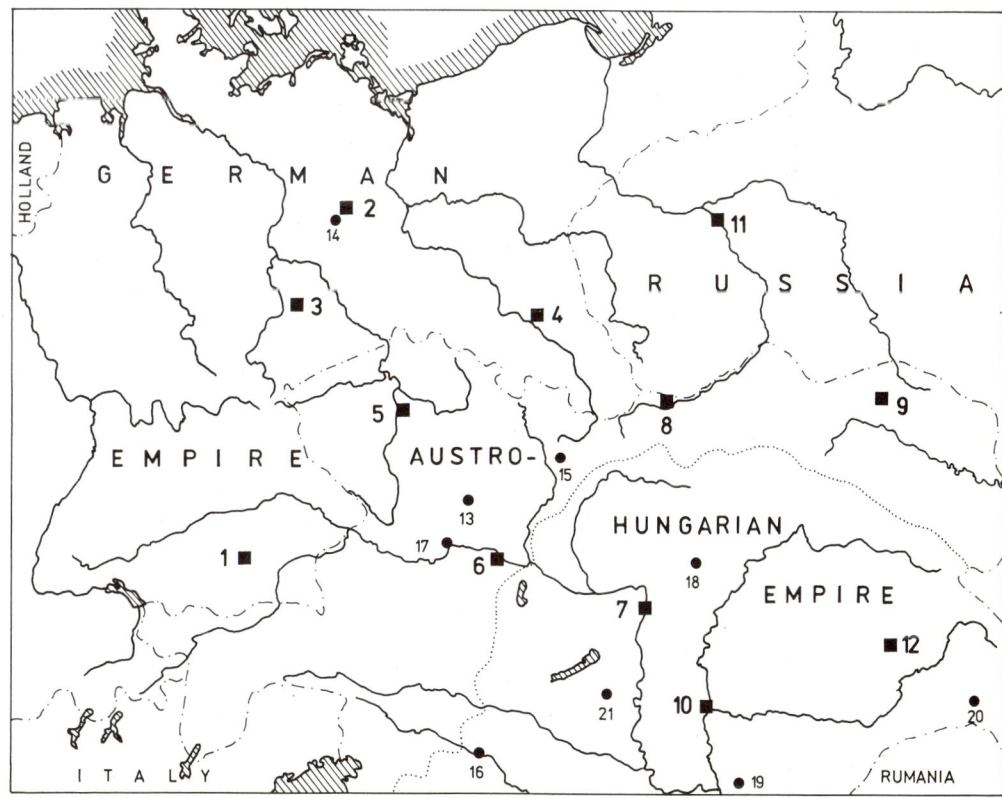

is thus only roughly that we can place a dividing line between the two phases about the beginning of the 1890s, when several of the older features slipped into the background and new traits suddenly made their appearance. With a certain amount of generalization we can formulate the differences between the two phases:

1890s

Analytical phase	Synthetical phase
The fight for the Three Age System dies out	The Three Age System generally accepted
Static division into periods	An attempt at a more complex view of evolution
Classification of cultures and groups	Their arrangement in systems
Mechanical-materialist approach (interest in basic economic phenomena)	Interest in social phenomena (religious ideas, art)
Culmination of mechanically conceived evolutionism	The theory is overcome
Positivism – concerned with things	First attempts to see the people behind the things
Tending towards the natural sciences	Return to the historical sciences
Integration in anthropology	Disintegration of anthropology
An international science	Rebirth of the idea of a 'national science'
Interest in humanity as a whole	Interest in the early stages of one's own nation's history
Predominance of analytical studies and those dealing with the material	Broad syntheses, lexicons

In what concerns the organization of research, the second phase of the archaeological period was not nearly so distinctive as the first. Most of the institutions were set up between 1870 and 1890, and there was little quantitative change afterwards. It is more to the point to trace changes in quality: in all the anthropological societies the short-lived integration fell apart and the original components emerged again. Prehistory was the most important of them, with a well-established hinterland of practical archaeologists in the field, and of collectors, while physical anthropology and ethnology had to rely on a few professionals usually engaged in purely theoretical study. This was the reason why prehistory finally came out on top in almost all these anthropologically-oriented societies, and left its mark on their activities. This even happened to the strongest of these societies, that of Germany, after the death of R. Virchow in 1902; his personality alone had held it together, the personification of tradition.

Since at the same time prehistory as a discipline was again viewed as a historical science, most scholars came to the conclusion that anthropology, in its earlier form, was finished. H. Seger, for example, said so at the Heilbronn congress in 1911. For this reason the archaeologists of Central Europe broke off their last bonds with the traditionally structured societies in the last few years before the war, the time when this process was coming to a head; instead they formed new societies concerned only with prehistory as a historical and national science. The central prehistory societies were of course of greater significance than the regional bodies (the Moravian Archaeological Club, 1906, the Czech Archaeological Club, 1910); with their specific aims, the former were deliberately formed as a counterweight to the old societies, and were informed with the attitudes of the synthetic phase. In Germany the new trend was headed by Gustaf Kossinna, a young scholar of Germanistic studies who acquired a great influence after the death of Virchow. In 1909 Kossinna set up the German Society for Prehistory, in Berlin, and founded the journal *Mannus*. The name of the new society, renamed more aptly in 1913 the Society for German Prehistory, shows its primarily nationalistic aims: for Kossinna prehistory was a historical science, and in particular 'eine hervorragend nationale Wissenschaft' (1911). A separate Prehistoric Society was also established in Vienna in 1913, catering for the whole of Cisleithania and publishing its own journal, the *Wiener Prähistorische Zeitschrift* (from 1914). The Society was close to university circles, and was headed by the finest Austrian prehistorian, Moritz Hoernes; the secretary was O. Menghin.

The rapid growth in the numbers of private collectors and amateur archaeologists, together with the membership of these and similar societies, shows how popular the subject had become with the middle classes of Central Europe. During the last two decades of the century the number of archaeological collections quadrupled, and this was due largely to private collectors. Nevertheless the museums were now definitely recognized as the home of archaeological finds and the institutions concerned with the protection and exhibition of material. Yet the museums were slow in developing during this period, especially central museums. The time when national museums were being established had passed (the proposal to set up a German–Austrian national museum in Vienna found little support in 1908); the complexity of this type of museum was soon seen to be an anachronism. In Central Europe, on the other hand, the time was not yet ripe for the formation of specialized central museums; when the Berlin Anthropological Society suggested setting up a national archaeological-ethnographical museum in 1891, the proposal was rejected by the German government because there was already a Germanic Museum in Nuremberg – although this institution was mainly concerned with archaeology from the point of view of art history.

The attitude of the German imperial government towards archaeology changed, however, with the times. It was not until the discipline acquired a political tinge under Kossinna that they began to take it into account, at first encouraging the study of Roman monuments in western Germany, which fitted in with the longing of the German Empire for grandeur. Kaiser Wilhelm II himself suggested that the Roman fort in Saalburg should be reconstructed; work went on from 1897 to 1907, creating an original open air museum. Investigation of the Roman frontier region was particularly favoured in Germany, partly thanks to the work of the 'Limeskommission', set up in 1892 with the historian T. Mommsen at its head, and partly thanks to the Central Romano-German Museum in Mainz, revived by K. Schumacher (1899) after the death of Lindenschmit. After complicated negotiations a Romano-German Committee led by H. Draggendorf also started work (1902).

The architecture of the museums of the time was far from ideal for their purposes; they were built for show, in imitation of Renaissance palaces (Vienna, Prague), Gothic churches (the Museum of the Mark of Brandenburg in Berlin), or Roman city gates (Halle), and not with regard for the requirements of the professionals who were to run them. This was partly due to the fact that there were as yet few professional archaeologists, and therefore few laboratories and storerooms were needed; they aimed at exhibiting as much of their material as possible, and the rest usually found a place on the lower shelves of the show-cases, there to form the rudiments of working collections consisting mainly of less attractive sherds.

Museum exhibits always reflect fundamental progress in both theory and technique; for this period typology showed the greatest advance, while here and there closed associations were put on show. As in the previous period of Romanticism, advances in museum technique came from Scandinavia, with occasional outbursts of traditional disdain for the German sphere. Like Worsaae in 1846, in the 1870s H. Hildebrand criticized German museums for exhibiting remnants of pagan culture instead of type series of artifacts. Towards the end of the century, however, there were a few attempts to improve the situation. Of the permanent systematic exhibitions we can mention that arranged by J. L. Píč in the Prague National Museum (1893 onwards), which was ahead of its time in emphasizing the ethnohistorical evolution to be traced in prehistory, rather than typology. Perhaps the most advanced of the short-term exhibitions was that of the excavation of an Iron Age settlement site at Buch near Berlin, presented by the head of the excavation work, A. Kiekebusch. Visitors to the exhibition of building techniques in Leipzig or to the special Buch exhibition arranged in the Museum of the Mark of Brandenburg in Berlin (1914) were the first to be given some idea of what excavation was really like, illustrated by plans and cross-section drawings and all kinds of artifacts and material brought to the museum from the field (post-holes, hearths and stratigraphical sections). The ground-plans were shown by means of models on the scale of 1:10 on an area of 4×1.2 metres. This exhibition foretold the nature of prehistorical exhibitions in the future: whereas the first period in archaeology displayed objects for their own sake, and the second period exhibited their relations in time, the third already demonstrated their spatial relations, reconstructing the life of prehistoric man (as well as the techniques of archaeological work). The numbers who visited the exhibition are a proof of its unusual character: there were 14,000 in the course of the first two months of the Berlin exhibition and the number had risen to 26,500 by the outbreak of the First World War.

An opportunity to display archaeological finds elsewhere than in the museum was presented by the great national and imperial exhibitions which were so popular a feature towards the end of the nineteenth century; in Central Europe for example, there was a Jubilee Exhibition in Prague, 1891, and the exhibition celebrating 1,000 years of the Hungarian state, held in Budapest in 1896.

Finally, attempts were made to lay the foundations of a separate discipline dealing with museums and museum practice (museology), to a large extent connected with archaeology. The first museological journal in the world began to appear, the *Journal of Czecho-Slav Museums and Archaeological Societies*, published by K. Čermák in Caslav, Bohemia, from 1896 onwards.

There were also significant advances to be observed in the universities. After the first wave of founding archaeological chairs towards the end of the Romantic period (after 1850), and the second wave deriving from anthropological-prehistorical attitudes (around 1870), the third and most widespread began about 1890 and persisted unweakened up to the outbreak of the First World War. By now of a remarkably high standard, these departments were concerned entirely with prehistory, while the work carried on was of course archaeological, in keeping with the times.

In the German-speaking sphere the first university teacher whose appointment specified lecturing in prehistory was Dr J. Heierli, Privatdozent at the Technical University of Zurich, in 1889. At the turn of the nineteenth and twentieth centuries there were 20 universities in the German Empire, of which only three boasted a chair of anthropology, only one of these with the standing of an Institute of Anthropology with a regular seminar (Munich, under Professor Ranke). The prehistory line came into its own with Professor G. Kossinna, who began lecturing on the subject in 1902, later with H. Schmidt as Reader. In the same year K. Weule became Professor of Ethnology and Prehistory in Leipzig; H. Seger lectured in Wrocław as Reader, from 1907. We should also mention the Honorary Professors Johanna Mestorf in Kiel (1899) and J. Naue in Tübingen (1901), both of an older, positivist generation.

Prehistory was accepted in the universities of Austro-Hungary earlier than in Germany. Four of the nine universities in existence at the turn of the century had prehistory in their syllabus: Prague, where L. Niederle became Reader in Prehistory and Ethnology in 1891, becoming Professor in 1898; Vienna, where M. Hoernes began lecturing in 1892 and became Professor in 1899, with O. Menghin as Reader from 1913; Budapest, where J. Hampel was Professor from 1890, although here prehistory was still only a part of the subject of classical archaeology; and Koloszvár (now Cluj) in Transylvania, with B. Pósta as professor from 1899. In 1905 this figure was raised by two universities in the Austrian-occupied part of Poland: Cracow, where W. Demetrykiewicz was Reader, and Lwow, where K. Hadaczek became Professor of Classical Archaeology and Prehistory. From 1906 L. von Marton was Reader in Szeged in Hungary.

It is important to look at conservation organization also: by the end of the previous period the first steps towards a more specific programme of protection for archaeological sites and finds had been taken. An important landmark in this development was the thesis by H. Seger dealing with methods of conservation work ('The protection of prehistoric monuments', 1903). In practice, however, the institutions and conditions of the second half of the century remained in force up to the First World War. In the Cisleithanian regions of the Austro-Hungarian Empire the archaeological aspects of conservation were entrusted to a network of curators and correspondents under the First Section (prehistory) of the Vienna Central Commission for the study and preservation of historical monuments and works of art. The regional Institute for Art Treasures in Hungary was reorganized in 1898 to become the Supreme Regional Office for Museums and Libraries, which also undertook archaeological work. Prussia too appointed provincial curators in 1891, and by the opening of the twentieth century most of the German states had followed suit. A provincial Office for the Preservation of Monuments was set up in Bavaria, with P. Reinecke as Chief Curator from 1908. These countries also passed conservation laws, and that adopted in Hessen in 1902 was the first German law to cover explicitly archaeological material not yet excavated. Yet the German Empire as a whole was one of the last civilized countries to legislate on the subject, in spite of the extent and renown of the work of German scholars in classical and Oriental archaeology, at home and abroad. In 1914 there was at last a law passed limiting the right to excavate sites, if nothing more, in order to prevent uninformed disturbance of archaeological sites.

From the part to the whole
The positivist age turned its attention so emphatically to study of the actual material that this firmly rooted tendency could not be shaken during the succeeding period. There were some changes in the focus of interest, due to improved methods, especially in typological determination, and stricter criteria. Certain types of find were given more importance, for example bronze fibulae, which became the favourite 'raw material' for typological treatment, although some scholars preferred pottery in this role because they considered pottery as a local, purely regional product, while the fibulae were thought to be imported. Nevertheless potsherds, established as the 'principal fossil' in archaeology during the preceding period, remained crucial in the determination of the culture represented by a site. This was in close connection with the expansion of the study of settlements, which became perhaps the most striking feature of work in the field during this stage. The first settlement sites with pits and post-holes were published (Grossgartach in Germany, by A. Schliz, 1901). Detailed stratigraphy of the different occupation levels and superpositioned artifacts was introduced, allowing conclusions to be drawn as to the relative chronology of a site (e.g. C. Koehl's excavations of Neolithic sites round Worms, or J. Palliardi's work on Eneolithic hill sites in southern Moravia). A. Kiekebusch's excavation of the Buch site, Berlin, 1910–14, was a remarkable achievement, particularly the exhibition which brought it to the notice of the public. It was in connection with this site that it was first stated explicitly (at the congress of the German Anthropological Society in Nuremberg, 1913) that settlement sites are more important than graves as a source for prehistory. This too was one of the turning-points between the old and the new era.

As a result of his work on this site Kiekebusch published the first introduction to archaeological fieldwork on similar sites (*Prehistoric Settlements and Methods of Investigating Them,* 1912), another step beyond the boundaries of the archaeological period.

In apparent contrast to these advances, there were no revolutionary changes in study of the separate periods of prehistory in the course of the synthetic phase. No new periods were distinguished; there were only new classifications within the recognized periods. Archaeological studies still moved along two parallel lines, study of the Paleolithic remaining largely the sphere of the natural sciences, while prehistory was the field dealt with by traditional archaeological methods.

The Paleolithic period was still the weak point of prehistoric studies in Central Europe, with the exception of Moravia, but even here a comparatively promising beginning was not fully followed up. It is true that lack of interest in the more fashionable subject of eoliths did no harm; only a few individual scholars like M. Verworn were interested in them in Germany, while in Bohemia and Moravia eoliths were not accepted. Paleolithic studies found a sounder basis for the chronology in the system of four glaciations, named after four rivers in the German Alps – Günz, Mindel, Riss and Würm respectively (A. Penck and E. Brückner, *The Alps in the Ice Age*, 1901–3). Significant anthropological finds stimulated Paleolithic studies, too, providing evidence of the presence and the appearance of Late Paleolithic hunters (particularly a common grave of 20 individuals in Předmostí, Moravia, excavated by K. J. Maška in 1894), of Neanderthal man (numerous finds, among them those in a cave near Krapina, Croatia, by K. Gorjanović-Kramberger in 1899) and even of earlier forms of man (the Mauer jaw – O. Schoetensack, 1907).

In spite of all this material there was very little interest shown in the Paleolithic. The few stone tools found in Central European sites were overshadowed by the famous sites of western Europe, except for a few rich sites, frequently exploited, like Předmostí in Moravia and Willendorf in Upper Austria. The French material was considered decisive and the conclusions drawn from it were accepted almost without opposition in Central Europe, and the French Paleolithic scheme was applied there without correction. In addition to the Moravian sites, research intensified in Germany at the outset of the twentieth century, because of its proximity to France: R. R. Schmidt should be mentioned in this context; O. Herman instituted excavations in the hilly country of northern Hungary (the Szeleta cave, 1907). For most regions of Central Europe, however, the accepted conclusion at the time was that they had not been settled in Paleolithic times – a conclusion which had total acceptance for the Lower Paleolithic. The theory that there had been a hiatus between the Paleolithic and the Neolithic, according to de Mortillet's French system as mechanically interpreted for Central Europe, still held good, while the first finds of Mesolithic stone industry (for instance, in southern Bohemia in 1907) were not recognized.

The Neolithic retained its crucial importance among the later periods. It was no longer a question of defending its existence; its opponents were by now an insignificant minority. The problems now were correct classification, relative chronology, and consequently the right approach to the evolution of Neolithic (and Eneolithic) agriculture. During the last quarter of the nineteenth century some idea of the basic cultural groups of this period of prehistory had already been formed, although still in terms of pottery groups; interpretations of their relative chronology and genetic relations varied a great deal. The foremost Neolithic scholar in Western Germany, C. Koehl of Worms, concluded in 1906 that the earliest (and original) prehistoric farmers were the people of the Linear Pottery culture (spiral-meander motif). In 1912 he distinguished four stages of Neolithic: Michelsberg 'pile-dwelling' pottery; Bandkeramik (i.e. Linear and Stroke-ornamented); Corded Ware; and 'Zonenbecher', a term used for Rhineland finds that corresponds roughly to Bell Beakers. A. Götze, the archaeologist of the Central German school, in Berlin, drew up a more complicated scheme which he presented at the Halle congress in 1900, applying it to the whole of Central Europe. He classified Corded Ware and Bell Beakers in the earlier complex, while the stages of the later complex were (in chronological order): Globular Amphorae and Bernburg pottery; Bandkeramik; and Rössenstyle pottery (*The Classification and Chronology of the Later Stone Age*, 1900). Reinecke agreed with him, with the reservation that Corded Ware and Bell Beakers could not be proved to be contemporary. A different conception, and one that seems more correct today, was elaborated by the Czech university school, and presented by K. Buchtela in his article 'The prehistory of Bohemia' (1899); here the cultures were placed in reverse order, with Linear pottery as the earliest and Corded Ware and Bell Beakers at the end of the series.

Problems of a different sort faced archaeologists in the middle Danube basin, where the Lengyel culture can be traced from Upper Neolithic times. Here the Moravian scholar J. Palliardi worked out a chronological sequence of late Neolithic and Eneolithic cultures which was not properly appreciated at the time; modern archaeological research, however, has confirmed his conclusions, which were based partly on his discovery of Moravian Painted pottery, and partly on a consistent application of stratigraphy in the excavation of the hill settlement near Jevišovice (published from 1897 onwards).

These details were of great importance for archaeology in Central Europe, but only of secondary significance compared with the general theory of the spread of agriculture and of Neolithic culture, which was elaborated at this time by European scholars; they saw these developments as a typical case of diffusionism, and assumed that the lands of the ancient East were more advanced in their culture than barbarian Europe. Although the role of the Near East was not yet clarified, the crucial importance of the Balkans for Central European culture was beginning to emerge; archaeologists there learned of significant results from Greece (where C. Tsountas published his finds from Sesklo and Dimini in 1908), from Serbia (where M. M. Vasić excavated the Vinča site near Belgrade the same year), and from Transylvania, where the results of ten years' digging on a Neolithic site at Ariuşd (Erösd) were published in 1914. Several important sites were already known in Hungary (Lengyel, published 1888–92), but these offered only isolated information. The links between the cultures of the Balkans and those of Central Europe north of the Danube had not yet been established.

The Bronze Age was traditionally much less problematical and gave rise to little discussion, scholars being mainly concerned to classify their knowledge under archaeological periods and phases. The Scandinavian model was followed for Central Europe by P. Reinecke (*On the Chronology of the Second Half of the Bronze Age in Southern and Northern Germany*, 1902); his system was reminiscent of that of Montelius, but more detailed and up-to-date, and is still used in outline today. He divided the Bronze Age into four stages, A–D. As far as Central Europe was concerned, however, Reinecke was closer to Undset and Tischler. Diffusionist theories were of course brought into play to interpret Bronze Age phenomena, displacing the simpler ideas of the migrationists. Like Undset before him, M. Hoernes stressed the importance of the Near East for the Bronze Age in Central Europe (*The Prehistory of Man*, 1892), as did Montelius, tracing the contacts for northern bronze industry to Italy. This point of view brought Montelius into conflict with the uncritical autochthonists of the North who declared bronze industry to be native to the North and invented a 'Nordic-Germanic bronze culture' to represent it (Montelius, *The Chronology of the Earliest Bronze Age*, 1900). His theory, which was widely recognized, assumed that during the first phase of the Bronze Age knowledge of the metal spread into Europe from the south-east. It should not be forgotten, however, that the Danish scholar S. Müller had already formulated this theory clearly in 1884; this Scandinavian contribution to archaeological knowledge met with fierce opposition from German scholars (M. Much and others) because they thought it depreciated the importance of the pure Germanic prehistoric culture.

The theories and arguments concerning the origin of bronze industry were parallelled by those concerning the beginnings of iron industry. Reinecke based his classification of the Hallstatt and La Tène periods into four stages (A to D), which gained increasing support in Central Europe, on the same principles as his classification of the Bronze Age. It was not until later that the difficulties his system presented, especially for the transition from the Hallstatt to the La Tène periods, became obvious.

Thus the main achievement of the phase of typological synthesis, in relative chronology, was the creation of graduated systems based on typology, systems comprising either a sequence of cultures or a series of chronological phases; the systems were then integrated to cover the development of material culture from the Neolithic up to the early historical period. It was no less important, however, that progress was also made in the sphere of absolute chronology, mainly thanks to the evolution of a method of historical dating based on comparative typology. As certain types of finds from neighbouring regions were gradually arranged in sequence, it became possible to link the evolution of most parts of Europe to the historical dating of the classical region of the eastern Mediterranean. The principal method used was that of synchronization, dating associations of finds with the help of imports from the 'historical' regions, or of forms and ornaments known from some specific ancient culture. The leader in this branch of research was again Montelius, who succeeded around 1900 in synchronizing the dating of European finds with Italian material, then Greek, and finally with Egyptian chronology as established by his precursor, W. Flinders Petrie. The results were not always perfect, and were criticized from various points of view, but nevertheless this was the only way to estimate the absolute chronological relations between the prehistoric cultures of Europe; it became the basic method of dating for the next half-century, right up to the 'radiocarbon revolution'.

The difference between the analytical and the synthetical approach to prehistory in Central Europe can best be seen reflected in the literature, and without attempting an exhaustive picture we can at least draw the outlines.

Typical of the period are the general surveys of prehistory and its civilization, in which we can trace the trend for taking the archaeological approach towards a historical interpretation – even though the result, where prehistory was concerned, was usually no more than a history of archaeological cultures, the evolution of objects, drawn up according to 'influences'. Syntheses of this type multiplied from the early 1890s: the Viennese scholar M. Hoernes was outstanding, with his *Prehistory of Man* (1892), *Prehistory of Mankind* (1895), and *Natural History and the Prehistory of Man* (1909), which was the greatest synthetic study of the period. The Prague scholar L. Niederle published *Man in Prehistoric Times* in 1893; in Germany there was J. Ranke's *Man* (1894), followed by R. Forrer's *Prehistory of European Man* (1908) and H. Hahne's *Prehistoric Europe*. C. Schuchhardt's *Ancient Europe* also belongs to this list, although it did not appear until 1919. Hoernes dealt with a specific aspect in his *Prehistory of the Arts* (1898), the first synthetical survey of knowledge on the subject.

Archaeological encyclopaedias made their first appearance at this time, at first short volumes like Forrer's *Encyclopaedia of Prehistoric, Classical and Early Christian Antiquities* (1908) or J. Schlemm's *Dictionary of Prehistory* (1908), followed by a more extensive collective work edited after the war by M. Ebert (*Encyclopaedia of Prehistory*, 1924–32), which comprised 15 volumes with contributions by 128 authors and covered primarily the material discovered during the archaeological period. L. Niederle's *Slav Antiquities* (from 1902) and *Life of the Ancient Slavs* (1911 onwards) were encyclopaedic surveys dealing with a specific ethnic group, like the *Encyclopaedia of Germanic Archaeology* edited by J. Hoops (1911–19).

Regional surveys of prehistoric and early historic settlement remained traditional in conception. G. Schwantes' *Prehistory of Germany* (1908) went through several editions, and J. Kostrzewski's *Greater Poland in Prehistoric Times* appeared in 1914. An older scholar, F. Pulszky, was the author of the *Archaeology of Hungary* (1897). During this time there were two synthetic studies published in Bohemia as part of the polemic between the two schools of thought: J. L. Píč's extensive *Antiquities of the Land of Bohemia* (1899–1909), which covered the entire archaeological material and attempted (not too successfully) a historical synthesis; and the *Handbook of Bohemian Archaeology* by L. Niederle and K. Buchtela (1910), which was an archaeological synthesis but more important for later developments, and which remained the theoretical foundation for the modern Czech school of archaeology until the middle of the twentieth century.

26. Archaeological publications in the nineteenth century: Hoernes' *Urgeschichte des Menschen* was the best synthesis of that time.

Publication of source material and catalogues, studies of individual
sites, etc., continued throughout the period; but this was not an
especially important feature of the time.

From national pride to chauvinism

Very briefly we have noted the progress made in archaeology and
archaeological classification in the narrower sense, and the fact that
some works published during the synthetic phase were already attempting a complex historical approach to the subject. What was the
situation with regard to those aspects which cannot be called strictly
archaeological?

The term 'diffusionism' has occurred several times in our account of
attempts to explain the evolution of prehistoric cultures. Evolutionary
theory had been applied to interpret archaeological developments in
specific regions, but the diffusionist theory made it possible to construct
a logical picture of the prehistory of Europe and neighbouring regions of
the Mediterranean. It was during the period we are now discussing that
diffusionism reigned supreme, and indeed it did not lose its crucial
significance for European research until the advent of the 'radiocarbon
revolution' in the 1950s.

At first it was possible to explain individual aspects of prehistory
simply, in terms of the migration of peoples and tribes, but in the
context of the whole of Europe and beyond, and in particular to explain
the emergence and spread of basic cultural achievements, a more
complex explanation had to be found. At this point the idea of cultural
diffusion came into its own, suggesting that influences, ideas and models
were passed on by more advanced peoples to the less advanced with
whom they came into contact, a process which produced the same
phenomena in different places sometimes sooner, sometimes more
slowly. In itself the idea was certainly sound, and was often justifiable,
but as so often with new and fashionable trends, it was generalized and
taken to extremes. For a long time the idea of 'influence', usually vague
and ill-defined, became the magic wand with which to explain why some
cultures seem related, why their material goods showed resemblances,
and how they came into being and developed into other cultures.

The first and most significant wave of diffusionism was represented by
the theory of 'Lux ex oriente', which assumed that the cultures of the
ancient Near East were always more advanced than those of prehistoric
Europe, and that all cultural achievements gradually spread over
Europe from the eastern Mediterranean region, passing over the
Balkans or through Italy. This theory was universally accepted as long
as its principal foundation held good – the 'short' chronology of
European prehistory. Montelius elaborated their chronology, becoming
the classic exponent of diffusionism; his *Earlier Cultural Periods in the
East and in Europe* (1902) was the keystone of the involved theoretical
basis for this school of thought. For Montelius, as for S. Müller and
others, particularly in Scandinavia, 'the civilization which was gradually
born over our continent, was for long but the pale reflection of Eastern
civilization'.

From the outset, however, critical voices were raised in opposition to
this 'Eastern miracle', voicing both objective reservations and – more
frequently – subjective, nationalist views. Many German scholars could

not accept an interpretation of prehistory which disparaged the nineteenth-century European's inborn feeling of superiority to the East, and rejected the idea that the greatest civilization in the world derived not only from beyond the Germanic North, but even from outside Europe. The theory that the cradle of Europe civilization was in the north of the continent was put forward to counterbalance the 'lux ex oriente' theory; among the foremost proponents of the former was the elderly Austrian scholar M. Much (*The False Reflection of Oriental Culture in Northern and Central Europe in Prehistoric Times*, 1907), while in Germany it was supported by G. Kossinna and his followers (G. Wilke, H. Hahne and others). In their eyes it was 'the heroic Indo-Germanic people of the North' who had invented megalithic monuments, metalworking, writing etc.

The forced nature of this explanation, which conflicted with a number of facts in relative chronology and in archaeological material, was responsible for its rejection even among German scholars, while elsewhere it found no favour. The idea of diffusion from the Near East, on the other hand, gradually gained universal acceptance mainly thanks to Montelius and his systematic comparative typological studies. By the end of the archaeological period it had become the foundation stone of European prehistory.

The actual mechanism of the presumed process, however, was far from clear. Of the forms of movement of cultural goods which could be archaeologically proved it was trade that enjoyed the greatest popularity, and hypotheses were put forward based on long-distance trade in amber, copper, bronze, flints and pottery (e.g. A. Götze, *On the Neolithic Trade*, 1896). Finally Montelius himself elaborated the theme in his *Trade in Prehistory* (1910).

Not even during this synthetic phase, however, was a broader and more generalized view of prehistoric economy worked out. The archaeological material remained the principal objective, and the presumed movements of peoples and of cultural achievements were expressed in terms of objects and forms. One of the few advances made in the archaeological attitudes of the day was that the old triple scheme of economic development, from hunting to pastoral life and then to settled farming, gave way to a simpler and more correct division into two stages, a non-productive one (hunting and gathering) and a productive one (farming and animal husbandry).

The social evolution of prehistoric man was studied by scholars of other related disciplines rather than by the archaeologists themselves. The ethnographical model which held the field during the archaeological period encouraged the wide application of the results of comparative ethnography (ethnology), from mechanical application to prehistoric conditions of ethnographical conclusions often drawn from unsuitable contexts, to serious attempts at a broad picture of prehistoric life in the spirit of social and cultural anthropology. Besides the classics of British scholarship, their German colleagues were active here, like H. Schurtz (*The Prehistory of Culture*, 1900), K. Weule and H. Klaatsch. In the German sphere another trend arose in opposition to the evolutionists; instead of chronological arrangement of the facts in time, these writers arranged them in space, creating a system of geographical regions (Kulturkreis) characterized by certain unchanging cultural phenomena which were secondarily transferred to other regions. Here cultural change was seen not as the result of evolution, but of migration or diffusion. The theory was elaborated by L. Frobenius and developed further in Germany particularly by the Cologne school under F. Gräbner, by F. Ratzel and A. Bastian, and by the Vienna school with the Austrian priests W. Schmidt and W. Koppers. To a certain extent they based their theory on the division of cultural history into three stages; for the stage of savagery they assumed a unified 'preculture', while the subsequent agricultural phase was divided into geographical regions.

Neither of these tendencies had any appreciable influence on archaeological thinking. 'Pure' archaeology went on along its own lines, in relative independence, and with little interest in matters not directly concerned with material finds. It was left for the next period to integrate the various viewpoints from which prehistoric society was being studied.

Yet if there was one aspect which interested the archaeologists of the day beyond their classification and systematization of the material, it was the ethno-historical approach to prehistoric culture. This fact has already been mentioned, and the reason why it was that just at the turn of the nineteenth to twentieth centuries that Central European archaeologists returned to the apparently out-dated attitude of the Romantics; at a time when one would expect the universal anthropological interest in Man during the 1870s and 1880s to produce a 'nameless' synthesis of the economic and social evolution of prehistoric man, these scholars used the methods and factual knowledge offered by the analytical phase in renewed efforts to trace the thread of 'national history' back into the prehistoric past, and once again to put the question: 'to which nation does this particular find belong?'

This did not apply to all archaeologists to the same degree; there were of course some who remained faithful to the anthropological approach, but nevertheless the historicizing approach became typical. On the one hand there were those who held a sober, 'anonymous' view (like Montelius and S. Müller), while those who took the 'pseudonymous' attitude were concerned with history only so far as it enabled them to attach the names of ancient tribes and peoples to a given culture and thus prove the greatest antiquity for the group to which they themselves belonged (like Kossinna and his followers in Germany, and to some degree J. L. Píč in Bohemia). This approach was the typical one for German archaeologists and even Virchow was forced to admit at the Lübeck congress in 1897 that the time for discussing the broad features of the history of the human race was past, and that it was now once again time to discuss primarily what concerned the history of the Germans themselves.

The nationalism of the Romantics had disappeared from the scene for a while, but it had not died out. It remained latent, only to be revived in the 1890s as an expression of the political forces of nascent imperialism; at times it became modern chauvinism, a dangerous ideological weapon. Everyone with the slightest acquaintance with the archaeological thinking of the time will at once think of Kossinna, who declared archaeology to be the most national of the sciences and the ancient Germani to be the worthiest representatives of prehistoric Europe and the only subject fit to be studied by serious archaeologists.

There was another difference between the old and the new Romantic-ism, in that the new trend in Central Europe not only produced no Celtomania, but even managed without the Celts as an ethnic group. Not that the scholars concerned denied the existence of the Celts; Virchow even chose (intentionally, one wonders?) the 'uncommitted' subjects of the Celts in Germany as the subject for his address to the Kassel congress in 1895, naming Bohemia as the crucial area to be studied in future when dealing with the question of the original Celtic homeland. But the question was not dealt with for a long time to come. For the moment the Celts were of no greater importance in the archaeology of Central Europe than the Illyrians, the Thracians or the nameless bearers of any of the prehistoric cultures. Once again the protagonists were the Germani and the Slavs – or those so regarded by the archaeologists of the day.

At the Kassel congress Kossinna attacked any surviving interest in the Celts, saying: 'The other face of the Celtic question, for the Germans, is the Germanic question. We therefore put the question thus: where in the prehistory of present-day Germany are we dealing with the Germani, and where with non-German peoples?'

Gustaf Kossinna was undoubtedly the most controversial personality in Central European archaeology, his 'popularity' putting in the shade some of his no less significant contemporaries, even perhaps better scholars such as C. Schuchhardt or M. Hoernes. Yet not even Kossina was without precursors, nor was his teaching without its roots. He derived not so much from the anthropologizing archaeological school of Virchow as from the historical-linguistic field of German philology. An important factor was the theory of the North as the cradle of European civilization, associated with the predominantly philological reconstruc-tion of the Indo-Germanic peoples. In the early years of the twentieth century this line of thought culminated in the formulation of the idea that the Indo-Germans, or the original Germans, could already be found in northern Europe in Neolithic times (the philologists J. Hoops and R. Hirt, 1905, and the archaeologist G. Wilke in his *Neolithic Pottery and the Aryan Question*, 1907).

As could be expected in view of the non-archaeological reasons accounting for the growth of these ideas, this theory did not find favour in northern Europe, but in the German Empire which proclaimed its Germanic character all the louder for the doubtful racial and tribal purity of its inhabitants, past and present. The work of the philologist K. Müllenhof, the first to combine philological and archaeological proof, was rounded off by F. Kauffmann in his *Science of German Antiquities* (1913). Kossinna, who was a disciple of Müllenhof, brought the ideas of philological Indo-Germanism into archaeology; the principal ideologist of the era of militant nationalism after the death of Virchow in 1902, he became the foremost representative of German archaeology in the synthetic phase, but without his predecessor's general renown.

Kossinna, who has been called 'a philologist playing the dilettante in archaeology', first put his views forward at the congress of the German anthropological society in Kassel in 1895, where he spoke on the extent of Germanic settlement in prehistory. As a professor at Berlin Univer-sity he published his theories systematically in his *Origin of the Germani* (1911) and *German Prehistory, an Eminently National Science* (1912).

This designation of prehistory, so much in keeping with the mood of the times, and usually linked with Kossinna's name, was not his invention; it can be found at the end of the nineteenth century in the work of Danish archaeologists.

It was, however, to the credit of Kossinna and his school that prehistory became an independent discipline. His approach was known as 'settlement archaeology' ('Siedlungsarchäologie') from the main principle that a clearly archaeologically defined prehistoric or proto-historic cultural entity ('province') also represents an ethnic (or racial) entity, and that the geographical limits of its distribution correspond to the area settled by that ethnic group. It was not settlement sites in the strictly archaeological sense that was meant here, of course, nor the settlement patterns in a given region; Kossinna and many of his disciples were not interested in the least in the results of field observations. What they aimed at was the determination of the historical 'settlements' of different ethnic groups on the map of Europe. This was the reason for the strong emphasis laid by Kossinna and his school on the mapping of the distribution of certain types of finds, chosen as representative of a certain (usually Germanic) ethnic group. These maps were called 'Siedlungskarten', although they were really only type distribution maps. It must be admitted, however, that although archaeological mapping was not a monopoly of the Germans (we should remember J. L. Píč, who supplied his *Antiquities of the Bohemian Land* with synoptic maps of various contemporary types), the settlement archaeology school must be credited with great improvements both in the quantity and the quality of prehistoric cartography.

In fact the methods used in settlement archaeology, proclaimed by Kossinna as his own, had already been used by Montelius and even earlier by J. E. Vocel; the aim was to trace a certain ethnic group back from proved early historical occurrences to prehistory by means of archaeological methods, particularly typology. Kossinna did not, however, respect the principle laid down by Montelius, that typology for this purpose must only be applied within one cultural region; Kossinna was interested in the results, not in the correct application of method. He was thus able to draw a continuous line of Germanic culture back into the Neolithic period in northern Europe, and to prove it the autochtonous culture of a much larger area than that covered by modern German settlement. His subjective and biassed approach and the far-reaching conclusions he based on insufficient factual evidence provoked considerable opposition among his contemporaries (S. Müller in Denmark, E. Majewski in Poland, M. Hoernes in Austria, Czech archaeologists). The one-sidedness of Kossinna's professional interests also aroused comment, itself contradicting the very basis of 'settlement archaeology': 'in his *German Prehistory* [Kossinna] did not illustrate a single house, a single grave, a single fort . . . Museum material was his province: vessels, tools, weapons and decorative objects' (C. Schuchhardt). Only once during his whole life did Kossinna do any excavating, in 1915.

German archaeology was the scene for more and more violent conflicts, as Kossinna's intolerance took the place of the openmindedness of Virchow in his later years. One feature of this intolerant attitude was the nationalists' hostility to the 'Römling' (the Romanized), a hostility which along with the name had been taken from the arsenal of the Romantics, and which rejected all scholarly interest in classical archaeology or that of the former Roman provinces as un-national if not downright treasonable. This attitude played no small role in Kossinna's dislike for the Berlin archaeologist C. Schuchhardt and his circle, centred around the journal *Praehistorische Zeitschrift*.

The basic tenet of 'settlement archaeology', the identification of culture with nationality, was known before Kossinna took it up. While L. Lindenschmidt still believed that there had only been Germani in Germany, Virchow had already reached the conclusion that the Fort 'Burgwall' culture of Greater Poland, Silesia and Pomerania was a Slav culture. For the prehistory of the eastern regions of the German Empire Kossinna admitted the presence of Thracians and Illyrians as well, but right up to the end of his era it was usual to attribute all non-Slav (and often Slav) monuments to the Germani. Kossinna also drew on the Indo-Germanic theory of the northern cradle of European civilization, setting out his views in *The Indo-Germanic Question Archaeologically Answered* (1902). Kossinna and his followers assumed that the Germanic element could be distinguished in northern Europe as early as the Stone Age, and that even then this element was the bearer of progress and creator of all great values (K. Penka, *The Emergence of the Neolithic Culture in Europe*, 1907, and other writers).

In Slav archaeology conditions were different. There was less chauvinist passion; autotochthonism lived on at the fringes of the discipline, and the social commitment of the discipline itself was different from that of German scholars – in direct correlation with the difference between the political ambition and opportunities of German imperialism and those of the subjugated Slav peoples. On the other hand, the economic potential and social organization of these peoples, and their cultural and political situation in Central Europe, were so far advanced in the majority of cases that archaeology no longer needed to play the role of defender of their very existence. Freed from these external pressures, Slav archaeology was able to work towards a more balanced synthesis, which found its classic expression in the work of the leader of the 'university school' in Czech archaeology, Professor Lubor Niederle.

Beginning as a cultural anthropologist in the Tylor manner, during the synthetic phase Niederle turned more and more to Slav archaeology with the intention of replacing Šafařík's *Slav Antiquities* by a more modern, more extensive and more thorough synthesis. He succeeded when (following preparatory studies like his *Origin of the Slavs*, 1896) he began in 1902 the publication of the many volumes of his still standard work; it bears the same title of *Slav Antiquities*. Niederle's principal contribution to the subject was the archaeological standpoint from which he treated it, for hitherto it had been mainly the domain of uncritical authors of the autochtonist school. Niederle followed the tradition formed by Šafařík of seeking the original Slav homeland to the east of Central Europe, whereas J. L. Píč placed it in the lower Danube basin. Both these trends in Czech archaeology agreed, however, that the Slavs could be archaeologically traced back to the Lusatian Bronze Age culture in Central Europe.

Only when the positivist analytical phase made it possible to distinguish Slav monuments from the rest of the archaeological material could Slav archaeology develop along truly scientific lines. It should be stressed, however, that this did not mean that the pre-Slav period was neglected either by the university school or by the more nationally-inclined 'museum school'. It was to the credit of both that at this time Bohemia became the focus of archaeological research on the Slav side of the national boundary, as Virchow declared in 1895. While Niederle and his followers laid the theoretical foundations of the Bohemian archaeological system, the material they used was mostly provided by the museum school led by Píč, which organized systematic surveys and excavation campaigns throughout the province. Compared to this advance, which Niederle dated from the year 1891, Moravian archaeology remained more or less at the analytical stage; this attitude also marked the work of the leading Moravian archaeologist I. L. Červinka, *Moravia in Prehistoric Times* (1902), although in theory it was close to the ideas of the Czech university school. For the time being unfavourable political conditions prevented the discipline from taking root in Slovakia; it was primarily Hungarians who made isolated, more or less amateur, efforts in that region.

In Polish territory there was a slackening of interest and intensity compared with the previous analytical phase, and here, too, the political situation was to blame, in particular in the German-occupied territory where nationalist oppression was intensified after 1900. Nevertheless it was the German-administered part of Poland that ultimately became the liveliest archaeological arena, with fierce rivalry between German and Polish scholars working on parallel lines especially in Poznań, the intellectual centre of the territory. In 1914 Józef Kostrzewski began working there, and soon became head of western Polish archaeology and the leading personality in the emergent Polish archaeological school. While the majority of Czech archaeologists stood aloof from the methods used by Kossinna, Kostrzewski adopted this manner of battle and used the same weapons; he had originally studied under Kossinna in Berlin, and was well aware of both the strong points and the weaknesses of settlement archaeology.

Besides Kostrzewski, and other less striking representatives of Polish archaeology in the easier circumstances of Austro-Hungary (W. Demetrykiewicz in Cracow and K. Hadaczek in Lwow), we must mention E. Majewski, who organized archaeological activities in Warsaw, then under Russian rule; Majewski was the first Polish scholar to criticize Kossinna sharply (in 1902), but himself sought the cradle of the Indo-Europeans in Europe and that of the Slavs in the Polish-German region (*The Ancient Slavs in the Territory of Present-day Germany*, 1899). The political situation in Russian-occupied Poland was not favourable for Polish scholars, although it improved when a measure of democracy was achieved in Russia after the 1905 revolution.

As so often before, the urnfields became a bone of contention in the Polish-German border regions. Virchow had once recognized the Slav affinities of the Lusatian urnfields of the Bronze Age and the Hallstatt period, before going over to the German hypothesis. Kossinna realized more clearly that it was not easy to determine the ethnic identity of such a large and varied cultural assemblage. He did not want to declare it German outright, yet he could not bring himself to accept it as Slav, and so he had recourse to other vague ethno-historical concepts: in 1899 he declared the people of the urnfields to be Thracians (as did Götze in 1900); in 1912 he described them as Illyrians (an ethnic entity introduced into archaeology by M. Hoernes in 1893, when he described them as the bearers of the Hallstatt culture in the southern half of Central Europe).

On the other side of the boundary, naturally, the idea that the people of the urnfields were Slavs was increasingly accepted. It took such firm root in Polish archaeology that it is still accepted today. During the synthetic phase both Czech schools of thought took it into account. J. L. Píč placed the Lusatian culture at the beginning of his 'people of the cremation graves' and attempted in a way not unlike the methods of settlement archaeology to trace the archaeological line backwards from the Slav cremation graves of the proto-historical period to the Lusatian culture. In the search for links in this chain true Slav graves of the Migration Period were discovered, known as the Prague type – today the earliest pottery in Central Europe reliably distinguished as Slav. The significance of these discoveries was not properly appreciated, however. When it was realized that cremation graves of the Roman Iron Age found in Bohemia were Germanic, this carefully constructed typological chain fell apart and the theory that the Lusatian urnfield culture was Slav was dropped.

The Slav monuments of the early historical period in Central Europe had already been precisely classified and were recognized in both camps. Fierce arguments still raged, however, over the extent of proto-historical settlement by Slav peoples in the border regions; these arguments were more violent in the Oder basin and in Silesia, and less so in Bohemia, where the archaeology of the German minority had little scientific standing, and where relations between Czech and German archaeologists were relatively good.

It is clear from this brief outline that conditions in Central European archaeology were by no means idyllic, particularly in the last decade of the archaeological period, and that they were far from the ideal of the previous generation of scholars, dreaming of a harmonious supranational community of scholarly anthropologists. The greatest blame for this situation must be laid on the rising tide of German chauvinism, which struck archaeology with full force. We must add that the objective archaeological arguments we have described were not the grounds for the importance Kossinna and his followers undoubtedly had in their day. Their social prestige and following accrued from their ability to place their professional teachings at the service of the German Empire, in the front ranks of the ideological spokesmen for its imperialist policies. It is in Kossinna's theories that the Germani appear for the first time as the 'Kulturträger' with the historical role of carrying their superior civilization to the inferior non-Germanic peoples, with the rights of the 'first-born among the Indo-Germanic peoples' to force their will on the others. Distribution maps of archaeological types became a convincing argument for expansionist aims: wherever a single find of a type designated as Germanic was found, the land was declared ancient German territory which the Empire held by divine right or else was entitled by divine right to win back, to 'liberate'. The most welcome aspect of Kossinna's ideology was his constant emphasis on the 'fact' that the archaeological evidence showed the Germans to have always been warriors, and therefore they should remain warriors in modern times, too. This explains the favours shown to archaeology in the pre-war period by a number of highly-placed personages, starting with Kaiser Wilhelm himself. And the Emperor's Commander-in-Chief, Field Marshal von Hindenburg, declared as he stood by the graves excavated during Kossinna's first and last campaign in the field (1915): 'As we gaze at this high Ancient German culture we must realize once again that we shall only remain Germans so long as we keep our swords keen and our young men battle-worthy!'

Thus archaeology added its mite, in Germany, to the hell let loose over practically the whole of Central Europe from 1914 to 1918, years which drained the area of its finest men and so changed it that it was barely recognizable.

The historical background II: Central Europe 1914–45
The First World War took great toll of lives in Central Europe, but on the whole the territory of these states was spared. Fierce fighting took place on the fringes; in the east the Russians first drove back the attacking Austro-Hungarian armies and advanced as far as Cracow and eastern Slovakia, but with the help of German forces the Austrian army drove them back into the Carpathians, where the front settled roughly along the line of the present Polish–Soviet border until it crumbled in 1917. The battlefields in the Balkans (Serbia and Rumania) as well as the Italian front which was opened in 1915 but hardly moved throughout the war, were also beyond the sphere of Central Europe.

The Central Powers differed, however, in the internal conditions prevailing, as one would expect from the differences in their pre-war development. Germany remained fairly stable and well-organized up to the end of the war, only to collapse all the more drastically after her defeat. In Austro-Hungary, on the other hand, the organization of the Empire soon disintegrated under the growing discontent of the non-Germans who formed the majority of the population and were forced to fight on the side of a government opposed to the national interests of the peoples concerned. In the course of the war the Czechs and Slovaks, Yugoslavs and to some extent the Poles formed units (Legions) to fight on the side of the Entente powers, and gradually the Allies recognized the political representatives of these nations in their activities in exile. Of decisive significance for the future of Central Europe were both the Russian Revolution of 1917 (which encouraged the revolutionary mood in Germany and Austro-Hungary), and the demand for self-determination included in the Fourteen Points put forward by Woodrow Wilson, President of the USA, in his peace proposals of 1918. At the last moment the new Emperor of Austro-Hungary, Karl (1916–18) tried to save the situation by offering a federal form of government to the peoples within the Empire, but a proposal which might have been favourably received before the war was now no longer sufficient to satisfy them.

While Germany was fundamentally little changed by the Treaty of Versailles (June 1919), Austro-Hungary paid for its part in the war by ceasing to exist. By the time peace was signed in September 1919 at St Germain near Paris (in the Paleolithic Hall of the Museum of National

Antiquities) the Hapsburg Empire had practically ceased to be. The independence of Czechoslovakia was declared on 28 October 1918; the Croats and Slovenes adhered to Yugoslavia, declared independent on 24 November; the Poles of the former Austrian, Russian and part of the German annexed territories were once more united in an independent Poland. What was left of Austria – the German Alpine provinces – was declared a republic on 12 November. Transylvania was turned over to Rumania and Hungary was left with the area ethnically Hungarian. A separate peace was signed with Hungary in July 1920, the delay being due to the particularly involved situation there.

Political and economic disruption, defeat, and the example of Soviet Russia contributed to the radical temper of the people and the wave of revolution that shook Central Europe for several years. Czechoslovakia was the first of the newly-formed states to achieve political and economic stability; but by the end of 1920 the struggle to determine the character of the régime was concluded in favour of a relatively moderate bourgeois democracy (the nation-wide enthusiasm at the accession of freedom played a consolidating role). Germany, by contrast, declared a republic on 9 November 1918, and was rocked by armed conflict between the revolutionary and the counter-revolutionary elements up till the end of 1923. The revolution was most successful in Hungary, where a 'Republic of Councils' was set up on the Soviet model; this government, however, rejected the partition of the territories traditionally ruled by Hungary, imposed by the peace terms. This served to justify military intervention by Czechoslovakia, Rumania and France, and allied with anti-revolutionary forces in Hungary itself they brought the Republic to an end in August 1919.

As the wave of revolution fell away all the states in Central Europe developed as bourgeois republics, but of very varying political shades. The democratic régime was most progressive and most stable in Czechoslovakia, where it had close ties with France; on the initiative of Czechoslovakia a 'Little Entente' was formed with Rumania and Yugoslavia, but the monarchist régimes in those two countries were a far cry from democracy. The Weimar Republic in Germany, profoundly affected by the humiliating peace terms, was never strong in the face of reaction at home, and the final result was Nazism, coming to power in 1933. There were fascist tendencies in Austria, too, underlined by the overthrow of the government in 1933, and close ties with the fascist Italy of Mussolini. Italian fascist influence was strongest, however, in Hungary. From the outset aggressively imperialist tendencies prevailed also in Poland, which gained considerable stretches of Soviet territory in the western Ukraine and White Russia in the fighting which went on until 1923.

This was the situation which led Hitler to choose Central Europe for his first steps towards world domination, encouraged by the short-sightedness of British and French foreign policy. Austria was annexed by the Third Reich in March 1938; when they signed the Munich Agreement in September 1938 the Western powers broke their pledges to Czechoslovakia, which lost its border regions to Germany, while the remainder of Bohemia and Moravia was occupied by the German army in March 1939 and called the 'Protectorate'; at the same time Slovakia was declared an 'independent' state under a fascist government. In

September 1939 Hitler attacked and occupied Poland. By this time the Western powers realized the significance of what had been going on in Central Europe, but it was too late. The Second World War had begun.

This second war, like the first, moved away from Central Europe after the fall of Poland, to return only at the very end. In all the territories occupied by the Germans, however, armed resistance flared up and culminated in the risings in Warsaw and in Slovakia in 1944; during all these years cruel reprisals were inflicted on the population. Poland and Czechoslovakia both had governments in exile in London, as well as units fighting alongside the Allies on practically all fronts. It was the end of the war which took the greatest toll in Central Europe, most of the area being liberated by the Soviet armies after heavy fighting, from the end of 1944 until May 1945, when the war ended with the fall first of Berlin and then of Prague. The Soviet and American armies met on the Elbe and in western Bohemia.

The six years of war were a grievous time for the peoples of Central Europe; Poland lost one-sixth of its population not only in the fighting, but in concentration camps and by firing squads. Once again the experiences of war led to a radicalization of broad strata of the population. Together with the victory of the Soviet army this created the conditions for the gradual establishment of socialist governments allied to that of the Soviet Union: in Poland in 1947, within somewhat different frontiers from those of the pre-war Poland (the western regions formerly under German rule were returned under the peace treaty, while Ukrainian and White Russian territory was returned to the Soviet Union); in 1948 in Czechoslovakia, in 1949 in Hungary. It was during this time that Germany was divided into two states, the German Federal Republic (1948) and the German Democratic Republic (1949). The organization and development of Central Europe has continued on these foundations up to the present day.

Archaeology between the two World Wars
The history of archaeology from 1918 onwards brings us up to the present day. It is always difficult to judge the present (besides being an ungrateful task); and it would take too long to assess the practical results of archaeological exploration, and the theories and methods employed, and so this most recent period will only be dealt with in outline.

The map of Central Europe was fundamentally redrawn after 1918; the old states disappeared and their place was taken by others, more numerous. The remarkable thing about archaeology at this time, however, was the contrast between institutional discontinuity and continuity in ways of thinking. Attitudes and approaches in archaeology had not changed. Undoubtedly this was primarily because the people concerned were still the same; the new chairs of archaeology, the new organizations and institutions were run by men trained in the pre-war period. The old traditions in heuristics, source criticism, methods and theory remained practically unchanged. The foundations for synthetic studies of periods and cultures, lands and regions, or ethnic entities, remained the same. We must therefore qualify this inter-war period (including the Second World War) as still belonging to the synthetic phase of archaeological history in its main outlines.

From the organizational standpoint developments were so marked that they deserve closer attention. Perhaps Poland showed the most striking advances, for here the pre-war partition under three foreign rulers acted as a brake on development. The economic and political situation of the new Poland was not easy, and difficulties arose in the effort to unify three such dissimilar regions, which were not by any means confined to the organization of research.

The capital of Poland was now Warsaw, and one would suppose that archaeology would find its centre there too, but being in the region formerly under Russian rule, the least developed region, Warsaw could not offer the right conditions. To make matters worse, Professor E. Majewski, the foremost archaeologist, was nearing his end. When in

Map 8. Central Europe between the two World Wars (c.1930).

Universities:	10 Vienna	19 Marburg	*Localities:*
1 Warsaw	11 Graz	20 Königsberg	23 Biskupin
2 Poznań	12 Innsbruck	(now	24 Gniezno
3 Cracow	13 Berlin	Kaliningrad)	25 Stehelčeves-
4 Lwow	14 Halle	21 Kiel	Homolka
5 Prague	15 Tübingen	22 Rostock	26 Dolní
6 Brno	16 Wrocław/		Věstonice
7 Bratislava	Breslau		27 Federsee
8 Budapest	17 Göttingen		28 Haithabu
9 Szeged	18 Heidelberg		29 Externsteine

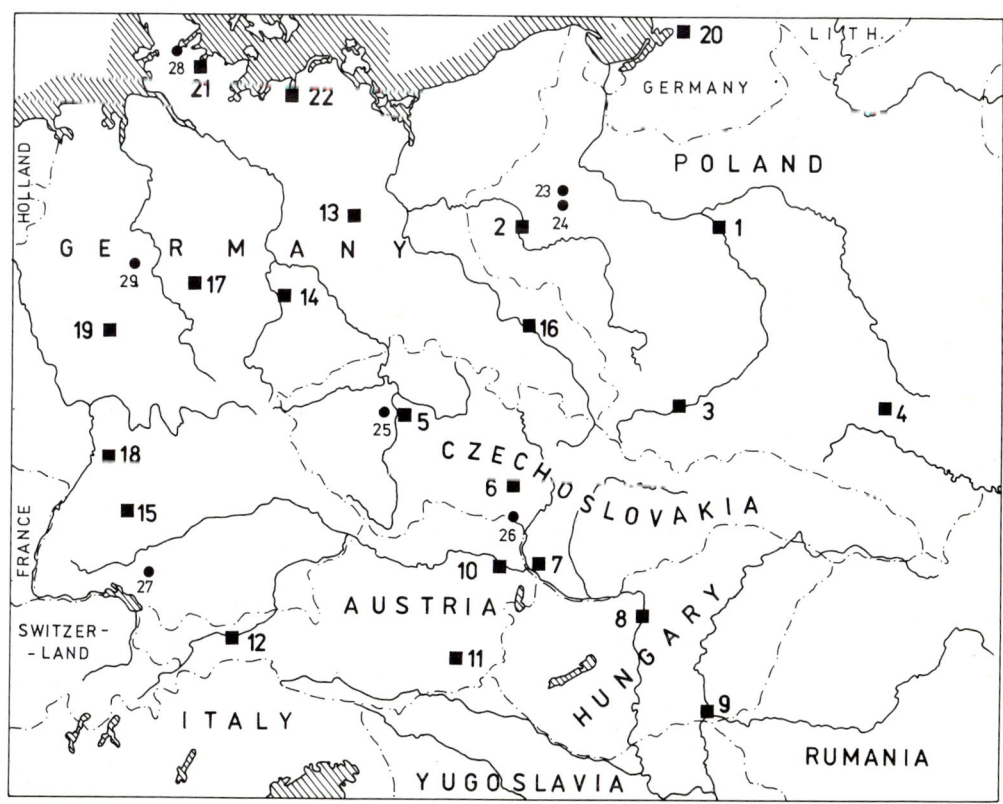

1920 a chair of prehistory was established in Warsaw University, W. Antoniewicz became Reader. The first central archaeological institution was also established the same year: the State Committee of Conservators of Prehistoric Monuments, whose work was taken over in 1928 by the newly-founded State Archaeological Museum under R. Jakimowicz. The Polish Prehistoric Society was also set up in 1920, and later organized two congresses (Poznań, 1927, and Cracow, 1935), but differences between the three parts of Poland could not be overlooked. The other centres, outside Warsaw, had their own traditions, their archaeologists, central organization, museums and universities: Poznań, Cracow and the less important Lwow, in Galicia.

Thanks to this background a new generation of archaeologists could be trained at four universities, each with a chair of prehistory: Warsaw, where E. Majewski as Honorary Professor prepared the way for the new department; Cracow, where the existing chair was held by W. Demetrykiewicz, followed by T. Sulimirski in 1936; Lwow, with L. Kozłowski in the chair from 1921; and finally Poznań, where a chair had been created for J. Kostrzewski in 1919. Kostrzewski, the founder of the Polish school of archaeology, soon became chairman of the Polish Prehistorical Society. He was the most striking and the most forceful personality in Polish archaeology, and made Poznań the centre of a stiff battle against Kossinna's German school of thought, for the correct interpretation of prehistoric developments east of the Oder – a battle which was expressedly political. On the other hand, Kostrzewski himself had been trained by Kossinna, and was a typologist in the narrower archaeological sense, unlike W. Antoniewicz, for example, who was broader in his interests.

The publication of archaeological papers centred round two new journals, *Przegląd archeologiczny* (*Archaeological Review*, Poznań, from 1919) and *Wiadomossci archeologiczne* (Archaeological Informations, Warsaw, from 1920). The restoration of an independent Poland necessitated a synthetic study of prehistoric times throughout the country; this was first provided by Antoniewicz (*Archaeology of Poland*, 1928). The progress made in the years between the two wars was presented in *The Prehistory of the Polish Lands*, by a group of authors, and Kostrzewski's *Prehistory of Poland*, on which he had been working since the late 1930s; both works appeared only after 1945.

The worst problem for Polish archaeology during this period – apart from personal conflicts which did not, however, break the united front against Nazi archaeology – was lack of funds. In 1928 a progressive law was passed to ensure the preservation of archaeological monuments, but it was poorly financed. It was not until the late 1930s that large-scale fieldwork was undertaken, mainly around Poznań (Biskupin, a unique timber-built fortress of the urnfield culture, was excavated from 1934 onwards, and the Old Slav fort of Gniezno was explored from 1936).

Czechoslovakia had inherited better opportunities for development than Poland, for scholarship had had a more favourable climate in which to flourish, but problems were not lacking where regions so long separated were united in one state. Slovakia had been retarded in both economy and culture by the stepmother attitude of the old Hungary, and everything had to start from the beginning. In 1919 a university was established in Bratislava, the capital of the region; the Czech archaeologist Jan Eisner, a disciple of Niederle, became Reader in 1924 and Professor in 1929; Eisner laid the foundations of Slovak archaeology, trained the first generation of Slovak archaeologists, and was the first to present the prehistory of Slovakia to the public in his book, *Slovakia in Prehistoric Times* (1933). Research was centred in Prague, and carried on the pre-war tradition of Niederle's 'university school'. He himself held the Chair of Prehistory at Charles University until 1929, when he was followed by A. Stocký; in 1935 J. Schránil became Professor, and in 1938 J. Filip became Reader. A third chair of prehistory was established at the new university of Brno in 1931, under Professor E. Šimek, and Prague acquired a second chair when L. Franz of Vienna was appointed by the Czechoslovak state to be the first Professor of Prehistory at the German University there, serving the German minority (1929).

Czechoslovakia made greater advances than the other new states, setting up a State Archaeological Institute in Prague, on the recommendation of Professor Niederle, as early as 1919; unlike the museums, this institution was primarily concerned with fieldwork. It was headed first by Niederle, followed in 1924 by his closest collaborator K. Buchtela, and in 1938 by J. Böhm. The Institute employed a network of conservationists throughout the country, who also collaborated with the government department for the conservation of historical monuments. Nevertheless no law was passed regulating these activities. Both the Institute and the two principal museums – the National Museum in Prague and the Moravian Museum in Brno – engaged in major archaeological campaigns, such as the excavation of an Eneolithic hill settlement at Homolka near Stehelčeves (where an expedition from Harvard University also worked, under Professor V. J. Fewkes, an American of Czech descent); and the earliest phase of occupation on the site of Prague Castle; in Moravia Professor K. Absolon excavated the Paleolithic site of Dolní Věstonice.

The Society of Czechoslovak Prehistorians was the organization embracing all archaeologists; founded in 1919, it published a new series of the journal *Obzor prehistorický* (*Prehistoric Review*); from 1922, which was second in importance only to the traditional *Památky archaeologické* (*Archaeological Monuments*), published by the Czech Academy of Science and the National Museum. The German minority had its own archaeologists, organized in the German Society for Prehistory in Czechoslovakia, which published a journal, *Sudeta* (from 1925). Archaeological publications followed the traditional lines both on form and content; in 1932 the first synthesis of the prehistory of the whole of Czechoslovakia appeared, the work of J. Schránil; in 1928 the same author published *The Prehistory of Bohemia and Moravia*, a purely archaeological study.

Czechoslovakia also contributed to the post-war revival of international co-operation in archaeology, taking part along with Poland, Yugoslavia and Rumania in the first meeting of the Institut international d'ánthropologie, which comprised representatives of several allied and neutral states and was held in Liège in 1921. The second meeting of the Institut was held in Prague in 1924. As the idea of reviving international archaeological congresses took root, a preparatory meeting in Bern in 1931 set up a permanent council of representatives of the 14 countries taking part. Besides Czechoslovakia and Poland some of the countries previously excluded from participation – Germany and Hungary – were now admitted.

Hungarian archaeologists were active in international archaeological affairs, and recognition of this was expressed when the proposal to hold the third international congress after the First World War in Budapest in 1940 was accepted. (The first had taken place in London in 1932, the second in Oslo in 1936). The third never took place because of the outbreak of war.

The post-First World War frontiers of Hungary limited it to the ethnic territory of the Hungarian people, thus freeing it from some of the problems experienced by other countries in Central Europe. Budapest remained the natural centre, with the National Museum where L. Marton, J. Hillebrand and F. Tompa all worked. Hillebrand had the title of Professor of Budapest University, while Tompa held the chair there from 1938. Up to this time, however, the university had meant little for the progress of archaeology. Prehistory was more alive at the university of Szeged, where L. Marton had been Reader before the war; Professor A. Buday, more of a classical archaeologist, held the chair here from 1924, while his assistant, the prehistorian J. Banner, took his place in 1937. The journal *Dolgozátok* appeared here from 1925 onwards.

Szeged developed into the cultural centre of southern Hungary after Koloszvár (now Cluj), the capital of Transylvania, became part of Rumania. In Cluj, too, research and publication activities revived before 1930, centred on the museum; the primary interest, however, was classical archaeology.

Neighbouring Austria was in much the same situation as Hungary. The city of Vienna was over-large for the little that was left of the former vast empire, and a certain degree of decay set in as far as the central institutions were concerned. Nevertheless they continued to function, as did the Anthropological and the Prehistoric Societies, together with their respective journals. In 1920 the Central Commission was renamed the State Department for the Preservation of Monuments; a law on conservation was passed in 1937. Museum work centred in the Natural Science Museum, where J. Bayer was in charge of prehistory. Hoernes' successor O. Menghin held the chair at Vienna University from 1919 throughout the period we are considering, and an independent Prehistorical Institute was established there in 1924. Besides Vienna, there were lectures on archaeology in Graz and Innsbruck. During the period between the two wars Austrian archaeology was not very lively, and both in theory and in practice remained within the framework valid for the previous periods. The Vienna ethnological school, with its 'cultural regions' ('Kulturkreis'), exerted a strong influence; Menghin belonged to this school of thought.

German archaeology under Kossinna and afterwards
There remains Germany, of the Central European states, and this country is particularly significant because of the direction taken by developments in prehistory there. Like archaeology elsewhere in Central Europe, in Germany neither the events of wartime nor the adjustment of frontiers affected the subject. Scholarship maintained its

continuity, including existing divisions into various schools of thought with that of Kossinna dominating. History gave Kossinna sufficient justification for a new call to arms addressed to the Germani. Archaeology soon began to play a role similar to that assigned to it after the Napoleonic wars, but this time the revival served somewhat different ends.

At first archaeological work was hindered by the economic disruption of the post-war years; the situation improved after the mid-1920s, only to be upset again by the economic crisis all over the world at the end of the decade, which provided fertile soil for the growth of Nazism in Germany. Once again the Kossinna school came into its own.

Kossinna – the 'Master' – himself did not live to see it, dying in 1931, but the attitudes he cultivated in his disciples were just right for the new political conditions in Germany. Archaeology turned its attention mainly to the past of the Germani, putting forward 'proof' that they were the 'firstborn' of all peoples, faultless and superior (Nietsche's 'superman'), proof that their original geographical distribution gave their descendants the right to rule over the whole of Europe. While one trend in European archaeology (e.g. Childe, *The Aryans*, 1926) turned eastward to seek the cradle of the Indo-European peoples, most frequently to the steppes of the Black Sea region, German archaeologists insisted on the Nordic origin of the 'Indo-Germans', now identified absolutely with 'Nordic race'. From here, they claimed the Indo-Germans, the 'master race', spread all over Europe, but through intermarriage with the inferior races they ruled over their racial purity was defiled; only in the original homelands of Germany and Scandinavia was the race intact. In all the writing on the subject the inevitable contrast to the German 'master race' was provided by the inferior Slavs.

This simple and attractive theory served Nazi archaeologists to flatter the conceit of the semi-educated petty bourgeoisie who formed the mainstay of the Nazi movement; the primitive racialist doctrine it implied was just what they wanted. Thanks to this fact archaeology was elevated to the rank of an official science in the Third Reich, and became part of the foundations of the Nazi ideology. It was, incidentally, archaeology that provided the Nazis with their symbol, the 'Aryan' swastika. The chief ideologist of the Party, A. Rosenberg, declared that the history of the German nation did not begin with Charlemagne, but with the ancient Germanic megaliths, and that belief in the value of racial purity and the Germanic race was the basis of the National Socialist world outlook.

All that did not fit into the new order was liquidated. Virchow's long-established German Anthropological Society disappeared, while Kossinna's Society for German Prehistory flourished (entitled the Reich Union for German Prehistory after the Nazis came to power). It was headed by the chief exponent of Nazism in archaeology, H. Reinerth, now professor at the University of Berlin and Rosenberg's deputy for these matters. Not only institutions disappeared; people who were found undesirable for political or racial reasons lost their positions and in many cases left the country (H. Kühn, G. Bersu, P. Goessler etc.).

For archaeology as part of the Nazi régime this was a a time of great prosperity compared to conditions in other countries. Germanic prehistory was taught in schools and in the army, as part of the offical propaganda machine; hundreds of popular pamphlets and articles vulgarized the discipline, and a foundation to support archaeological work was endowed, under the direct auspices of the SS: Ahnenerbe (The Heritage of our Forefathers), with its own journal, *Germanen-Erbe*. On the other hand, a number of new chairs were established at German universities. There were a number of lecturers on the subject during the 1920s, like H. Schmidt, A. Kiekebusch, and Kossinna's successor M. Ebert in Berlin, H. Hahne in Halle, H. Kühn in Cologne, R. R. Schmidt and H. Reinerth in Tübingen, H. Seger in Breslau (Wrocław), K.-H. Jacob-Friesen in Göttingen, E. Wahle in Heidelberg; but it was not until 1928 that the first regular chair of prehistory was established in Germany (Marburg, under Professor G. von Merhart of Austria). In the first two years after the Nazis came to power (1933–5) eight new chairs were created: in Berlin (H. Reinerth), Königsberg (now Kaliningrad) under another leading Nazi, the Prussian Baron von Richthofen, Halle (H. Hahne), Wrocław (M. Jahn) and others. Other chairs were established later, like Kiel (G. Schwantes, 1937) and Rostock (E. Petersen, 1939).

These were mainly disciples or followers of Kossinna and published their work in the journal *Mannus* or in another of Kossinna's publications, the *Nachrichtenblatt für Deutsche Vorzeit* (*Newsletter for German Prehistory*), established in 1925. Many more of Kossinna's school found places in museums, of which there were dozens. Public financial support made it possible for many of these institutions, both universities and museums, to undertake large-scale exploration work such as the excavation of the Neolithic site in Köln-Lindenthal, Buchau and other sites on the Federsee, or the Viking trading post of Haithabu. The results of some of these campaigns were used for reconstruction of prehistoric sites and monuments, life-size, as at Federsee, Unteruhldingen and Rössen. The regional and local museums were less notable but came into existence in large numbers, for the role of archaeology in the spirit of Nazi ideology and education was constantly emphasized. It was no wonder, in this mental climate, that the wildest of amateurs found an outlet for their fantasy, as in the case of the Externsteine affair (this site, in fact medieval, was transformed by uncritical propaganda into a prominent sanctuary of Ancient Germans), as well as forgers who cashed in on the political advantages of archaeology. Historical anthropology sank even lower during this period, degraded by its protagonists, who were often totally unqualified, to the level of maid-of-all-work for politics. One typical example was H. Günther's *Racial Doctrine of the German Nation* (1922), which had appeared in ten editions by 1926. This shows how early the ground was being prepared for Nazi ideology.

It must be said, however, that even at this time there were still archaeologists who did not identify with this attitude, especially those influenced by Kossinna's traditional opponent C. von Schuchhardt of Berlin. He enjoyed great authority and his works continued to be reprinted (*Ancient Europe*, originally published 1919; *The Prehistory of Germany*, 1928), although on some points they opposed the views of the Kossinna school. As late as 1943, in the fifth edition of his *Prehistory of Germany* we can still read, though in more moderate terms, the words of the Introduction to the first edition (1928), that 'we lack a real history of prehistoric Germany. The works which bear these or similar titles in reality only present the prehistory of the Germani, as chauvinistic in their attitude as possible'. Schuchhardt was also interested in non-German ethnic groups, although more in the archaeological material itself than in the questions it raised. On the contrary, the prehistorians of the younger generation ardently pursued such questions, naturally in the spirit of Kossinna and his teachings. The few voices raised in criticism of their methods (e.g. by E. Wahle, himself a disciple of Kossinna, in 1941) could avail nothing. The broad stream of literature aimed at prehistoric synthesis in this spirit, but actually producing only ideological dogma, culminated in 1940 with the publication of three long volumes of H. Reinerth's *Prehistory of the Germanic Tribes*, in which the interpretation of the source material was made completely subservient to the needs of Nazi teaching.

The work of these Nazi archaeologists was of considerable political significance, but none played such a role as the writings of the 'Grand Master' Kossinna himself, both his earlier works and those of more recent date like his *Heights of the Ancient Germanic Culture* (1927). These became the gospel of the official Nordic-Aryan myth. The archaeological literature of the 1930s joined in the political offensive against Poland, concentrating on proofs of the age-old Germanic character of Silesia, Greater Poland, and Pomerania. This campaign, mainly a pamphlet war, was led by von Richthofen, whose chief opponent was J. Kostrzewski. In his counter-arguments the latter revived the old theory that the Lusatian culture of the Bronze Age and the Hallstatt period was a Slav culture. Another theory long advanced by the German side, i.e. that the Slavs had come from the Pripet Marshes to the east of Poland, could be disproved by the complete lack of evidence for settlement of this area between the Neolithic and the proto-historic periods.

Von Richthofen's vicious campaign, which had only a formal connection with scholarship, was not very successful; at first he had recourse to deliberate falsification of the evidence, and finally took steps to ensure diplomatic pressure on the Polish government, to force it to silence the Polish archaeologists on pain of bringing down the wrath of the Reich on their country. This all helped to unite the Polish scholars and to persuade others, among them some Czech archaeologists, to reconsider the possibility of the Slav character of the Lusatian culture.

In themselves, these German-Polish polemics were peripheral, but they presaged a future in which Hitler's Germany would reach for more effective weapons. If the shortsightedness of Polish policy, hoping to draw advantage from alliance with Hitler (one of the supporters of this policy was the statesman and former archaeologist Professor L. Kozłowski), was not yet evident, the events of 1 September 1939 made it clear.

On the threshold of a new epoch

The Second World War left indelible marks on archaeology in Central Europe, and the conditions under which it developed in each country concerned diverged widely. For a few years the archaeologists of Nazi Germany carried on a feverish, unnatural activity, following in the wake of Hitler's armies; they formed part of the administration of the occupied territories, often wearing the uniforms of the SS or serving as officials of the Gestapo. They tracked down important finds for transport to the Reich, set up archaeological inspection bodies, became directors or inspectors of museums large and small. They occupied chairs at the German and Germanized universities, while the universities of the subjugated nationalities were closed down as part of the plan to deprive the countries of their intellectual leaders and transform them into a reservoir of manpower for the German armaments industry.

The worst effects of Nazi occupation were felt in Poland, where one-sixth of the population and one-quarter of the archaeologists lost their lives in battle or in concentration camps and prisons. Kostrzewski survived, living as an agricultural labourer under an assumed name, in a remote village; his son was executed. It goes without saying that the Polish archaeologists were not allowed to carry on their work. Copies of some Polish journals and other publications deliberately destroyed after the occupation of the country, are today bibliophiles' treasures. Headed by Professor E. Petersen, Nazi archaeologists liquidated the State Archaeological Museum in Warsaw; the Poznan museum did not survive the end of the war, when the German soldiers defending their positions in the city used the archaeological collections to barricade the windows of the building. Cracow fared better, having been the centre of German archaeological activity in occupied Poland. Evidence which needs no comment is the deliberate destruction of the extensive remains of the wooden fort of Biskupin, the best-known archaeological site in Poland; this vandalism came under the heading of 'archaeological research by the SS'.

The Czech nation was 'placed under the protection of the Führer' by the establishment of the Protectorate of Bohemia and Moravia, which meant that conditions were less severe. In spite of the fact that Czech archaeologists had always consistently opposed Kossinna's conception and his abuse of the discipline, and although the Czech Academy of the Sciences had published in 1934 (in French in 1935) a study entitled *The Equality of all the Races of Europe*, as part of an open polemic with racist theories, during the early years of the war work was allowed to continue in institutes and museums, although of course to a very reduced extent and only under the tutelage of German specialists. The Czech universities were closed in the first months of the war. For those parts of the country annexed by the Reich a Department of Prehistory was set up, while in the Protectorate the work of Czech archaeologists was followed very carefully by archaeologists sent from Germany to occupy key positions. Chief of these was Professor L. Zotz, appointed to the Prague German University. In Moravia, where Professor K. Absolon was not even allowed to keep his own library, his work on the Dolní Věstonice site was carried on for a time by A. Bohmers. It was only in the fascist state of Slovakia that conditions were more favourable, since during the first years of the war this region was not occupied. In 1942 a State Archaeological Institute was set up here.

Even those archaeologists who were 'approved' could only write in the spirit of Nazi ideology or at least not in opposition to it. When I. Borkovský managed to publish a book, in 1940, proving that the Prague type pottery dating from the period of the migration of the peoples was Slav, and the earliest archaeological evidence of their presence in Central Europe, the publication was seized and destroyed. The ancient

Slavs had no right to any culture whatever. The decisive aspect was declared by one of the rulers in the Protectorate, K. H. Frank, in 1941, to be that the Germans gave the primitive Slav newcomers 'their first social values . . ., teaching them to use the plough and thus giving them bread.'

In 1942 even such limited opportunities were withdrawn, and all archaeological activity was concentrated in the hands of the Germans. Even their journals ceased to appear, however, for the twilight of the 'thousand year Reich' was approaching. The end of the war brought damage to archaeological material in Czechoslovakia, too, particularly when the German army retreating through southern Moravia set fire to the castle of Mikulov, destroying great classical collections representing nearly a hundred years of investigation into the Moravian Paleolithic, from Předmostí, Dolní Věstonice and elsewhere.

Today all this is in the past – although it is a past which is both instructive and cautionary, warning against senseless destruction of lives and cultural values by war, and against the abuse of archaeology for

Map 9. Central Europe after 1945.

Aa = important archaeological institutes and their branches
Mm = important central and regional archaeological museums or museum
      departments
U   = universities with departments or chairs of prehistory

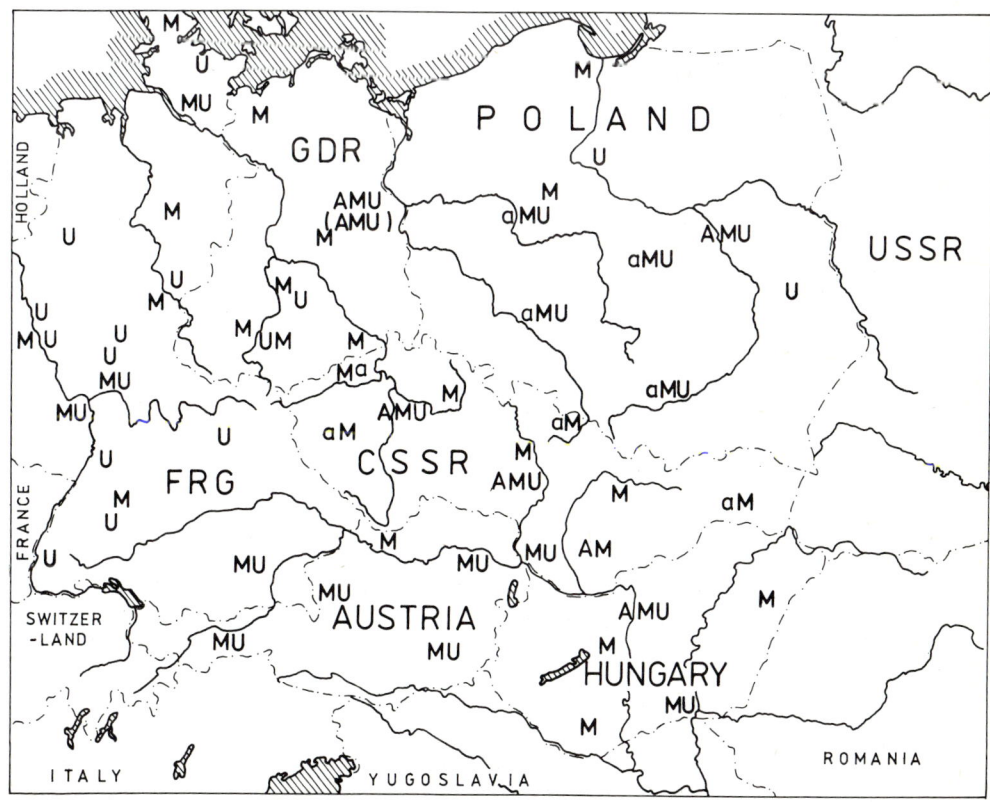

purposes which have nothing to do with scholarship. Central Europe after 1945 changed even more radically than after the Great War – but we have already spoken of the external aspect of these changes, and the archaeological aspect will remain untouched here. The Marxist, materialist historical approach to source materials on the one hand, and the 'radiocarbon revolution' or the methods of the 'new archaeology' on the other, together with other factors have contributed to place post-War archaeology in Central Europe on new foundations. The 'archaeological' epoch, still surviving in the first post-War years in synthesizing studies which matured before and during the War, is now over. A new epoch is opening, one we can perhaps call historical, for it will result – we may be allowed to hope – in a complex view of the economic, social and cultural history of prehistoric man in the context of his environment. Besides archaeology, many other social and natural sciences will contribute to this synthesis. Meanwhile, although we may attempt partial syntheses while keeping our ultimate aim in mind, we are still in the first, analytical phase of this new period. This is the present, whose history will be written by others, after us.

Original Titles of Works Mentioned in the Text

The titles of publications in Central European languages have been translated into English for the sake of clarity. The following list gives their titles in the original, in the order in which they appear in the text. Latin and French titles have not been translated.

1 Thunderstones and Magic Crocks: the Age of Antiquarianism

Hájek z Libočan, V., *Kronika česká* (Prague, 1541).
Kuthen, M., *Kronika o založení země české* (Prague, 1539).
Büttner, D. S., *Beschreibung des Leichenbrands und Toden- Krüge . . .* (Halle/S., 1695).
Treuer, G., *Kurtze Beschreibung der Heidnischen Todten-Töpffe . . .* (Nuremberg, 1688).
Albinus, P., *Meissnische Chronica . . .* (Dresden, 1589 [1590]).

2 The Clear Light of Reason: the Age of Enlightenment

Schmidt, M. I., *Geschichte der Deutschen* (Ulm, 1778–85).
Herder, J. G., *Ideen zur Philosophie der Geschichte der Menschheit* (1784–91).
Dobrovský, J., 'Ueber die Begräbnissart der alten Slawen . . .', *Abhandlungen d. kgl. Ges.d.Wissenschaften* (1786) (Prague).
Naruszewicz, A. S., *Historya narodu polskiego* (Warsaw, 1780–86: II–VII; 1824: I).
Hummel, B. F., *Bibliothek der deutschen Alterthümer* (2 vols., Nuremberg, 1787, 1791).
Kluk, K., *Rzeczy kopalne* (Warsaw, 1781).
Biener von Bienenberg, K. J., *Versuch über einige merkwürdige Alterthümer im Königreich Böhmen* (Hradec Králové, 1778–85).
Kant, I., *Muthmasslicher Anfang der Menschheitsgeschichte* (1786).

3 Our Glorious Pagan Forefathers: the Age of Romanticism

Gaisberger, J., *Die Gräber bei Hallstatt* (Linz, 1848).
Sacken, E. von, *Das Grabfeld von Hallstatt in Oberösterreich und dessen Alterthümer* (Vienna, 1868).
Gruner, H., *Die Opfersteine in Deutschland* (Berlin, 1881).
Klemm, G. F., *Allgemeine Kultur-Geschichte der Menschheit* (10 vols., Leipzig, 1843–52).
Sacken, E. von, *Ueber die vorchristlichen Kulturepochen Mitteleuropas* (Vienna, 1862).
Sacken, E. von, *Leitfaden zur Kunde des heidnischen Alterthumes* (Vienna, 1865).
Büsching, J. G. G., *Abriss der deutschen Alterthumskunde* (Weimar, 1824).
Klemm, G. F., *Handbuch der germanischen Alterthumskunde* (Dresden, 1836).
Wagener, S. C., *Handbuch der vorzüglichsten, in Deutschland entdeckten Alterthümer aus heidnischer Zeit* (Weimar, 1842).
Kalina von Jäthenstein, M., *Böhmens heidnische Opferplätze, Gräber und Alterthümer* (Prague, 1836).
Vocel, J. E., *Grundzüge der böhmischen Alterthumskunde* (Prague, 1845).
Vocel, J. E., *Pravěk země České* (Prague, 1866–8).
Pauli, Z., *Starożytności Galicyjskie* (Lwow, 1840).
Tyszkiewicz, E., *Rzut oka na zrzódla archeologii krajowej* (Wilnius, 1842).
Preusker, K. B., *Blicke in die vaterländische Vorzeit . . .* (Leipzig, 1841–4).
Büsching, J. G. G., *Die heidnischen Alterthümer Schlesiens* (Leipzig, 1820–4).
Kruse, F. K., *Deutsche Alterthümer* (Halle/S., 1824–8).
Lisch, G. C. F., *Friderico-Francisceum, . . .* (Leipzig, 1837).
Kruse, F. K., *Budorgis, oder über Schlesiens Alterthümer* (Leipzig, 1819).
Wagner, F. A., *Die Tempel und Pyramiden der Urbewohner auf dem rechten Elbufer . . .* (Leipzig, 1828).
Schmitt, A. P. *Archaeologická mapa království Českého* (Prague, 1856).
Lindenschmit, L., *Die Alterthümer unserer heidnischen Vorzeit* (5 vols., Mainz, 1858–1911).
Vocel, J. E., *Archaeologische Parallelen* (2 vols., Vienna, 1853, 1855).
Keferstein, C., *Ansichten über die keltischen Alterthümer . . . in Deutschland* (Halle/S., 1846).
Adelung, J. C., *Älteste Geschichte der Deutschen* (Leipzig, 1806).
Grimm, J., *Deutsche Mythologie* (Göttingen, 1835).
Zeuss, J. C., *Die Deutschen und ihre Nachbarstämme* (Munich, 1837).
Surowiecki, L., *Śledzenie początku narodów slawiańskich* (Warsaw, 1824).
Chodakowski, Z. D., *O Słowiańszczyźnie przed chrześcijaństwiem* (Krzemieniec, 1818; Lwow, 1819).
Kollár, J., *Staroitalia Slavjanská* (Vienna, 1853).
Šembera, A. V., *Západní Slované v pravěku* (Vienna, 1868).
Šafařík, P. J., *Slovanské starožitnosti* (Prague, 1836–7).
Palacký, F., *Geschichte von Böhmen*, I (Prague, 1836).
Worbs, J. G., 'Sind die Urnenbegräbnisse, die man im östlichen Deutschland findet, slavischen oder deutschen Ursprungs?', in Kruse, F. K., *Deutsche Alterthümer*, I. 1 (Halle, 1824).
Adler, G. W., *Grabhügel und Opferplätze im Orlagau* (Saalfeld, 1836).
Tomíček, J. S., *Doba prvního člověčenstva* (Prague, 1846).

4 Tracing the Evolution of Things: the Age of Positivist Analysis

Hoernes, M., 'Grundlinien einer Systematik der prähistorischen Archäologie' *Zeitschrift für Ethnologie* (1893) (Berlin).
Bibra, E. von, *Die chemische Analyse als Hülfsmittel für den Archäologen* (1872).

Voss, A., *Merkbuch Alterthümer aufzugraben und aufzubewahren* (Berlin, 1888).
Baer, W., and Hellwald, F. von, *Der vorgeschichtliche Mensch* (Leipzig, 1874).
Čermák, K., *Pravěk lidstva evropského* (Prague, 1887).
Hellwald, F. von, *Kulturgeschichte in ihrer natürlicher Entwicklung bis zur Gegenwart* (Augsburg, 1875).
Sadowski, J. N., *Wykaz zabytków przedhistorycznych na ziemiach polskich*, I (Cracow, 1877).
Šnajdr, L., *Počátkové předhistorického místopisu země České* (Pardubice, 1891).
Penck, A., 'Mensch und Eiszeit', *Archiv für Anthropologie* (1884) (Braunschweig).
Haeckel, E., *Natürliche Schöpfungsgeschichte* (1868).
Pulszky, F., *Die Kupferzeit in Ungarn* (Budapest, 1884).
Hampel, J., *Alterthümer der Bronzezeit in Ungarn* (Budapest, 1887).
Much, M., *Die Kupferzeit in Europa und ihr Verhältniss zur Kultur der Indogermanen* (Vienna, 1886).
Undset, I., *Études sur l'âge du bronze de la Hongrie* (Christiania, 1880).
Undset, I., *Das erste Auftreten des Eisens in Nord-Europa* (Hamburg, 1882).
Hehn, V., *Kulturpflanzen und Haustiere* (Berlin, 1870).
Schrader, O., *Sprachvergleichung und Urgeschichte* (Jena, 1883).
Poesche, T., *Die Arier* (Jena, 1878).
Penka, K., *Origines Ariacae* (Vienna, 1883).
Nowacki, A., 'Über die Entwicklung der Landwirtschaft in der Urzeit', *Landwirtschaftliche Jahrbücher* (1880).
Schaaffhausen, H., 'Über die Methode der vorgeschichtlichen Forschung', *Archiv für Anthropologie* (1872) (Braunschweig).
Bachofen, J. J., *Das Mutterrecht* (Stuttgart, 1861).
Marx, K., *Zur Kritik der politischen Oekonomie* (Berlin, 1859).
Engels, F., *Der Ursprung der Familie, des Privateigentums und des Staates* (Hottingen and Zürich, 1884).

5 Tracing the Evolution of Cultures: the Age of Typological Synthesis

Penck, A., and Brückner, E., *Die Alpen im Eiszeitalter* (Leipzig 1901–3).
Götze, A., 'Über die Gliederung und Chronologie der jüngeren Steinzeit', *Verhandlungen der Berliner Anthropolog. Gesellschaft* (1900).
Buchtela, K., 'Die Vorgeschichte Böhmens', *Věstník slovan.starožitností* (1899) (Prague).
Reinecke, P., 'Zur Chronologie der zweiten Hälfte des Bronzealters in Süd- und Norddeutschland', *Corresp.-Blatt der Deutschen Anthrop.Gesellschaft* (1902) (Munich).
Hoernes, M., *Die Urgeschichte des Menschen* (Vienna, Budapest and Leipzig, 1892).
Montelius, O., *Die Chronologie der ältesten Bronzezeit in Norddeutschland und Skandinavien* (Braunschweig, 1900).
Hoernes, M., *Urgeschichte der Menschheit* (Stuttgart, 1895).
Hoernes, M., *Natur- und Urgeschichte des Menschen* (Vienna, 1909).
Niederle, L., *Lidstvo v době předhistorické* (Prague, 1893).
Ranke, J., *Der Mensch* (2 vols., Leipzig, 1886–7).
Forrer, R., *Urgeschichte des Europäers* (Stuttgart, 1908).
Hahne, H., *Das vorgeschichtliche Europa* (Bielefeld and Leipzig, 1910).
Schuchhardt, C. von, *Alteuropa* (Berlin, 1919).
Hoernes, M., *Urgeschichte der bildenden Kunst in Europa* (Vienna, 1898).
Forrer, R., *Reallexikon der prähistorischen, klassischen und frühchristlichen Altertümer* (Berlin, 1908).
Schlemm, J., *Wörterbuch zur Vorgeschichte* (Berlin, 1908).

Ebert, M. (ed.), *Reallexikon der Vorgeschichte* (Berlin and Leipzig, 1924–32).

Niederle, L., *Slovanské starožitnosti* (Prague, 1902–19).

Niederle, L., *Život starých Slovanů* (Prague, 1911–34).

Niederle, L., *Manuel de l'antiquité slave* (2 vols., Paris, 1923, 1926).

Hoops, J. (ed.), *Reallexikon der germanischen Altertumskunde* (Strassburg, 1911–19).

Pulszky, F., *Magyárország archaeologiája* (2 vols., Budapest, 1897).

Schwantes, G., *Aus Deutschlands Urgeschichte* (Leipzig, 1908).

Kostrzewski, J., *Wielkopolska w czasach przedhistorycznych* (Poznań, 1914).

Píč, J. L., *Starožitnosti země České*, I.1–III.1 (Prague, 1899–1909).

Niederle, L. and Buchtela, K., *Rukověť české archaeologie* (Prague, 1910).

Montelius, O., *Die älteren Kulturperioden im Orient und in Europa*, I: *Die typologische Methode* (Stockholm, 1903).

Much, M., *Die Trugspiegelung orientalischer Kultur in den vorgeschichtlichen Zeitaltern Nord- und Mitteleuropas* (Jena, 1907).

Götze, A., *Uber neolithischen Handel: Bastian-Festschrift* (1896).

Montelius, O., 'Handel in der Vorzeit', *Praehistorische Zeitschrift* (1910) (Berlin).

Schurtz, H., *Urgeschichte der Kultur* (Leipzig and Vienna, 1900).

Wilke, G., 'Neolithische Keramik und Arierproblem', *Archiv für Anthropologie* (1908) (Braunschweig).

Kauffmann, F., *Deutsche Altertumskunde* (Munich, 1913).

Kossinna, G., *Die Herkunft der Germanen. Zur Methode der Siedlungsarchäologie* (Würzburg, 1911).

Kossinna, G., *Die deutsche Vorgeschichte, eine hervorragend nationale Wissenschaft* (Würzburg, 1912).

Kossinna, G., 'Die indogermanische Frage archäologisch beantwortet', *Zeitschr. f. Ethnologie* (1902) (Berlin).

Penka, K., *Die Entstehung der neolithischen Kultur Europas* (Leipzig, 1907).

Niederle, L., *O původu Slovanů* (Prague, 1896).

Červinka, I. L., *Morava za pravěku* (Brno, 1902).

Majewski, E., *Starożytni Słowianie w ziemiach dzisiejszej Germanii* (Warsaw, 1899).

Antoniewicz, W., *Archaeologia Polski* (Warsaw, 1928).

Eisner, J., *Slovensko v pravěku* (Bratislava, 1933).

Schránil, J., *Vorgeschichte Böhmens und Mährens* (Berlin, 1928).

Schuchhardt, C., *Vorgeschichte von Deutschland* (Munich and Berlin, 1928).

Reinerth, H., *Vorgeschichte der deutschen Stämme* (3 vols., Berlin, 1940).

Kossinna, G., *Altgermanische Kulturhöhe* (Leipzig, 1927).

Weigner, K. (ed.), *L'Égalité des races européennes* (Maestricht, Paris and Bruxelles, 1935).

Select Bibliography

Abbreviations:
BRGK   *Bericht der Römisch-Germanischen Kommission*
BSPF   *Bulletin de la Société Préhistorique Française*
MAGW   *Mitteilungen der Anthropologischen Gesellschaft in Wien*
SbNM   *Sborník Národního muzea v Praze* [*Procs. Nat. Museum Prague*]

Austria

Barb, A. A., 'Geschichte der Altertumsforschung im Burgenland bis zum Jahre 1938', *Wiss. Arbeiten aus Burgenland, H. 4* (1954).

Franz, L., 'Aus der Geschichte der ur- und frühgeschichtlichen Bodenforschung in Österreich', in Franz, L., and Neumann, A., *Lexikon ur- und frühgeschichtlicher Fundstätten Österreichs*.

Franz, L., Mitscha-Märheim, H., 'Die urgeschichtliche Forschung in Österreich seit 1900', *BRGK, 16* (1925–6), 1–34.

Hirschberg, W., '100 Jahre Anthropologische Gesellschaft in Wien', *MAGW, 100* (1971), 1–10.

Meister, R., *Geschichte der Akademie der Wissenschaften in Wien 1847–1947* (Wien, 1947).

Niegl, M. A., *Die archäologische Erforschung der Römerzeit in Österreich* (Wien, 1980).

Pauli, L., *Die Gräber vom Salzberg zu Hallstatt. Erforschung – Überlieferung – Auswertbarkeit* (Mainz, 1975).

Pittioni, R., 'Fünfzig Jahre Lehrkanzel für Urgeschichte an der Universität Wien', *Archaeologia Austriaca, 4* (1949), 1–4.

Zagiba, F., 'Die erste Lehrkanzel für slawische Archäologie an der Universität Wien errichtet 1849', *Slavia antiqua, 12* (1965), 143–152.

Czechoslovakia

Böhm, J., 'Sto let Památek archeologických', *Památky archeologické, 45* (1954), 1–34. ['A hundred years of the journal *Památky archeologické*': German summary.]

Filip, J., 'Lubor Niederle – učitel, archeolog a organizátor', *Archeologické rozhledy, 19* (1967), 143–6. [French summary.]

Grolich, V. [ed.], *Jindřich Wankel, otec moravské archeologie* (Blansko, 1971). [*J. Wankel, the Father of Moravian Archaeology:* German summary.]

Maška, O., *Karel Jaroslav Maška* (Brno, 1965).

Nekuda, V., *150 let Moravského muzea v Brně* (Brno, 1969).

Niederle, L., *Albín Stocký* (Praha, 1934).

Neustupný, J., 'Josef Ladislav Píč', *Časopis Národního muzea, 116* (1947), 1–12.

Neustupný, J., 'Pravěké oddělení', in *Národní Museum 1818–1948* (Praha, 1949), 69–86. ['Department of Prehistory in the National Museum, Prague': French summary.]

Neustupný, J., '150th Anniversary of the National Museum in Prague', *Current Anthropology, 9* (1968), 221–4.

Pavel, J., 'Dějiny památkové péče v českých zemích v 19. století', *Sborník archivních prací, 25* (1975), 143–293.

Sklenář, K., 'Život a dílo Václava Krolmuse', *SbNM, 10–C* (1965), 187–217. ['Life and work of V. Krolmus': German summary.]

Sklenář, K., 'Archeologický sbor Národního muzea', in *150 let Národního muzea* (Praha, 1968), 91–101.

Sklenář, K., 'Nástin vývoje prehistorického bádání v Čechách do roku 1919', *Zprávy Čs.spol.archeologické při ČSAV, 11* (1969), 1–91. ['An outline of the development of prehistoric research in Bohemia until 1919': German summary.]

Sklenář, K., 'Archeologické spisy Josefa Dobrovského a jejich prameny', *Sborník Národního muzea v Praze, 24–A* (1970), 245–95. ['Archaeological works of Josef Dobrovský and their sources': German summary.]

Sklenář, K., 'Počátky české archeologie v díle M. Kaliny z Jäthensteinu', *SbNM, 30–A* (1976), 1–136. ['The place of M. Kalina of Jäthenstein in the history of Bohemian archaeology': English summary.]

Sklenář, K., 'Archeologická činnost Josefa Vojtěcha Hellicha v Národním muzeu', *SbNM, 34–A* (1980), 109–234. ['The first professional archaeologist at the National Museum in Prague: J. V. Hellich, 1842–1847': English summary.]

Sklenář, K., 'První profesura archeologie na Karlově univerzitě v Praze,' in *Varia archaeologica, 2* [*Praehistorica,* VII] (Prague, 1981), 13–17. ['The first archaeological professorship at the Prague University': English summary.]

Sklenář, K., *Jan Erazim Vocel* (Praha, 1981).

Sklenář, K., 'The history of archaeology in Czechoslovakia', in Daniel, G. [ed.], *Towards a History of Archaeology* (London, 1981), 150–8.

Sklenář, K., 'Vývoj poznání pravěku a rané doby dějinné v českých zemích', in Bouzek, J. *et al.*, *Dějiny archeologie* (Praha, 1983).

Skutil, J., 'Les débuts de la préhistoire nationale en Tchécoslovaquie', *BSPF, 50* (1953), 112–23.

Stocký, A., 'Le développement de la science préhistorique tchéque', *Anthropologie, 2 – Supplément* (Prague, 1924), 45–57.

Vignatiová, J., 'Přehled vývoje archeologického bádání na Moravě do začátku XX. století', *Zprávy Čs.spol.archeologické při ČSAV, 17* (1975), 93–125. ['Development of archaeology in Moravia up to the beginning of the twentieth century': German summary.]

Vývoj archeologie v Čechách a na Moravě 1919–1968 (Archeologické studijní materiály 10; Praha, 1972–5). [*The Development of Archaeology in Bohemia and Moravia 1919–1968:* English summary.]

Germany (Federal Republic of Germany/German Democratic Republic)

Andree, C., 'Geschichte der Berliner Gesellschaft für Anthropologie, Ethnologie und Urgeschichte 1869–1969', in *Festschrift zum hundertjährigen Bestehen der BGAEU* (Berlin, 1969–71).

Andree, C., *Rudolf Virchow als Prähistoriker* (Köln and Wien, 1976).

Behm-Blancke, G., *Die Entwicklungsgeschichte des Museums für Urund Frühgeschichte Thüringens 1892–1945* (Weimar, 1967).

Behrens, H., '150 Jahre prähistorische Sammlungs- und Forschungstätigkeit in Halle a.d. Saale', *Jahresschrift für mitteldeutsche Vorgeschichte, 57* (1973), 7–10.

Coblenz, W., 'Paul Reinecke, ein Wegbereiter der modernen Ur- und Frühgeschichtsforschung', *Zeitschrift für Archäologie, 6* (1972), 240–9.

Coblenz, W., 'Sammlung über die Geschichte der Arbeit': Zur Entwicklung des Landesmuseums für Vorgeschichte Dresden', *Ausgrabungen und Funde, 19* (1974), 66–9.

Dannheimer, H., '90 Jahre Prähistorische Staatssammlung München', *Bayerische Vorgeschichtsblätter, 40* (1975), 1–33.

Ebert, M., 'Schweriner Altertümersammlung 1835 bis 1925', *Vorgeschichtliches Jahrbuch, 1* (1926), 117–20.

Franz, L., 'Zur Geschichte des vorgeschichtlichen Sammelwesens in Leipzig', *Sachsens Vorzeit, 3* (1939), 101–14.

Gummel, H., *Forschungsgeschichte in Deutschland* (Berlin, 1938).

Hühns, E., and Kavalir, G., '150 Jahre Staatliche Museen zu Berlin', *Neue Museumskunde, 23* (1980), 247–69.

Klejn, L. S., 'Kossinna im Abstand von vierzig Jahren', *Jahresschrift für mitteldeutsche Vorgeschichte, 58* (1974), 7–55.

Krämer, W., 'Fünfundsiebzig Jahre Römisch-Germanische Kommission', *BRGK, 58* (1977) Beiheft, 5–23.

Neumann, G., 'Alfred Götze. Eine Würdigung seiner wissenschaftlichen Persönlichkeit', *Jahresschrift f. mitteldeutsche Vorgeschichte, 34* (1950), 185–7.

Schlette, F., 'Die Universität Wittenberg und ihr Beitrag zur Frühgeschichtsforschung in Deutschland während des 16. bis Anfang des 19. Jahrhunderts', *Wiss. Zeitschrift der Univ. Halle-Wittenberg, 28* (1979), 21–7.

Schlette, F., 'Büsching, ein Pionier der Urgeschichtswissenschaft', *Ethnographisch-archäologische Zeitschrift, 20* (1979), 523–32.

Schott, L., '125 Jahre Neandertaler', *Ethnographisth-Archäologische Zeitschrift, 22* (1981), 703–12.

Smolla, G., 'Das Kossinna-Syndrom', *Fundberichte aus Hessen, 19–20* (1979–80), 1–9.

Stemmermann, P. H., *Die Anfänge der deutschen Vorgeschichtsforschung* (Leipzig, 1934).

Unverzagt, W., 'Zur Hundertjahrfeier der Prähistorischen Abteilung des Staatlichen Museums für Völkerkunde in Berlin', *Nachrichtenblatt für Deutsche Vorzeit, 6* (1930), 146–50.

Wahle, E., 'Der Prähistoriker: Zur Geschichte seines Berufstandes im deutschen Sprachraum', *MAGW, 100* (1971), 129–37.

Wittenberg, M., 'Alte Beiträge zur Vor- und Frühgeschichte in deutschen Zeitschriften bis 1750', *Bonner Hefte zur Vorgeschichte, 7* (Bonn, 1973).

Hungary

Castiglione, L., 'Hundert Jahre der Ungarischen archäologischen und kunsthistorischen Gesellschaft', *Acta archaeologica Acad. Scient. Hung., 30* (1978), 437–9.

Fülep, F. (ed.), *Das Ungarische Nationalmuseum* (Budapest, 1978).

Tompa, F., '25 Jahre Urgeschichtsforschung in Ungarn 1912–1936', *BRGK*, *24–5* (1934–5), 27–127.

Poland

Abramowicz, A., *Wiek archeologii, Problemy polskiej archeologii dziewiętnastowieczniej* (Warszawa, 1967). [*A Century of Archaeology. Problems of Polish Archaeology in the Nineteenth Century:* French summary.]

Abramowicz, A., 'Tournant positiviste en archéologie polonaise', *Archaeologia Polona, 11* (1969), 131–41.

Abramowicz, A., *Dalecy i bliscy* (Łódź, 1974). [*Lointains et proches:* French summary.]

Abramowicz, A., *Urny i ceraunie* (Łódź, 1979). [*Urns and Thunderstones:* French summary.]

Blaszczyk, W., *120 lat w słuzbie narodu – Muzeum archeologiczne w Poznaniu [1857–1977]* (Poznań, 1979). [*120 Years of the Archaeological Museum at Poznań.*]

Hensel, W., 'Z historii zbiorów archeologicznych w Polsce', in Jażdżewski, K. [ed.], *Liber Iosepho Kostrzewski . . . dicatus* (Wrocław, Warszawa, and Kraków, 1968), 574–7. ['History of archaeological collections in Poland'.]

Jamka, R., 'Archeologia Polski w Uniwersytecie Jagiellońskim,' *Zeszyty naukowe Uniwersytetu Jagiellońskiego, 139* (1967), 267–85.

Jażdżewski, K., '50 lat dzialalności Polskiego Towarzystwa Archeologicznego oraz jego wspólzałożyciela i prezesa Józefa Kostrzewskiego', *Nauka polska, 18* (1969), 90–100. ['50 years of the activity of the Polish Archaeological Society and its President J. Kostrzewski'.]

Kostrzewski, J., *Dzieje polskich badań prehistoricznych* (Poznań, 1949). [*History of Polish Prehistoric Researches:* French summary.]

Kostrzewski, J., *Z dziejów badań archeologicznych w Wielkopolsce* (Wrocław, 1958). [*History of the archaeological Researches in Greater Poland.*]

Kowiańska-Piaszykowa, M., 'Pamięci prof. J. Kostrzewskiego', *Fontes Archaeologici Posnanienses, 21* (1970), 1–13.

Kramarek, J., 'Z dziejów archeologii na Śląsku', *Silesia Antiqua, 11* (1969), 225–43; *12* (1970), 197–224; *13* (1971), 223–54; *14* (1972), 207–28. ['History of archaeology in Silesia': French summary.]

Maślanka, J., *Zorian Dolęga-Chodakowski* (Wrocław, Warszawa, and Kraków, 1965).

Nosek, S., *Zarys historii badań archeologicznych w Malopolsce* (Wroclaw, Warszawa, and Kraków, 1967). [*An Outline of the History of Archaeological Researches in Little Poland:* French summary.]

Sarnowska, W., 'Dwudziestopieciolecie Muzeum archeologicznego we Wrocławiu', *Silesia Antiqua, 14* (1972), 7–34.

Twardecka, J., 'Eiazm Majewski jako pierwszy polski krytyk tez Gustafa Kossinny', *Archeologia Polski, 22* (1977), 399–420. ['E. Majewski as the first Polish critic of Kossinna's theses'.]

Tymieniecki, K., 'Prof. Dr Józef Kostrzewski', in *Liber Iosepho Kostrzewski . . . dicatus* (Wrocław, Warszawa, and Kraków, 1968), 8–16.

Yugoslavia
(Croatia, Slovenia)

Gabrovec, S., 'Sto petdeset let arheologije v Narodnem muzeju', *Argo, 10* (1971), 35–48. ['150 years of archaeology in the National Museum at Ljubljana': French summary.]

Kos, J., 'Za stoletnico prvih arheoloških izkopavanj na Ljubljanskem barju', *Poročilo o raziskovanju paleolita, neolita in eneolita v Sloveniji, 6* (1978),

43–59. ['A century of archaeological excavations at Ljubljana [Laibach] Moor': German summary.]

Lauer, R., 'Politische und literarische Aspekte der illyrischen Idee bei den Südslaven', in *Slavjanskite kultury u Balkany* (Sofia, 1978), 113ff.

Petru, P., 'Misli ob stopetdesetletnici Narodnega muzeja', *Argo, 10* (1971), 3–34. ['150 years of the National Museum in Ljubljana': French summary.]

Saria, B., 'Vor- und Frühgeschichtsforschung in Südslavien', *BRGK, 16* (1925–6), 86–118.

Index

of personal and place names